THE MASTER DICTIONARY OF
FOOD & COOKERY

THE MASTER DICTIONARY OF

FOOD

& COOKERY

AND MENU TRANSLATOR

by

HENRY SMITH, F.H.C.I.

*Winner of many Gold, Silver and Bronze
Medals, etc., awarded at
London, International and Provincial
Exhibitions*

PHILOSOPHICAL LIBRARY
NEW YORK

ABBREVIATIONS

Fr.	=	French
Ger.	=	German
It.	=	Italian
L.	=	Latin
Rus.	=	Russian

MADE AND PRINTED IN GREAT BRITAIN
BY
THE BURLEIGH PRESS
LEWIN'S MEAD
BRISTOL

The Master Dictionary of
FOOD & COOKERY

A

Aal à la Danube
A famous Austrian dish consisting of eels cooked in wine and served with a butter sauce containing chopped hard - cooked eggs.

Aalsoep
Name of a Dutch eel soup. One of the greatest national Dutch dishes.

Aarfugl
A Norwegian dish of black game; cooked in the same manner as ptarmigan.

Abaisse(Fr.)
Thinly rolled pastry crust.

Abalone
A large sea snail with a flattened shell. Eaten fresh and dried by Chinese and Japanese. Only the central muscle is used, as with the scallop.

Abatis (Fr.)
Giblets and winglets of a bird.

Abats (Fr.)
Offal (liver, lights, heart, head, feet and tail of an animal).

Abattoir
A building in which the slaughter of animals is concentrated.

Abavo
An Indian pumpkin used extensively in soup, noted for its fine flavour. Also for vegetable curries when the abavo is mixed with brinjaul (Indian egg plant).

Abd-el-Kader
Often misspelt on the menu, Ab-del-Kader. The great opponent of the conquest of Algeria by France, born near Mascar, 1808. Many culinary dishes bear his name—as Oeufs Abd-el-Kader.

Abelavis
Name of an Egyptian melon which, because of its good travelling qualities, is exported in considerable quantity. A variety of musk melon.

Abendmahl
German supper.

Abernethy Biscuits
Biscuits named after the famous doctor. Digestive biscuits.

Able (Fr.)
A species of salmon, but smaller, caught off the Swedish coast.

Abricot (Fr.)
See Apricot.

Abricotine (Fr.)
A French apricot brandy.

Absinthe
A strong, bitter cordial, pale green in colour, 50% to 70% alcohol. First made in Switzerland about 1740. It became popular in France in 1844, as an antidote to fever. Later, its use was forbidden, because of its detrimental effects when taken in excess. Contains extracts of wormwood, fennel, anise, parsley and marjoram. Its bitterness is its principal merit.

Acacia
There are about 550 species of acacia, widely scattered over the warmer regions. True gum arabic is the product of Acacia senegal. Acacia arabica is the gum arabic tree of India, yielding a gum inferior to the true gum arabic.

Accola (It.)
A pickled fish of the tunny species, used for hors d'œuvre.

Acetic Acid
The organic acid which gives vinegar its characteristic sharp taste.

Aceto-Dolce (It.)
Denoting Italian produce, as Antepast for hors d'œuvre.

Achaja
Name of a sweet Greek wine.

Achilles
Son of Peleus and Thetis, in Greek legend. Many culinary dishes bear his name. There is no particular type of garnish, the name being used to denote " of good finish ".

Acid (Aigre, Fr.)
The name loosely applied to any sour food or drink.

Acorn
The fruit of the oak tree, used extensively in the manufacture of " ersatz " coffee and credited with much of the fame of the Westphalia ham.

Acre (Fr.)
Of sharp character.

Adet
A cognac, bottled in two colours, white and dark.

Adragant (Fr.)
See Gum Tragacanth.

Adschempilavi
A Turkish dish, consisting of preserved meats cooked with rice.

Advocaat
A Dutch liqueur made with brandy and eggs.

Aerated Water
Distilled water to which purified, filtered air has been added, to improve its flavour. The term is often confused with carbonated waters (see Carbonated Beverages).

Affriolé (Fr.)
Appetising. This term appearing on the menu usually denotes first, fresh, early produce.

Affrité (Fr.)
Prepared for frying.

Africaine, à l' (Fr.)
African style. Applied to many dishes containing horseradish, curried chicken, or chicken with rice ; Consommé a l'Africaine being a chicken consommé flavoured with curry and garnished with rice. As a garnish for joints, it comprises sliced aubergine, small tomatoes and oil, and château potatoes.

Agar-Agar, or **Kanten,** or **Japanese Gelatine**
A vegetable gelatine made chiefly from gelidium seaweed. Used extensively in the manufacture of jams and jellies. It is pearly white, semi-transparent, tasteless and odourless, and is marketed in stick and block form.

Agaric (Fr.)
A type of edible mushroom used extensively in cooking.

Aggekage
A Dutch pork pancake, which enjoys immense popularity.

Agneau (Fr.)
See Lamb.

Agnès Sorel
Name of a French cream soup, Crème Agnès Sorel. Its base is a rich creamy chicken soup which is garnished with mushrooms, chicken and tongue, all cut julienne style.

Agoursis (Fr.)
A type of hors d'œuvre consisting of Russian cucumbers, sliced and salted.

Agriote (Fr.)
The French wild cherry.

Aïda Salade (Fr.)
Name of a salad which contains curled chicory, sliced tomatoes, artichoke bottoms, pimientos, whites of hard-boiled egg, and dressed with French dressing.

Aiglefin or Aigrefin (Fr.)
See Haddock.

Aiglefin (or Aigrefin) Fumé (Fr.)
See Findon Haddock.

Aigre (Fr.)
See Acid, also Vinegar.

Aigrette (Fr.)
Of acid or sour character.

Aiguillette (Fr.)
A long strip or slice of cooked fish, meat, poultry, etc.

Ail (Fr.)
See Garlic.

Aile (Fr.)
The wing of poultry or game birds.

Ailerons Consommé (Fr.)
Name of a chicken consommé, garnished with boned and stuffed chicken wings and boiled rice.

Aïole Sauce (Fr.)
A cold sauce, made from a base of pounded potato, clove, yolk of egg and seasoning, reduced with oil and lemon juice.

Airelle Myrtille (Fr.)
See Bilberry and Blaeberry.

Airelle Rouge (Fr.)
See Cranberry.

Aitch Bone (Culotte, Fr.)
The rump bone of an ox.

Akala Berry
A large juicy berry, native to Hawaiian Islands. Round, small-seeded berries, somewhat similar in appearance to raspberries, which reach up to 2 inches in diameter. They vary in colour from orange to dark purple.

Â la (Fr.)
An ellipsis of à la mode de — in the fashion (or style) of.

Â la Carte (Fr.)
Foods prepared to order.

Albacote
A species of tunny fish.

Albert (Fr.)
Name of a rich butter sauce, flavoured with horseradish, mustard and vinegar, thickened with breadcrumbs and bound with egg yolk. Also Potage Albert, which is a potato soup garnished with a julienne of vegetables.

Albion (Fr.)
Name of a chicken consommé garnished with asparagus tips, cocks' combs and truffle cut julienne style.

Albufera Sauce (Fr.)
Name of a suprême sauce mixed with meat glaze and purée of pimentos.

Albumen
A simple protein widely distributed in both vegetable and animal matter. The best natural example is the white of an egg, which is really pure albumen and water. When chemically pure, it is almost colourless, odourless and tasteless.

Alcohol (Alcool, Fr.)
Also called grain alcohol, root alcohol, spirit of wine, etc., according to the source. A colourless, volatile, inflammable liquid, produced by fermentation and contained in distilled and fermented liquors. When taken, usually as an ingredient of beverages, it undergoes no digestive process in the intestines and is rapidly absorbed in the blood stream. In small doses, it can act as a stimulant on certain tissues of the body, but on the brain it is depressant. The word is of Arabic origin. (See also Denatured Alcohol.)

Alcool (Fr.)
See Alcohol.

Alderman's Walk
The best part of the undercut (fillet) of a sirloin of beef. City Aldermen showed a special liking for this cut and would always walk to the carving table to witness the carver cut this special fillet to their own particular liking. Some apply it to a haunch of mutton, others to a haunch of venison.

Ale
A fermented beverage made with an infusion of hops and malted barley. Contains 3% to 4% alcohol. A pint yields approximately 250 calories.

Alecost or **Costmary** (Baume-Coq, Fr.)
A perennial herb with a slightly bitter, minty flavour. It stands the winter well and makes a good winter substitute for mint sauce.

Alevins (Fr.)
See Elvers.

Alewife
A fish allied to the shad and of great gastronomic value.

Alexandra
Name of a chicken consommé garnished with rice, brunoise and diced chicken.

Algérienne, à l' (Fr.)
Originating from Algeria—Algerian style. As a garnish, it comprises small tomatoes (chats) blanched and cooked in olive oil with croquettes of sweet potatoes ; usually served with roasts of meat.

Allegretti Pecan Cakes
Name given to frosted or iced pecan nut cakes with a top coating of bitter chocolate icing.

Allemande, à l' (Fr.)
German style. From the French word for German. The name is much used in culinary works—as Sauce Allemande. Allemande Sauce is one of the four mother sauces, and consists of veal stock thickened with roux, cream and yolks of eggs, flavoured with nutmeg and lemon juice. It goes back to the days when it was spelled " Almayne ", a term that included Holland as well as many German States.

Also applied to dishes finished or garnished with sauerkraut, smoked sausage, pickled pork or noodles tossed in butter.

Allerlei Leipziger (Ger.)
A German dish of macedoine of spring vegetables and mushrooms cooked in butter with a little sugar and a few prawns.

Alligator Pear (Avocado Pear)
A tropical fruit, native to Mexico, Central America, and northern South Africa. The Californian Fruit Growers' Association have coined the name Calavo, to distinguish their fruit from all others.

The fruit is big and heavy, weighing up to 4 lbs., consists of a large rugged seed wrapped in a membranous cover, inside a firm buttery flesh of bright greenish-yellow. The outer skin is tough and leathery. Shape oval, and colour usually of bright green. The word " avocado " is Spanish for lawyer.

Allspice (Ground Pimento)
The dried, unripe berry of the pimento or allspice tree, not to be confused with mixed spice. Also known as Jamaica pepper.

Allumettes (Fr.)

"Matches"—as applied to straw potatoes.

Allylic (Fr.)

Resembling garlic or onions.

Alma

A river of Russia. It gives its name to a famous victory gained over the Russians on 20 September, 1854, in the Crimean War. Many dishes bear its name, chief of which is Alma Pudding.

Almavica

An Italian luncheon sweet made of semolina.

Almeria

Maritime province in Southern Spain, noted for its White Almeria Grapes, from which many dishes take their name when incorporating grapes in their composition.

Almond (Amande, Fr.)

The fruit of the almond tree. The bitter almond is rather broader and shorter than the sweet almond, and may yield from 6% to 8% of prussic acid. The most sought-after sweet almond is the Jordan almond, used extensively for salted almonds and sugared almonds. Other varieties are the Valencia, Majorca and those exported from Malaga. Jordan almond means garden almond, just as the best green peas are referred to as garden peas ; Jordan being a corruption of the French "jardin".

Almond, Green

See Pistachio Nut.

Almond Oil

The commercial oil is prepared from the kernels of the bitter almond, which yield 35% to 45% of oil. The oil is pale yellow in colour, and possesses a bland, nutty flavour. For edible purposes, almond oil should be prepared from sweet almonds only.

Almond Paste (Pâté d'Amandes, Fr.)

An amalgamation of ground almonds, sugar and eggs.

Aloes

A medicinal substance used as a purgative, being the expressed juice of the leaves of the aloe plant.

Alose (Fr.)

See Shad.

Alouette (Fr.)

Another name for the lark, the other French name being mauviette. (See Lark).

Aloyau (Fr.)

See Sirloin of Beef.

Alphabétique (Fr.)

Italian paste used principally in clear soups. It is stamped out in small letter form.

Alphénic (Fr.)

See Barley Sugar.

Alsacienne, à l' (Fr.)

The name given to dishes originating from Alsace, a territory which has been the subject of many disputes between French and Germans. Alsatian style. As a garnish, it comprises artichoke bottoms filled with mushroom purée and served with Sauce Madère.

Altar Bread
Bread prepared for the Eucharist.

Alum
The double sulphate of aluminia and potash. A powerful astringent used for curing skins and sugar boiling.

Alvéole (Fr.)
Wax cell of a honeycomb. (Honeycomb—Rayon de Miel, Fr.). See Honeycomb.

Amalgamer (Fr.)
Amalgamate. To mix together. To combine several substances.

Amande (Fr.)
See Almond.

Ambassadeur (Fr.)
Ambassador style. A garnish similar to Alsacienne, comprising artichoke bottoms filled with a purée of mushrooms and sprinkled with grated horse-radish with Sauce Madère.

Ambiqu (Fr.)
A light, buffet style of lunch.

Amé
A Continental sweetmeat used by Chinese and Japanese to spread on bread, or it is eaten alone.

Amer, Amère (Fr.)
See Bitter.

Américaine, à l' (Fr.)
American style. Tomatoes or lobster generally form part of the garnish or sauce. (See also Armoricaine.)

Amer Picon
A bitter liqueur wine.

Amidon (Fr.)
See Starch.

Amiral, à l' (Fr.)
Admiral style. When used as a garnish for fish, it is chiefly composed of mussels, shrimps and crayfish.

Amontillado
A dry type of sherry, of light colour, exported from Spain, which derives its name from the town of Montilla. (See Sherry.)

Amoroso
A sherry wine, darker in colour and slightly sweeter than Amontillado, and with a fuller flavour. (See Sherry.)

Amourette (Fr.)
A French liqueur.

Amphitryon (Fr.)
The host.

Ananas (Fr.)
See Pineapple.

Anchois (Fr.)
See Anchovy.

Anchovy (Anchois, Fr.)
The anchovy is a small, herring-like fish, and is that essential adjunct required in making delicious anchovy essence, so often used in fish sauces. The best anchovies are those which are small and plump. The fish is about $6\frac{1}{2}$ inches in length, the form rather slender, especially towards the tail, the head long and sharp-pointed, the colour of the head and back greenish-blue, nearly all other parts silvery-white.

Anchovy Essence

No longer do chefs or cooks have to spend hours pounding and simmering these little fish to obtain anchovy essence. Modern manufacturers now make this product readily available to us in bottles, obtainable at almost any good grocer. Avoid anchovy essence if it shows a clear liquid at the bottom of the bottle, as this is a sign of staleness.

Anchovy Pear

The russet brown fruit of a tall slender tree cultivated in the West Indies. It measures 3 inches in length and is eaten pickled.

Anchovy Toast

A savoury toast, made by spreading anchovy butter or paste on hot toast.

Ancienne, à l' (Fr.)

In ancient style. As a garnish, it consists of beans, cooked lettuce, and hard-boiled eggs.

Andalouse (Fr.)

French term for dishes originating from Andalusia, one of the old provinces of Spain, broken up in 1833. Andalusian style. Andalouse Sauce is mayonnaise sauce blended with tomato purée and chopped red sweet peppers.

Andouille (Fr.)

A large type of hog's pudding, usually served as hors d'œuvre. The best variety is that made at Vire, in Normandy.

Aneth (Fr.)

See Dill.

Angel Fish

The name given to a species of fish found in tropical seas. It takes its name from its large wing-like pectoral fins.

Angel Food Cake

Name given to a variety of very light spongy cakes originating from America. This type of confection was first introduced to England in 1934. There were many failures in its manufacture in the earlier days, due to the fact that a special soft flour was required to ensure lightness and soft eating qualities.

Angelica (Angélique, Fr.)

A plant of the parsley family, native to the Alps. It is used as a flavour for gin, vermouth, benedictine, and other wines, and sometimes in medicine. The young and tender leaf stalks and midribs are candied for sale as confectionery and used extensively for decorating cakes and chocolates.

Angels on Horseback (Huîtres à Cheval, Fr.)

A savoury, consisting of oysters rolled in bacon slices, grilled and served on toast.

Anglaise, à l' (Fr.)

English style. Foods cooked and served without elaborate garnish. Simple, plain cooking, as boiling or steaming. Not altogether a compliment to the Frenchman's idea of English cooking.

Angostura

A popular brand of bitters. Rum is used as its basis, which is infused with a number of aromatic herbs and roots. Also, the name of the bitter bark of the Cusparia tree.

Anguille (Fr.)

See Eel.

Anguilles Fumées(Fr.)

Fillets of smoked eel, usually dressed on a serviette.

Animelles (Fr.)

See Lamb's Fry.

Anis (Anise, Fr.)

A plant cultivated in Egypt for medicinal purposes. Its fruit is known by the name of aniseed, from which the well-known flavour is extracted.

Aniseed

The seed of the anis. (See Anis.)

Anisette (Fr.)

A liqueur of aniseed flavour.

Anjovislada

Name of a Swedish anchovy omelette, which is baked with potatoes, more like a cake than an omelette.

Annato or **Annatto**

A yellowish-red dye used in colouring butter and cheese, obtained from the annato tree.

Antepast (It.)

(L. ante—before, pastas—food). A foretaste, appetizer.

Anversoise

Name of a style of garnish, comprising small tartlet cases filled with hop shoots mixed with cream accompanied with small boiled potatoes.

Aouded

A North African wild goat used as food.

Aperitif (Fr.)

A short, strong and often bitter drink, taken before meals to create an appetite, so it is supposed. An appetizer.

Apfel

German for apple. Apfel Strudel—a delicate apple confection.

Apfelsinnenbiscuittorte Ungefullt

Name of a delicious German orange cake, much enjoyed by the tourist.

Apfelsuppe

A German apple soup, very pleasing and refreshing.

Apician

Meaning dainty, or expensive cookery. (See Apicius.)

Apicius

The name of three celebrated Roman epicures. A collection of receipts ascribed to Cascius Apicius is founded on Greek originals, and belongs to the 3rd century A.D. The name is applied to many elaborately finished French dishes.

Appetiser

That food or drink which creates an appetite. Cocktails and hors d'œuvre of all kinds.

Appetite (Appetit, Fr.)
The natural desire for food, not necessarily hunger. Appetite is stimulated by a good chef; he does not regulate it. A good chef can constantly entice one's appetite; it is up to the diner to regulate it. (See also Hunger.)

Apple (Pomme, Fr.)
Apples are palatable, healthful and comparatively inexpensive as food. Apples that are good to eat raw are not necessarily good for cooking. Of the present varieties there are several thousands. Because of their pectin content, vast quantities are employed in jam and jelly making. A ripe, raw, good quality fruit, if well masticated, digests in about ninety minutes. Unless well masticated, it is likely to undergo fermentation. An apple a day will keep the doctor away, if ripe, of good quality, and well masticated.

Apple Brandy
Distilled cider.

Apple Butter
Apples boiled or otherwise evaporated, with cider or vinegar, to a semi-solid consistency, with added sugar and spice.

Apple Fool
See description under Gooseberry Fool.

Apple Gin
Gin combined with the soluble ingredients of the apple, greenish in colour.

Apricot (Abricot, Fr.)
A fruit which in appearance suggests a small peach. The apricot is a stone fruit used extensively in preserves and in tarts. It has long been cultivated in Armenia, but now California produces some 300,000 tons per annum, used for canning and drying, of which some 100,000 tons are exported annually.

Apricot Brandy
An apricot liqueur. Tawny in colour, and usually quite sweet.

Apricot Gin
A liqueur flavoured with apricot.

Aqua d'Orott
An expensive Italian liqueur flavoured with rose petals and rosemary.

Aquavit (Fr.)
A colourless strong spirit, distilled from potatoes and flavoured with caraway seeds.

Arabique (Fr.)
Arabic. In Arabian style—gracefully or tastefully finished.

Arachide (Fr.)
See Pea-nut.

Arenburg
Formerly a German duchy of the Holy Roman Empire. Many culinary dishes bear this name. Garnishing of dishes is chiefly composed of shredded artichoke bottoms or sauerkraut.

641.03 Sm58m

Argenteuil (Fr.)
A town of Northern France, and a name applied to many French dishes, Argenteuil being famous for its market gardens and vineyards. As a garnish, it is chiefly applied to asparagus.

Arille Fr.)
See Mace.

Arlésienne (Fr.)
The French term for dishes originating from the district of Arles, formerly known as the dukedom of Burgundy. As a garnish, it is chiefly composed of tomatoes, onions and aubergines, fried in oil.

Arménienne, à l' (Fr.)
Armenian style. With rice, grains, semolina or maize.

Armenonville (Fr).
French term for a garnish comprising sliced artichoke bottoms, quartered tomatoes, French beans, with small potatoes in cream sauce.

Armoricaine (Fr.)
Not to be confused with Américaine (being the French for American style). Armorica is the Roman name derived from two Celtic words meaning " seaside ", for the land of the Armorici, roughly the peninsula of Brittany, à l'Armoricaine being applied to many French dishes originating from Armorici—as Fillet of Sole Armoricaine, poached fillets garnished with poached oysters, soft roes and coated with Sauce Américaine.

Aromates (Fr.)
Aromatic herbs. Roots and herbs with a tasty flavour.

Aromatique (Fr.)
Aromatic. With fresh herbs— finely flavoured—a mingling of flavours. Sauce Aromate consists of a rich white sauce blended with aromatic herb purée.

Arome (Fr.)
Aroma—of delicate bouquet.

Arrack (Arac, Fr.)
A potent spirit made from coco-nuts and rice.

Arrowroot (Fécule de Marante, Fr.)
One of the most easily digested starch products. The true arrowroot is a starch obtained from the rootstock, shiyome, of a West Indian plant, Maranta arundinacer. Its name has been attributed to the Indian practice of using the fresh roots to cure the wounds made by poisoned arrows. A smooth jelly-like custard is made from it, which is particularly good in infant feeding and diets for disturbed digestive tracts. It keeps better than cereal starches.

Arroz con Pollo
A Spanish dish of rice and chicken.

Artichaut (Fr.)
See Artichoke.

B

Artichoke (Artichaut, Fr.)
The Globe Artichoke is a plant resembling a large thistle, cultivated for its flowering head, which, gathered before the flower expands, is used as a vegetable. It has good keeping qualities, remaining fresh for two weeks or longer. The novice is sometimes in doubt as to the proper method of eating a whole artichoke.

The Jerusalem Artichoke has no relation to the true artichoke, it being a tuber of a species of sunflower, the tuber resembling the potato in general characteristics, but being sweetish in flavour and more watery. It is round, knobbly and white. Its food value is low. (See also Jerusalem Artichoke.)

Artois (Fr.)
A name applied to many French dishes, originating from this ancient province of France. Chiefly of flour confectionery, such as light puff pastry or sponge goods, used as luncheon or dinner sweets.

Asado
A very popular dish of the Argentine, consisting of lamb roasted on a spit.

Ascorbic Acid
An organic acid first known in lemon and lime juice, called anti-scorbutic acid. Now known to be present in many fresh fruits and vegetables and known as vitamin C.

Ashberry
The berry of the mountain ash, from which a tart jelly is made which is best when served with game, known as Rowanberry Jelly.

Asiatique (Fr.)
Asiatic.

Asparagus (Asperges, Fr.)
A valuable vegetable plant, native of Europe, which was a favourite vegetable of the Ancient Romans. The spears are cut when a few inches above the ground, by cutting the stalks well below the surface. Fresh asparagus should be eaten as soon after being gathered as possible, for it quickly loses its delicate flavour. In cooking, the best method is to stand the bunch on end, leaving about 1 inch of the tops above the surface of the water. In this way, it is possible to cook the spears thoroughly without destroying the appearance of the tips. That grown in Argenteuil, near Paris, is prized for its size and quality.

Asperges (Fr.)
See Asparagus.

Aspérule Odorante (Fr.)
See Woodruff.

Aspic Jelly
A clear, savoury jelly. Derived from a word meaning " spike jelly ", i.e. jelly flavoured with " spike " or " French " lavender, at one time a popular desert, now a clear savoury jelly made from fish, fowl or meat.

Assaisonner (Fr.)
To flavour or season or mix.

Assiette (Fr.)
A small entrée or hors d'œuvre, not more than a plate will contain.

Assorti (Fr.)
Assorted—mixed.

Assyrienne, à l' (Fr.)
Assyrian style.

Ãtelet (Fr.)
See Hâtelet.

Athénienne, à l' (Fr.)
Athenian style. As a garnish, it is chiefly comprised of stuffed aubergines set in madeira sauce.

Atkafish
An excellent food fish of the North Pacific. Its average weight is from 2 to 3 pounds.

Attereaux (Fr.)
Pieces of meat cooked together on a skewer.

Au (Fr.)
With, in, of.

Auberge (Fr.)
An inn.

Aubergine (Fr.)
See Egg Plant.

Aubergiste (Fr.)
Hotel or inn keeper.

Aubergiste, à l' (Fr.)
Proprietor's or innkeeper's style —the special dish of the house.

Au Beurre (Fr.)
With, or cooked in, butter. As Sauce au Beurre Blanc (white butter sauce), melted butter with finely-minced shallot, flavoured with lemon juice.

Au Bleu (F.)
A French term applied to fish, simmered in white wine, with herbs. As Truite au Bleu— Trout au Bleu. The essential factor in presenting this dish correctly is that the trout be alive when they reach the kitchen. Stun the fish and clean quickly, plunge them into boiling Court Bouillon and simmer to the exact degree of done-ness—12 minutes for a 6 oz. to 8 oz. fish. Dress on a dish with parsley, and serve with melted butter and plain boiled potatoes.

Audit Ale
A strong ale, originally brewed at Oxford and Cambridge Universities, which was drunk at the feasts held on audit-day.

Au Maigre (Fr.)
A French expression applied to Lenten and other fast day dishes—dishes prepared without meat. As an adjective it denotes thin, poor or scanty.

Aumale Oeufs (Fr.)
Name given to a dish of scrambled eggs, which are mixed with tomatoes, diced kidney, and flavoured with madeira wine.

Au Naturel (Fr.)
Plain and simple cookery. Foods plainly and quickly served, or served uncooked, as Huîtres au Natural—oysters served in the deep shell.

Aurore (Fr.)
Of a yellow colour, dished up high. Bold and yellow in colour. Sometimes dome-shaped foods are masked with Béchamel and sprinkled with paprika.

Aurum
A delicately flavoured orange liqueur made in Italy.

Autrichienne, à l' (Fr.)
Austrian style. Paprika, caraway seeds, sausages and stuffed cabbage usually form part of the garnish to Austrian dishes.

Aveline (Fr.)
See Filbert.

Avignon (Fr.)
A city of France well noted for its food. A name applied to many French dishes, to denote their gastronomic value.

Avocado Pear
See Alligator Pear.

Avoine (Fr.)
See Oats.

Azote
Nitrogen.

Azyme (Fr.)
Denoting the absence of a ferment—unleavened.

B

Baba
A light yeast cake, usually flavoured with rum or kirsch, like a tipsy cake, the difference being that a baba usually contains butter and is fruited, whilst a tipsy cake does not. The baba is made from a rich fermented dough, while the tipsy cake is made from sponge cake.

Babassu Nuts
Nuts of the babassu palm, which grows abundantly in Brazil, the oil from which greatly resembles coco-nut oil and is used in similar ways.

Babawte
An African curry of baked minced beef.

Babeurre (Fr.)
See Buttermilk.

Baby
The name given to the quarter-sized bottle of mineral water, or quarter bottle of champagne. A nip.

Bacalao
A Spanish fish dish, usually made of salt cod with a savoury sauce.

Bacardi
A popular brand of rum.

Bacchus
The god of wine.

Backhuhner
An Austrian dish of fried chicken, garnished with anchovies—as Wiener Schnitzel.

Bacon (Lard, Fr.)
The salted, or smoked, meat product which is prepared from the sides of hogs.

Badger (Blaireau, Fr.)
The common badger is 25–29 inches long, with a tail of about 8 inches. A mature badger will weigh 28–35 lbs. In colour it is grey above and black below, with a white head, on either side of which is a black stripe. The old "sports" of badger drawing and badger baiting were prohibited in Great Britain about the middle of the 19th century. Badger can be cured by salting, the hams being exceptionally good fare.

Badoise
Name of a French garnish, consisting of red cabbage cooked with diced bacon and served with creamed potatoes.

Bael or **Bengal Quince**
A fruit of the orange family, used as a preserve in jam or it is crushed for its luscious juice.

Bagasse (Fr.)
See Sugar Cane.

Bagration (Fr.)
Name of a Russian general who fought in the Napoleonic wars. A monument was erected in his honour on the battlefield of Borodino. His name appears frequently in French dishes, no doubt due to the fact that his chef was the celebrated A. Carême. Bagration—in honour of this general. Potage Bagration — see Master Book of Soups.

Bain-Marie (Fr.)
A water bath with its set of saucepans, in which sauces, etc. are kept just off boiling point without reducing by evaporation.

Baissière (Fr.)
Wine sediment.

Baisure (Fr.)
A dainty thin crust.

Bake, to
To cook in a dry heat, as in an oven, or on a stove.

Bakehouse
A house or building for baking.

Baker (Boulanger, Fr.)
The name applied to one engaged in the business of baking bread, biscuits, cakes or rolls.

Bakery
A place where baking is concentrated.

Baking
The action of the verb to bake.

Baking Powder (Poudre de Levure, Fr.)
A mixture of chemicals to replace yeast in baking, its principal ingredients consisting of sodium bicarbonate (baking soda) and cream of tartar, usually blended 2 parts cream of tartar to 1 part sodium bicarbonate.

Baking Soda
See Bicarbonate of Soda.

Bald Pate
The common name for a North American duck.

Ballotines (Fr.)
Small balls of meat, fowl or fish. Also applied to small game birds stuffed with force-meat.

Ball Supper (Souper de Bal, Fr.)
A cold supper usually served after the twelfth dance marked on the dance card. Some such suppers are very elaborate meals, running into six or sometimes eight courses, all of a very light nature.

Balm (Mélisse, Citronelle, Fr.)
Not to be confused with Barm, which see. A wild, nettle-looking plant. The leaves are very aromatic and are used for seasoning and in the manufacture of scents.

Balm, Garden
A term applied to balm mint or lemon balm. An aromatic herb with a marked lemon odour, used for general culinary purposes, and its oil in scent manufacture.

Balthasar
A bottle holding $2\frac{3}{4}$ gallons, equal to 16 ordinary bottles. See Bottle.

Balyx
A Russian term for salted or smoked sturgeon.

Balzac (Fr.)
Name of a veal consommé garnished with shrimps, peas and diced turnip.

Bamboo Shoots
A favourite vegetable of China and Japan. The young shoots of the bamboo plant are banked up as in asparagus cultivation, and are cut as soon as the tips show above the surface. Good specimens measure several inches in diameter and weigh several pounds. They may be boiled or fried and have a flavour similar to that of the artichoke.

Banana
A plant closely allied to the plantain, cultivated for its delicious soft fruit. Bananas grow on a plant which resembles a palm tree. The fruit grows out of the stalk, forming an elongated bunch. They are always harvested green, even for local consumption. Their food value and flavour are governed by the care taken of them during the ripening process.

Banbury Cake
A flat, round, spiced puff pastry confection, with a filling of spiced, sugared fruits.

Bang
A mixture of spiced ale and cider, with a small addition of whisky and gin.

Bangou
See Egg Plant.

Bannock
A flat, round cake, made of oat, rye or barley meal. They are baked on a hearth or on a griddle over the fire. (See also Pitcaithly Bannock.)

Banquet (Fr.)
A feast or entertainment. To feast; to fare sumptuously. Originally a little bench or table.

Banqueter
One who takes part in a banquet; a feaster.

Bantam Fowl
A small breed of domestic fowl supposed to be named after Bantam, in Java.

Bap
A soft, flat, white, floury-coated Scottish breakfast roll.

Bar (Fr.)
See Bass.

Baraquine (Fr.)
Name of a veal consommé garnished with strips of truffle, chicken and tapioca.

Barbadoes Sugar
The cultivation of sugar was introduced to Barbadoes in the middle of the 17th century, and it is now the staple product of the island. Considered one of the finest of cane sugars.

Barbeau (Fr.)
See Barbel.

Barbecue
From the Spanish " barbacoa ". Originally a tripod or frame-work for holding whole animals over an open fire for roasting. Americans apply the word to open-air feasts where whole animals are roasted out in the open like the roasting of an ox in England. To dress and roast whole. Barbecued steak—steak cooked over an open fire.

Barbel (Barbeau, Fr.)
This fish deserves very little notice. When cooked it is tasteless and woolly. It some-times measures 3 feet in length and weighs up to 18 lbs. It takes its name from the cirri or barbels at its mouth. The best method is to score the fish and soak it in olive oil for half an hour, sprinkle it with salt and pepper and broil each side gently over a moderate fire. Serve with Maître d'Hôtel Butter. France takes more kindly to this fish than we do. The general colour of the upper parts is greenish-brown, be-coming yellowish-green on the sides; belly white; irides yellow; lips pale flesh colour. It spawns in May and June. (See also Barbillon, below.)

Barberry Fig
See Prickly Pear.

Barbillon (Fr.)
A small or young Barbel (which see).

Barbue (Fr.)
See Brill.

Barcelona Nuts
Spanish nuts similar in charac-ter to the English filbert, cob-nut or hazel-nut.

Bard (Barder, Fr.)
The covering of birds for roast-ing with thin slices of fat bacon or pork.

Bardane Géante (Fr.)
See Burdock.

Bar de Mer (Fr.)
See Bass, Sea.

Barding, Application of
To bard means to cover breasts of poultry or game birds, or other types of game, with thin slices of fat. This is usually applied to small birds such as snipe, woodcock, larks, etc., which need to be roasted in a sharp oven in the least possible amount of time. Or in the case of plovers or quails, to save time in basting, which must otherwise be done.
Thin slices of fat ham or bacon are laid completely over the bird and usually tied upon the bird. Where small birds are wrapped in vine leaves, the slice of bacon then encloses the whole.

Barigoule, à la (Fr.)
A style of garnish, incorporating artichokes and mushrooms dressed in Espagnole Sauce.

Bar-le-Duc (Fr.)
This preserve was once famous for being made of whole white currants with the seeds removed by hand, in Bar-le-Duc, France. It is now made from currants, strawberries, raspberries and gooseberries, with the seeds not removed.

Barley (Orge, Fr.)
A species of grain used for food and especially for making malt. Pearl barley is the grain with the germ and most of the bran removed.

Barley Corn
A grain which at one time was used as a measure, three of which (sometimes four) were considered to make up an inch.

Barley Sugar (Alphénic, Fr.)
Sugar boiled till it is brittle, formerly with a decoction of barley.

Barley Water
A decoction of pearl barley used in medicine.

Barmaid
A maid or woman who serves at a bar where intoxicants are served.

Barman
A man who performs similar duties to a barmaid (which see).

Barm-Yeast (Levain, Fr.)
The scum formed on the top of malt liquor when fermenting ; yeast to set up fermentation in liquor or used to leaven bread. (See also Yeast.)

Baron of Beef
The name applied to two sirloins of beef not cut asunder. The joint of beef similar to a saddle of mutton.

Barquette (Fr.)
Boat-shaped.

Barquettes (Fr.)
Boat-shaped pastry shells usually filled with caviare, oysters, etc., and served as an hors d'œuvre or savoury.

Barracouta
The name given to snoek in Australia and New Zealand. (See Snoek.)

Barracuda
A long, slender fish, found off the coast of California. It is popular as a big game fish.

Bar Rayé (Fr.)
Striped bass.

Barrel
A wooden cask which contains 26¼ gallons of ale or beer by English measure.

Barsac
A very popular type of French white wine, most important varieties of which are Château Contet and Château Climens.

Barsez
Name of a Polish soup, similar in character to the Ukrainian national beetroot soup.

Barthou, Jean Louis
A French politician born at Oloron-Sainte-Marie, 25 Aug., 1862. Many culinary dishes bear his name.

Basil (Basilic, Fr.)
A cultivated aromatic pot herb, with a pleasant spicy flavour, used for flavouring dishes, especially turtle soup. Basil vinegar is made by steeping the leaves in vinegar.

Basin (Bassine, Fr.)
A deep, hollow, circular vessel or dish, suitable for holding liquids.

Bass, Sea (Bar, Loup de Mer, Fr.)
There are other types of bass, but as they are not available to us in these Isles, let us dwell on the type that is. Sea bass is a striped fish with a large head, which grows to 2 to 3 pounds in weight, and as its name denotes, is never found in fresh water. It is caught by sea anglers in the brackish waters of estuaries during the spawning season, May to August. Gastronomically, it is the best of the tribe. Other types of bass are black bass, black sea bass, Ross bass, all of which are available to the Americans.

Basset (Fr.)
A name used in some parts of France for the Tourne-broche (see Turnspit). Basset hounds were chiefly used for turning the spit because of the hound's long body and short legs.

Bassine (Fr.)
See Basin.

Baste
To drip fats or liquids which have oozed from foods over them during the cooking process, or to coat with additional fats or liquids during the cooking process, to prevent a hardening of the outer casing or skin.

Bâtarde (Fr.)
Name of a thin cream sauce, flavoured with lemon juice and bound with yolks of eggs.

Batelière (Fr.)
A garnish for fish, comprising glazed onions, chopped fried egg, sliced mushrooms and crayfish tails.

Bath Bun
A kind of light sweet bun, of irregular shape, containing butter and currants. It takes its name from the city of Bath, where it originated.

Bath Chap
The cheek of a pig salted and smoked like bacon. The city of Bath still enjoys the honour of " the know-how " in curing the pig's cheek to perfection.

Bath Olivers
A famous type of biscuit, first made at Bath, attributed to a Dr. Oliver. Its secret is said to be the stout with which the biscuits are mixed.

Bâton (Fr.)
In the kitchen, a stick or slice of food.

Batter
A mixture of flour, milk, eggs and water, used for frying or baking. Butter is sometimes added to enrich it.

Batterie de Cuisine (Fr.)
A complete set of cooking apparatus.

Baudroie (Fr.)
See Rockling.

Baume-Coq (Fr.)
See Alecost.

Baume Saccharometer
The following table gives the amount of sugar dissolved in 1 pint of water and the reading as shown by the saccharometer at a temperature of 60°F.

Ounces of Sugar dissolved in 1 Pint of Water	Readings on Saccharometer at 60° F.
2	5 degrees
4	8 ,,
6	12 ,,
8	15 ,,
10	18 ,,
12	21 ,,
14	23 ,,
16	24.5 ,,
18	26 ,,
20	28 ,,
22	29 ,,
24	30 ,,

(See also Saccharometer.)

Bavaroise (Fr.)
Almond-flavoured cream stiffened with gelatine and set in fancy-shaped moulds.

Bavaroise, à la (Fr.)
Bavarian style or fashion. Sauce Bavaroise—enriched Hollandaise garnished with crayfish tails.

Bavière (Fr.)
Name of a veal consommé garnished with quenelles made of semolina and flavoured with marsala.

Bayard, Pierre Terrail
A great French soldier. Knighted after the battle of Fornova (1495) where he had captured a standard. Many French dishes bear his name. The name Bayard, when applied to garnishing, comprises sliced truffles, mushrooms, artichoke bottoms and foie-gras served in madeira sauce.

Bayeux
Town of France situated on the Aure, 5 miles from the English Channel. À la Bayeux—in the style of Bayeux.

Bay Leaf (Laurier, Fr.)
The aromatic leaf of the sweet-bay. It is usually cultivated, but in some parts it grows wild. The leaves may be used fresh or dried for flavouring purposes. N.B.—The sweet-bay and its leaves have no connection with " bay rum ". That owes its name to the original manu-facture by distilling rum with the leaves of the bayberry.

Bayonnaise, à la (Fr.)
Bayonne, town of France. Bayonnaise style, being gar-nished with gherkins, braised onions and anchovy fillets.

Bay Rum
Not edible, being a fragrant liquid cosmetic. See Bay Leaf for fuller explanation.

Bay Salt
Coarse-grained salt, obtained by the natural evaporation of sea water.

Beaker
A large, wide-mouthed drink-ing cup.

Bean Feast
Theory connects the phrase with a feast on Twelfth Night, at which a cake with a bean buried in it was a great feature. The person who received the slice with the bean in it was the Bean King. Now the term is applied to annual dinners or outings, at which a meal is served to the gathering. (See also Twelfth Cake.)

Beans (Fèves, Haricots, Fr.)
The seed of certain leguminous plants, planted for food all over the world. This group (beans, peas, lentils) is richer in protein than any other vegetables. The many varieties are too numerous to mention. Beans appear to have been cultivated long before the commencement of recorded history. (See also French Beans, Kidney Beans, Runner Beans.)

Béarn
Formerly a small frontier pro-vince in the South of France. (See Béarnaise below.)

Béarnaise (Fr.)
Name of the now well-known sauce, originally made in the province of Béarn, birthplace of King Henry IV. There is the generally known Béarnaise Sauce, Béarnaise Brune, which has meat extract added to give it colour, Béarnaise Tomate— Béarnaise Sauce enriched with tomato purée.

Beaucaire
Town of France on the right bank of the lower Rhone. À la Beaucaire—Beaucaire style. Anguille Beaucaire — boned, stuffed eel, braised in brandy and white wine, garnished with mushrooms and onions.

Beauharnais (Fr.)

Name of a garnish consisting of stuffed mushrooms and sliced artichoke bottoms cooked in oil, served with tournedos and noisettes. After Josephine Beauharnais, the first wife of Napoleon Bonaparte.

Beaujolais

A red wine produced in South-Eastern France.

Beaune

A town of France, the centre of the wine trade of Burgundy.

Beauvais

A town of north France, lying at the foot of hills on the left bank of the Thérain, known for its market gardening. À la Beauvais—from the Beauvais market.

Beauvilliers, Antoine

Author and French restaurateur, born 1754, died 1811. He gave his name to a number of French dishes.

Bécasse (Fr.)

See Woodcock.

Bécassine (Fr.)

See Snipe.

Bec-figue (Fr.)

See Fig-bird.

Béchamel (Fr.)

Name of one of the four mother sauces (white). Veloutée sauce enriched with cream. Invented by Louis de Béchamel (Marquis of Nointel) while he was maître d'hôtel to Louis XIV.

Beech Nut

The nut of the beech tree. The kernel is tender and has a good flavour. The nuts grow in pairs inside a prickly burr.

Beef (Bœuf, Fr.)

Flesh from mature cattle used as food. It contains the highest form of protein for human consumption. The flesh of an ox, bull or cow, when killed. In free, open market, it is sold as prime, choice, good, medium and manufacturing. The flesh of the adult steer is the most important of meats.

Beef Extract

An extract of the soluble constituents of beef. It is used to give piquancy to gravies, soups and other dishes.

Beef Marrow (Moëlle de Bœuf, Fr.)

A fatty substance found in the larger bones of animals killed for beef. (See also Marrowbone.)

Beefsteak Pie (Pâté de Bifteck, Fr.)

The vexed question of how much kidney should one mix with steak for a pie is best answered by—kidney is 12 times stronger in flavour than beef, so to balance the flavours use 12 lbs. of steak, 1 lb. kidney ; more kidney for more flavour.

Beefsteak Society

A society founded in London in 1745, which remained in vogue for 132 years. Founded by one John Rich.

Beef Tea
A nutritious broth made from beef, suitable for invalids and convalescents. When made from a good rich beef, it is said it makes the hale and hearty envy the sick.

Beer (Bière, Fr.)
A beverage made by the alcoholic fermentation of crushed cereal. Records show that beer made from barley was brewed 5,000—6,000 B.C. Bread and beer-making have always been closely connected in their manufacture.

Beestings
The first milk given by a cow after calving — Beesting Custard.

Beetroot (Betterave, Fr.)
One of the most important food roots. The red beet are distinguished for their individual flavour and for being more colourful than other root vegetables. When pickled, the acid of vinegar tends to soften the fibre and thus aids digestion.

Beignets (Fr.)
Food dipped in batter and fried —fritters.

Beignets de Fromage (Fr.)
Cheese fritters.

Belle Hélène (Fr.)
A French garnish comprising grilled mushrooms filled with tomato purée and topped with peas and very small young carrots ; served with croquette potatoes.

Benedictine (D.O.M. or Deo Optimo Maximo)
The name means, To God Most Good, Most Great. A famous aromatic liqueur made at Fécamp on the coast of Normandy. Considered by some as the only rival to the old Chartreuse. The present distillery buildings occupy the grounds which belonged to the old abbey of Fécamp. First made by the very learned monk named Dom Bernardo Vincelli.

Benzoate of Soda
One of the least harmful food preservatives, used in preserving sauces, relishes and fruit pickles.

Bercy
Name of a noted French sauce ; Espagnole enriched with wine and butter, with lemon juice, shallots, parsley and meat glaze to give added flavour.

Bergamot
A perennial herb valued for its aroma, which resembled the bergamot orange. Known in the U.S.A. as Oswego tea, a beverage at one time quite common.

Berny (Fr.)
Name of a French garnish, comprising potato croquettes and small tartlet cases filled with a purée of lentils and topped with shredded truffle.

Berrichonne (Fr.)
A garnish comprising small onions, chestnuts, sliced bacon and Brussels sprouts.

Betel Nut
The seed of the betel palm tree, chewed for its pungent taste in the East Indies. It stains the lips, teeth and mouth. It is about the size of a nutmeg.

Betterave (Fr.)
See Beetroot.

Beurre (Fr.)
See Butter.

Beurre, au (Fr.)
See Au Beurre.

Beurre Blanc (Fr.)
White butter (sauce).

Beurrée (Fr.)
Buttered.

Beurre Fondu (Fr.)
Melted butter.

Beurre Noir, au (Fr.)
Cooked in butter until browned.

Beverage
That which is commonly drunk, any pleasant mixed liquor.

Bicarbonate of Soda
Sodium carbonate or baking soda. Bi—twice ; carbonate— a salt formed by the union of carbonic acid with a base. (See also Carbonated Beverages.)

Bière (Fr.)
Beer.

Biestings
Same as Beestings (which see).

Bifsteck (Ger.)
Beefsteak.

Bifteck (Fr.)
Beefsteak.

Bigarade (Fr.)
Name of an orange sauce made with Espagnole flavoured with the juice and rind of bitter oranges.

Bigarreau (Fr.)
White-heart cherry.

Bigarreaus Confits (Fr.)
Preserved cherries with the stalks left on. They are marinated in boiled vinegar and salt for 3 weeks and served as an hors d'œuvre.

Bigorneau (Fr.)
See Periwinkle.

Bilberry (Myrtille, Fr.)
A dark-blue, or almost black berry, being the fruit of a small shrub, the whortleberry or blaeberry. Large quantities are gathered on the Surrey and Sussex Downs. See also Blaeberry.

Bill of Fare
The menu (which see).

Bin
A place where bottled wine is stored and kept in a cellar.

Bind
To moisten with liquids, eggs or melted butter, to hold it together.

Bird's Nest
An ingredient of certain Eastern soups. The nests consist essentially of mucus secreted by a small species of swallow, found chiefly among the islands of the Indian Ocean and along certain parts of the Chinese coast. The value depends upon the colour and purity—those silvery-white and free from feathers being most sought after.

Biriani
A dish of Indian lamb stew.

Biscaïenne, à la (Fr.)
Biscay style. Morue Salée Biscaïenne—salt cod cut in dice, partly fried in oil with garlic, chopped onions, tomatoes, dressed in layers with pimiento and garnished with croûtons.

Biscuit
(1) A kind of brittle, small, flat cake or bread.
(2) Thin, dry, brittle cakes.
The term " biscuit " is a French word which signifies twice-cooked, as in the operation of making rusks to give length to their keeping qualities.

Biscuit Glacé (Fr.)
Ice cream wafer, or biscuit.

Bishop
Port and sugar made hot with spices and orange steeped in it. A favourite drink of the Middle Ages.

Bisk
In ancient times a dish made of wild and tame birds mixed with aphrodisiac accompaniment—no longer sought after.

Bismark Herring
See Herring.

Bisque (Fr.)
Name applied to a wide variety of shellfish soups or stews.

Bitokes (Bitochky)
Russian meat cakes or balls.

Bitter (Amer, Fr.)
Acrid to the taste.

Bitters
Aromatised alcoholic beverages containing a bitter substance or substances, used as tonics, appetisers or digestives. The bitterness being imparted by such substances as cascarrilla, angostura, quinine, quassia, cinchona, bitter orange rind, rhubarb and gentian, the most common in use being angostura bitters (which see).

Bivalve
Having two shells which open and shut, as the oyster, cockle, etc.

Blackberry (Mûre de Ronce, Fr.)
A plant of the bramble species, being a prickly shrub, its fruit being of black colour when ripe ; the berry itself is used for jams, jellies and pies.

Blackbird (Merle, Fr.)
Blackbirds are in season November to the end of January. They are seldom eaten in England to-day, being one of the foods which were only tolerated for want of a wider range of fare. Guests of the Middle Ages would not have been surprised at four and twenty blackbirds fluttering from a pie, as after all they were not baked—only the crust would be baked and the live birds placed in afterwards. Pies were baked in such manner for this favourite conceit. Sometimes the pie would contain a dwarf, who stepped out to amuse the company by his antics.

The male bird is recognisable by its black plumage and orange bill, the female being a dusky brown and the beak also dark. Blackbirds should be skinned and not plucked. The skin is slit down the backbone and around the leg and wing joints. The skin is then removed complete with feathers.

Black Cock (Coq de Bruyère, Fr.) The black cock, black game or black grouse, is abundant in the Scottish Highlands. At first, the plumage is the same in both sexes, but later the cock changes to a rich, glossy black, shot with blue and purple, the eyebrows being a bright vermilion and destitute of feathers. It reaches a weight of about 4 lbs. The female usually only weighs 2 lbs. and is known as the grey hen or brown hen. Its plumage is of a russet brown colour, irregularly barred with black.

If not well hung, the bird is hard, dry and flavourless, but the flavour is remarkably fine when it has been kept until it shows the symptoms of being hung long enough. Pick and draw, but do not wash the inside. A dry cloth will be all that is necessary. Truss as a fowl.

Blackcurrant (Groseille Noire, Fr.) A bush fruit, bearing a small black fruit of the grape class. (See currant.)

Blackfish
The name applied to various dark-coloured fishes. In England it is a scombroid fish, shaped like a perch and reaching 2 feet in length. (Scombroid—fishes typical of the family to which mackerel and tunnies belong.)

Black Game, Black Grouse
See Black Cock.

Black Jack
Burnt sugar—boiled with water to form a black syrup for colouring soups and sauces. See Caramel.

Black Pudding (Boudin Noir, Fr.) Sausage made of pig's blood, suet and oatmeal.

Blackstrap
Molasses of a poor grade. (See Molasses.)

Blackthorn
The sloe (which see).

Blaeberry
Blae is Icelandic. In Scotland, the iceberry. (See Bilberry.)

Blaireau (Fr.)
See Badger.

Blanc (Fr.)
White. (See Blonde de Veau.)

Blanc, au (Fr.)
White, with white sauce.

Blanch (Blanchir, Fr.)
(1) To remove skins from fruit or nuts by allowing them to stand in boiling water from 1 to 5 minutes, then draining, rinsing in cold water, and slipping off skins.
(2) To reduce strong flavour or set colour of food by plunging into boiling water.

Blanchaille (Fr.)
See Whitebait.

Blanchir (Fr.)
The slow simmering of liquid foods to throw off the scum.

Blancmange
A white sweetmeat composed of arrowroot, milk, sugar and flavouring substances.

Blanquette (Fr.)
A veal or poultry stew served in a white sauce.

Bleak
A small, fresh-water fish of the carp family.

Bleu, au (Fr.)
See Au Bleu.

Blinis
A buckwheat cake served with caviare, peculiar to Russia.

Bloater
The larger-sized fat herring salted, smoked and half dried. Smoking fish consists chiefly of hanging salted fish in wood smoke. No additions can be made to kippers and bloaters, save pats of fresh butter and perhaps mustard sauce for the bloaters. These fish are best when grilled over an open fire. They are also good when properly fried.
A Yarmouth bloater is considered better than any other, because the herrings are in prime condition during October and November, the time they arrive at Yarmouth during their travels along the East Coast.

Bloater, Red (Hareng Saur, Fr.)
See Herring, Red.

Bloater, White (Hareng Salé, Fr.)
See Herring, White.

Blond (Fr.)
Light-coloured, as Blonde de Veau, white broth.

Blonde
A large type of ray, common to the south coast of England.

Blonde de Veau (Fr.)
Highly concentrated veal broth, used for the better white soups and sauces. A white stock.

Blook Pudding
See Black Pudding.

Blubber
The fat of whales and other sea animals.

Blueberry
The name given in North America to the bilberry, huckleberry or whortleberry. (See Bilberry.)

Blue Cheese
See Danish Blue cheese.

Blue Dorset, Blue Vinney
A hard, white cheese, with a blue vein right through. Made in Dorsetshire from skimmed cow's milk.

Blue Points
A large type of oyster, best suited for cooking.

Boar
The name given to the male of the domestic pig.

C

Boar's Head (Hûre de Sanglier, Fr.)
A traditional English Christmas dish, served at Court and other banquets for many years. Now no longer boned and stuffed when sold commercially, but cooked in moulds. (See Hûre de Sanglier and Wild Boar.)

Bœuf (Fr.)
Beef.

Bœuf Braisé (Fr.)
Braised beef.

Bœuf Fumé (Fr.)
Smoked beef.

Bœuf Fumé de Hambourg (Fr.)
Smoked Hamburg beef sliced thinly like smoked salmon.

Bohémienne, à la (Fr.)
Bohemian style. As a garnish it comprises stoned olives, mushrooms, button onions, olivette potatoes, served in Poivrade sauce.

Boil, to (Bouillir, Fr.)
To cook in liquid, usually at boiling temperature. The boiling point is reached when bubbles rise continuously and break at the surface. The boiling point of water varies with altitude. At sea level it is 212°F., and decreases about 1°F. for every 500 feet of elevation. For instance, at 1,000 feet elevation, water boils at 210°F.; at 3,000 feet elevation, 206°F.; at 5,000 feet elevation, 202°F. The boiling point increases under pressure of enclosed steam, and foods cook in less time at 5 lb. pressure, when boiling point is 228°F. At 10 lb. pressure it is 240°F. At 15 lbs. pressure, it is 250°F. (See also Boiling.)

Boiler
A vessel in which anything is boiled in large quantities.

Boiling
In the general culinary acceptance of the word, this is the simplest and (when properly performed) the most economical method of cooking, as the cooked flesh and accompanying broth represent practically the entire nutritive value of the raw food.
In the cooking of meats, boiling should be restricted to the first 5 minutes only—after that it should be reduced to slow simmering at a temperature of 180°F. to 190°F. The first few minutes boiling coagulates the albumen in the surface of the meat, forming a kind of protective envelope, which prevents the escape of an excessive amount of the minerals, blood, etc., into the water. Then the simmering cooks it sufficiently, but leaves it tender ; the heat which reaches the centre is sufficient to develop the flavour but is not high enough to harden it. Only just sufficient water to cover the food should be used, and the pan should always have its lid on, in order to prevent loss by evaporation, as the food must be kept fully covered with water.

Simmering of sauces takes place at 205°F. to 210°F. or just below boiling point, which is 212°F.

No exact rules can be given as to time required to boil foods properly, as size, age, and heat generated, all take their part, but moderate care and judgment will nearly always suffice as guides.

When a strong broth, such as a chicken broth, is desired more than the meat itself, the meat or bird should be put into cold water, to allow the flavour and nutritive ingredients to escape into the water. The water is then brought to the boil slowly and thereafter simmered until the meat is cooked. So remember—to retain the flavour in the meat, plunge into boiling water, allow to reboil, then lower to simmering point ; to produce broth, start off in cold water, bring slowly to the boil, then reduce to simmering point (See also Boil, to.)

Boitelle (Fr.)
This French term, when coupled with the name of any fish, denotes that chopped mushrooms have been cooked with it.

Bologna Sausage
An Italian sausage speciality made of veal and pork. Principally made at Bologna, from whence it takes its name.

Bombay Duck
A familiar name for the bummalo, a small fish about the size of a smelt. It is caught in great quantities off the Indian coast, and dried and used with curry dishes, also canned as a relish.

Bombe Glacée
A pudding or ice cream frozen in moulded form, usually in the shape of a melon or bomb.

Bonbons (Fr.)
Small sugared confections.

Bond
A store in which goods are kept under Customs and Excise supervision before duty has been paid.

Bon Goût (Fr.)
Good taste. Denoting highly flavoured.

Bonne-bouche (Fr.)
A small savoury or cocktail dainty.

Bonne Femme (Fr.)
Good woman — housewife style. Crème Bonne Femme consists of leek and sorrel soup garnished with chicken quenelles.

Bonnefoy (Fr.)
Name of a French sauce, comprising Sauce Bordelaise with chopped tarragon added at the moment of serving.

Bonvalet (Fr.)
Name of a cream soup. Crème Bonvalet, which is a cream of turnips garnished with green peas, haricot beans and leeks cut julienne style.

Borage (Bourrache, Fr.)
A herb with hairy leaves and stem, bearing bright blue flowers, used principally in salads and the "cup which cheers". Allied to the forget-me-not.

Bordeaux (Fr.)
City and seaport of South-West France. This city is the centre of the trade in Bordeaux wines and is the fourth largest town of France. "À la Bordeaux" usually conveys flavoured with the wine of Bordeaux.

Bordelaise, à la (Fr.)
A rich brown sauce flavoured with Bordeaux wine.

Bordure, en (Fr.)
With a border—of rice, mashed potato, etc.

Borecole
Borecole and kale are the same ; a popular winter green. (See Kale.)

Borshch (Borscht, Bortch, Borsch, Bortsch)
The name of the Ukrainian national soup, made with soured beetroot. Often confused with the Russian national soup, which is Shchi. The Russian Embassy in London give the correct spelling " Borshch ".

Bottle (Bouteille, Fr.)
A container to store or carry liquids. The generally accepted standard of contents is of $26\frac{2}{3}$ fluid ounces for wine, or 6 to the gallon.

2 bottles	=	1 Magnum
4 ,,	=	1 Jeroboam
6 ,,	=	1 Rehoboam
8 ,,	=	1 Methuselah
12 ,,	=	1 Salmanazar
16 ,,	=	1 Balthazar
20 ,,	=	1 Nebuchadnezzar

Bouchées (Fr.)
Tiny savouries and hors d'œuvre titbits, to be eaten in one mouthful. The centres of the small pastries are scooped out and filled with fish, poultry, meat or game.

Boudin Noir (Fr.)
A very small French black pudding type of sausage.

Bouillabaisse
A famous French (Provençal) fish stew, made of several kinds of fish, cut into small pieces and stewed with olive oil and a variety of herbs and spices.

Bouilli (Fr.)
Meat stewed with vegetables ; boiled or stewed meat of any kind. From the French bouillir, to boil.

Bouillon (Fr.)
A liquid extract made from beef, veal or fowl, and widely used as an appetiser. Usually left unclarified. Bouillon, French for broth (which see).

Bouillon Cube
A small cube of meat or chicken extract used with water to make bouillon.

Boulanger
The Frenchman who establish-
ed the first restaurant in France.
Also the French equivalent for
baker. (See Introduction to the
Master Menu and Recipe Book.)

Boulangère (Fr.)
Style of garnish consisting of
Lyonnaise Potatoes cooked
with the food.

Boule (Fr.)
Ball.

Boulettes (Fr.)
Very small meat balls.

Bouquet Garni (Fr.)
Bouquet of herbs. A small
bundle or " faggot " of various
pot herbs such as thyme, parsley, marjoram, tarragon, bay
leaves, tied together during
cooking, to assist their easy
removal after use.

Bouquetière (Fr.)
Style of garnish which calls
for as many fresh young vegetables as possible arranged in
groups alternately round the
dish of a large roast.

Bourbon
Whisky distilled from maize.

Bourdalouse, à la (Fr.)
Bourdalou style.

Bourgeoise (Fr.)
A style of garnish for roast
joints, consisting of small
shaped carrots, glazed onions
and chopped bacon.

Bourgeoise, à la (Fr.)
" Citizen cooking ". In simple,
family style.

Bourgogne, à la (Fr.)
Burgundy style. Usually with
Burgundy wine.

Bourguignonne, à la (Fr.)
Style of a garnish incorporating
braised button onions, mushrooms with rolled and grilled
bacon, served in Burgundy
or Bordeaux wine sauce (which
see).

Bouride (Fr.)
A soup similar in character to
the Bouillabaisse, strongly
flavoured with garlic, but containing no saffron, as in the case
of Bouillabaisse.

Bourrache (Fr.)
See Borage.

Bouteille (Fr.)
Bottle (which see).

Brabançonne, à la (Fr.)
Brabant style. Brabant Potatoes—small pared potatoes parboiled in salt water, drained and
baked in a moderate oven,
basting frequently.

Brabant
A duchy which existed from
1190 to 1430, later united with
the Duchy of Burgundy. À
la Brabant—Brabant style. (See
also Brabançonne, à la.)

Brace
A pair, a couple. A brace of
birds usually comprises 1 hen
and 1 cock bird.

Bragance (Fr.)
Style of garnish—small tomatoes (chats) filled with Sauce
Béarnaise and served with croquette potatoes.

Bragget
An old-fashioned spiced ale.

Brains (Cervelles, Fr.)
All kinds of animals' brains are esteemed as delicacies, the calf's being those most sought after.

Braise (Braiser, Fr.)
To smother. All foods cooked gently, with little added water, in a closely covered pot. In this way the food flavour and juices are retained. A combination of roasting and stewing.

Braising
Braising is a popular French method of cooking foods, first brought to England by the celebrated chef A. Carême, in the early part of the 19th century. It is a combination of roasting and stewing. At one time, special braising pans were used, and considered the only proper method of braising foods. To-day, with modern stoves, all this hocus-pocus has changed.
Small joints or birds are first heated and browned on all sides in hot fat and the pan usually lined with a " Mire-poix ", a layer of diced or sliced bacon or ham, vegetables, herbs, etc. Stock or water is then added sparingly, the pan closely covered, sometimes by a sheet of buttered paper, or by strips of paste, to prevent the escape of steam. The whole may be left, as a stewpan, almost to take care of itself, in a slow oven. The result is a very savoury and aromatic dish.

The gravy or juices obtained by this method of cooking should always be strained and used as the foundation for the sauce to accompany the meat to table.

Bramble
See Blackberry.

Bran
The ground husk of the grain used as a feeding stuff for cattle and horses.

Brander
The name given to the gridiron in Scotland. Brandered Haddie —grilled haddock.

Brandy (Cognac, Fr.)
A spirit distilled from wine of the grape. (See also Liqueur Brandy and V.S.O.)

Brandy Snaps
Very thin gingerbread biscuits rolled on sticks while hot, when cold removed from the sticks and filled with brandy cream.

Brasserie
A popular type of restaurant. In France, any beer garden or saloon.

Brassica
The family name for all vegetables of the cabbage variety— cabbage, cauliflower, broccoli, sprouts, etc.

Brawn
Usually pork trimmings, seasoned and spiced and cooked in a mould ; other meats may be treated in the same manner but are considered inferior to pork brawn. Always eaten cold.

Brazil Nut (Noix de Brésil, Fr.)
The seed of a large tree which grows throughout tropical America to a height of some 130 ft. The seeds are triangular in form, enclosing the " kernel ", each of which contains 18 to 25 nuts.

Bread (Pain, Fr.)
The name given to the staple food product prepared by the baking of flour, water, yeast and salt, with the addition of malt, fat, milk and other improvers in the more civilised parts of the world. The earliest forms of bread were prepared from crushed acorns and beech nuts and certain Indians do to this day eat a cake prepared from crushed acorns.

Bread, Pulled (Pain Tiré, Fr.)
The crumb of a loaf of bread, pulled to convenient sized pieces while it is still hot, and baked in a hot oven until golden crisp.

Bread, to
To cover with breadcrumbs, preparatory to cooking.

Bread Fruit
A globular fruit of the bread-fruit tree, which when roasted forms an excellent substitute for bread. In size, it is nearly as big as a man's head.

Bread-nut
The fruit of a tree common to Jamaica, which when roasted is used as bread.

Bread Sauce
The typical English sauce served with almost all poultry and game birds. Made with milk, onion, seasoning, butter, and thickened with fresh breadcrumbs. When cloves are added, they drown all other flavours.

Breakfast (Déjeuner, Fr.)
The first meal of the day—a break or breaking of a fast.

Bream (Brème, Fr.)
The carp bream is a handsome fish, but of very little gastronomic value, being a freshwater fish. The Sunday Express of 15 November, 1948, contained an account of a bream being caught in the Thames weighing 8 lb. 3 oz. reputed to be the largest caught to date.
The sea bream is a very delicate fish and is usually served grilled or broiled, as it does not take too well to boiling.

Breast (Poitrine, Fr.)
Part of the animal immediately below the neck or throat.

Brehan (Fr.)
Style of garnish for joints—artichoke bottoms filled with a purée of broad beans, and small pieces of cauliflower masked with Hollandaise, placed alternately around the dish.

Brème (Fr.)
See Bream.

Brésilienne, à la (Fr.)
Brazilian fashion or style.
Potage Brésilienne—leeks, turnips, carrots, onions, tomatoes, chopped and cooked in butter, moistened with veal stock and mixed with a purée of black haricot beans and garnished with rice.

Bressans
A goat milk cheese, best served February to September.

Breteuil, Baron de
A noted epicure of the reign of Louis XVI. Many French dishes bear his name.

Bretonne, à la (Fr.)
As originating from Brittany. Brittany style. A garnish consisting of haricot beans in parsley sauce. Bretonne Sauce consists of minced onion sauté, reduced with white wine, flavoured with tomato purée, garlic and parsley.

Brew
To prepare a liquor as from malt and other materials.

Brewer
One whose business is to brew malt liquors.

Brewing
The manufacture of the alcoholic beverage beer, mainly from malted barley, hops, sugar and water. In the Middle Ages it was the chief drink for breakfast, dinner and supper—tea, coffee and cocoa being very little known at that time, and not at all in England.

Brewis
Dry crusts of bread soaked in salted hot milk and beaten up.

Bride or **Wedding Cake** (Gâteau de Noce, Fr.)
The cake which is served out by the bride's parents for the guests at a wedding.

Brie (Fr.)
A fermented and refined soft French cheese. Made in the Brie district of France. Excellent in the winter months, but not usually served in summer.

Brill (Barbue, Fr.)
A flat fish closely resembling the turbot. It is of real gastronomic value, but is generally regarded as inferior to the turbot. When served whole, it can be treated in the same manner as turbot ; and in the same manner as sole, fried or poached, when served as fillets. Brill is also good served cold with mayonnaise.

Brillat-Savarin
See Savarin.

Brin (Fr.)
Sprig.

Brindisi (It.)
A toast—a drinking song. A call often made in Italy and often mistaken for the name of a drink.

Brine (Marinade, Fr.)
Water strongly impregnated with salt, for the salting or pickling of meats.

Brinjaul
See Egg Plant.

Brioche (Fr.)
A popular French breakfast bun. The lightness encourages its use in England for use as savoury filled rolls.

Brioche, American
Unlike the French brioche rolls the American brioche is more of a sweet rich cake and is flavoured with crushed cardamon seeds, in appearance more like Danish pastry, being brushed over with hot water icing or hot jelly or preserve.

Brisket (Brisquet, Fr.)
The breast of an animal, usually applied to beef. It is one of the choice cuts for pickling and pressing.

Bristol Cream
A fine Oloroso sherry.

Bristol Milk
Extra superior golden sherry.

Brittany Sauce (Sauce Bretonne, Fr.)
See Bretonne.

Broad Beans (Fèves de Marais, Fr.)
The broad, flat, furry pods contain 5 or 6 kidney-shaped beans, and when cooked and dressed in parsley sauce go well with a dish of home-cured ham. They are excellent served cold with salad.

Brocard (Fr.)
The young roebuck.

Broccoli (Brocoli, Fr.)
The winter cauliflower. It is less compact than the true cauliflower and the leaves are smaller.

Broche, à la (Fr.)
Roasted or broiled on a skewer.

Brochet, (Fr.)
Pike (which see).

Brochette, en (Fr.)
Cooked on a skewer before an open fire, or cooked on a skewer under the grill.

Broil
To dress or cook over a fire, either directly or on a gridiron. To subject to strong heat as on a grill.

Broiling, Application of
Only small or very young tender birds or parts of meat are suitable for this type of cooking, which is the principle of old-fashioned roasting applied to smaller pieces of meat or poultry. Broiling requires a utensil called a "gridiron", still to be found in many Scottish hotels, where kippers are cooked over an open coal fire, but south of the Border, usually found in antique shops. The gas or electric grill has been found to answer the city dweller's requirements. The important points to be taken into consideration are:
1. The gridiron must be kept dry, clean, and well greased. It is seldom washed, being wiped with clean paper to remove any bits and pieces and then rubbed over with a butter paper before putting it away.
2. The fire must be clear and bright, not a trace of smoke should be seen. Thus, the timing in stoking the fire plays a great part.

3. Sprinkle the meat or poultry with seasoning before putting it on the gridiron and brush with melted butter or good culinary oil.

4. Cook the outer shell quickly, to seal the food on all sides, to avoid loss of juices. Do not used a fork for testing the meat.

5. Avoid excessive fat dropping into the fire, or this results in spluttering, smoky flames which are liable to spoil the flavour of young birds or game.

6. Do not overcook—which tends to dry the food with resultant loss of flavour.

Brose
A Scottish dish, made by pouring hot water or milk over oatmeal and stirring till it has the consistency of Hasty Pudding, being a thin type of sweetened porridge.

Broth (Bouillon, Fr.)
A liquid obtained by boiling or stewing meat, poultry or game in water, always unclarified (see Bouillon).

Brouillé (Fr.)
Mixed, scrambled.

Brown Butter (Beurre Noir, Fr.)
Butter heated till it is nut brown.

Browning
Usually caramel made by boiling sugar till brown, or flour browned in the oven.

Brûlant (Fr.)
Alight, burning hot, to set aflame.

Brûlé (Fr.)
Burnt. Usually applied to caramelised sugar. As Crème Brûlée, being a gelatinised cream with a caramelised sugarcoating.

Brun (Fr.)
Brown.

Brunoise (Fr.)
From Brunoy, a district in France noted for its healthy spring vegetables. Garnished with finely cut spring vegetables, for soups, sauces, or garnitures.

Brussels Sprouts (Choux de Bruxelles, Fr.)
Records indicate the sale of Brussels sprouts in the markets of Belgium as early as the year 1213. It is a variety of cabbage which develops small heads or sprouts along the stem, about 1 inch in diameter. Now a very popular vegetable in England.

Brut (Fr.)
Natural, raw, unsweetened.

Bruxelloise, à la (Fr.)
Brussels fashion or style. As a garnish, it contains Brussels sprouts and braised chicory in rich brown gravy. Bruxelloise Sauce—a popular melted butter sauce which has lemon juice and chopped hard-boiled egg added to it.

Bubble-and-Squeak
Originally composed of minced salt beef mixed with chopped left-over cabbage and potato, and fried in cakes. To-day the beef has disappeared.

Bucherome (Fr.)
A garnish served with meat or poultry, consisting of small mushrooms, sliced pickled pork and boiled potatoes.

Buck
The male of the fallow deer and of rabbits, hares and goats.

Bucklings
Austrian smoked herring.

Buck Rarebit, or **Golden Buck**
A Welsh Rarebit topped with a poached egg. (See Welsh Rarebit.)

Buckthorn
A shrub reaching 10 ft. in height, bearing a fruit black and globose, which contains 4 seeds. The fruit has purgative properties.

Buckwheat
A herbaceous plant, native of Central Asia. The seeds are employed as human food, chiefly in the form of buck-wheat cakes. It resembles the beech nut in shape.

Buffet
A refreshment bar.

Bull
The name chiefly applied to the uncastrated male of the domestic ox.

Bullace
A small, wild plum, the colour of a damson, but smaller in size.

Bullace Gin
A gin flavoured with bullaces.

Bullock
A castrated bull; a full-grown steer.

Bull's Eyes
An old-fashioned peppermint flavoured sweetmeat, striped black and white. A favourite sweet for English children.

Bully Beef
A term applied to canned corned beef.

Bumbo
An American punch made of spirits, etc.

Bun
A class of small, light, sweet cakes, usually of the fermented character, such as Bath Buns, Swiss Buns, Chelsea and Hot Cross Buns.

Bung
A large cork or stopper used for closing the hole in the side of a cask.

Bung-hole
The hole in the side of a cask through which it is filled, the bung or stopper being thrust home to close it.

Burbot (Lotte, Fr.)
See Lote.

Burdock (Bardane géante, Fr.)
A dock with a prickly head; the juice extracted from the seed case is used for dandelion and burdock wine.

Burdwan
An Indian dish of curried poultry, meat, or game.

Burgundy

Burgundy is the name applied to both red and white wines made within the limits of the Côte d'Or, the Saône et Loire and the Yonne, which at one time were within the province of Burgundy in France. (See Bourgogne.)

Burgundy Sauce (Sauce Bourguignonne, Fr.)

Minced shallots, parsley, thyme, bay leaves, mushroom stalks, reduced with red wine and thickened.

Burnet (Pimpernelle, Fr.)

A herb the leaves of which have a flavour suggesting cucumber, used for flavouring soups and salads.

Burnt Sugar

Sugar treated for making colouring—Black Jack.

Burton

The name applied to beer or ale brewed at Burton-on-Trent. A Burton.

Bushel

A dry measure capacity of 8 gallons or 4 pecks. Used for measuring corn, potatoes, etc. The weight legally established in Great Britain is equal to 80 lbs. distilled water determined at 62°F. with the barometer at 30 in.

Bustard

A large game bird.

Butcher

One thoroughly experienced in the handling of meats, with a knowledge of the different qualities, for cutting and trimming meat for cooking.

Butler

One who acts as the chief male servant of a household.

Butt

A cask of 108 English gallons.

Butter (Beurre, Fr.)

The fatty substance obtained from cream or milk by churning. Melted butter (beurre fondu, Fr.) is used in many sauces. (See also Au Beurre.)

Butter Fat

The fatty constituent of cow's milk.

Butter Fish

A small fish caught along the Atlantic Coast of the U.S.A. Being of very delicate flavour, it is much esteemed.

Butterine

A name sometimes applied to butter substitute, such as margarine.

Buttermilk (Babeurre, Fr.)

The liquid remaining after the removal of the butter from cream by the churning process.

Butter Nut

The fruit of the North American white walnut. It has a pleasing buttery flavour and is used extensively in the manufacture of caramels and candies.

Butter-Scotch
A kind of toffee containing butter.

Buttery
Formerly a house for storing butts of wine (boterie, Fr.). In recent years, by confusion with "butter", it has become a place for storing food, and now the name is applied to a place where food is served.

Buvette (Fr.)
Refreshment bar or room.

Byrrh
A French aperitif or tonic wine.

C

Ca Banh Ran
A famous Indo-China dish, consisting of fish roes, steeped in wine and fried as fritters.

Cabaret (Fr.)
A tavern; a house where liquors are retailed. An inn.

Cabbage (Choux, or Chou, Fr.)
Cabbage is a leaf vegetable available all the year round in every part of the country and probably comes next to the potato in the quantity consumed. It is found in more than 70 varieties. All members of the cabbage family contain 91% to 92% of water. Compared with other green vegetables, they are relatively high in protein. Those with green leaves have a good percentage of vitamin A. (See also Savoy Cabbage.)

Cabbage, Red (Chou Rouge, Fr.)
A dark red cabbage chiefly used for pickling, rarely used as a vegetable as in most European countries which we might well copy.

Cabillaud, (Fr.)
See Cod.

Cabus (Fr.)
Headed, as applied to cabbages. (See Broccoli.)

Cacao
The scientific name for the bean of the cacao tree. From its seed the products cocoa and chocolate are made.

Cacciatori (It.)
Name of an Italian dish of chicken, jointed and cooked in casserole, well-flavoured with onion and garlic and served in a rich tomato sauce.

Cachou
A small, scented sweetmeat.

Caddy
A small package of tea. A small box for keeping tea.

Café (Fr.)
Coffee. Also name at one time given to a coffee house, now applied principally to places where light refreshments are served, ironically enough generally a tea-shop and not a coffee-shop. (See Coffee.)

Café au Lait (Fr.)
Coffee served with hot milk.

Café Noir (Fr.)
Black coffee.

Caffeine (or Thein)
The stimulating principle of coffee, tea, made cocoa, etc. It is interesting to note that native races widely separated on the face of the globe, discovered and adopted a beverage containing the same stimulant.

Caffeol
An aromatic oil developed during the roasting process of coffee.

Caille (Fr.)
See Quail.

Caisse (Fr.)
Case (soufflé or ramekin case). Served in a paper case.

Cake (Gâteau, Fr.)
The ingredients determine the nutritive value of cakes, but all are high in caloric value. Generally a mixture of flour, eggs and sugar for sponge cakes, with butter and dried fruits added for richer cakes. Usually sponge cakes are devoid of baking powder. (See also Wedding Cake.)

Calamondin
A citrus fruit resembling a small tangerine, with a delicate pulp, more like the lime in flavour.

Calf
The young of the cow.

Calf's Foot Jelly
A jelly made from the gelatinous substance extracted from the calf's feet, by long simmering. It is a delicate and stimulating jelly, especially when flavoured with brandy or wine.

Calf's Liver (Foie de Veau, Fr.)
See Liver.

Calf's Sweetbreads (Ris de Veau, Fr.)
See Sweetbread.

Calf's Tail (Queue de Veau, Fr.)
See Tail.

Calipash, Calipee
See Turtle.

Caloric
A punch made and bottled in Sweden.

Calory
The large or kilo calory: the amount of heat needed to raise 1 kilogram of water from Zero to 1°C.
The small calory: the heat needed to raise 1 gram of water 1 degree centigrade.

Calvados
Fine apple brandy.

Cambacérès (Fr.)
Jean Jacques Regis de Cambacérès, Duke of Parma (1753–1824), was a famous French statesman and celebrated gourmet. His dinners were utilised by Napoleon as a useful adjunct to the arts of statecraft. Crème à la Cambacérès is a rich creamy soup of pigeon and crayfish.

Camembert (Fr.)
Cheese made in the district of Camembert, France, being of the fermented and refined variety.

Campari Bitters
Extract of capsicum, not so pungent as angostura.

Canapés (Fr.)
Tiny sandwiches, open, closed or rolled, or bits of bread toasted or fried, combined with piquant foods. Much used for hors d'œuvre and savoury dishes.

Canard (Fr.)
See Duck.

Canard Sauvage (Fr.)
See Wild Duck.

Cancale (Fr.)
A fishing port of north-western France much noted for its oysters. À la Cancalaise—in the style of Cancale. Consommé à la Cancalaise—a fish consommé, garnished with oysters, julienne of sole, and quenelles of whiting.

Candied Peel
The sugared and candied skins of lemon, orange or citron.

Candy
The American term for all types of sugar and chocolate confectionery. There are the hard-boiled candy, such as barley sugar and lemon drops ; open fire candy, as pulled sugar rock ; creams, such as low-boiled sugar beaten to a creamy consistency ; caramels and nut candy ; fudges, plain or with fruit or nuts. The American candy shop is the equivalent to the English sweet shop.

Cane Sugar (Sucrose)
Cane was originally the only source from which this widely known form of sugar was obtained. First grown in India and frequently mentioned in the sacred writings of the Hindus. (See also Sucrose and Sugar.)

Caneton (Fr.)
See Duckling.

Canneberge (Fr.)
See Cranberry.

Canned
Foods preserved in cans and sterilised by heat — canned goods.

Cannelle (Fr.)
See Cinnamon.

Cannelons (Fr.)
Savoury rolls of puff pastry filled with fish, meat, poultry or game.

Cantaloup
A variety of musk melon. See also, Melon, Sugar.

Canteen
At first a travelling store or shop selling drink and food to troops. Canteens are now established in ships, factories and large offices.

Canvas Back Duck
A North American wild duck. Its name refers to the zigzag white, grey and black feathers on its back.

Capercailzie (Capercalzie, Fr.)
The capercailzie (cock o' the woods) is quite plentiful in northern Scotland. It is the largest member of the grouse family, but unfortunately has a habit of feeding on pine needles, which give it a turpentine flavour. The young birds, after feeding on the fruit and leaves of the bilberry and other such plants, and before the pine needles begin to fall, are at their best September to November. They should be drawn as soon as shot and hung at least a week—longer in cold weather. The male bird is remarkable for its size and dark plumage, with the breast metallic green. The hen bird is much smaller and mottled in colour. In season August to December.

Capers (Câpres, Fr.)
The flower buds of the caper bush growing in Mediterranean countries. After picking, they are carefully dried and stored in barrels of brine or vinegar with herbs. They are later bottled and used in flavouring sauces and pickles. The bush itself resembles a bramble.

Caper Sauce (Sauce aux Câpres, Fr.)
Creamy sauce to which white wine, vinegar and capers are added.

Capilotade (Fr.)
A culinary term for a mixed hash or stew. Generally a stew of cooked chicken.

Caplin or **Ice Fish**
A small fish very abundant off the shores of Newfoundland. It is principally used for bait in cod-fishing, some are dried for human consumption.

Capon (Chapon, Fr.)
A male chicken castrated when young to improve its weight and the flavour of its flesh. Capons grow larger, with well rounded bodies. They can be distinguished by the pale and shrivelled appearance of the combs and the undeveloped condition of the spurs. They are usually superfed in solitary confinement and killed when not more than 9 months old. Spring-reared birds are at their best for the Christmas table. Some farmers specialise in caponization and can arrange regular supplies.

Capons, to be tender, should be killed a day or two before they are dressed, and in cold weather 3 to 4 days should be allowed in between killing and cooking. When the feathers can be pulled out easily, the bird is ready for the oven. They should be prepared in the same way as turkeys, for cooking, stuffings and sauces.

Câpre (Fr.)
See Capers.

Capricot
Apricot brandy liqueur, of golden colour.

Capsicum

The capsicum includes several varieties of large and small peppers—red pepper, paprika, the small kind known as chili and numerous others. The fruit is extremely pungent and is used in sauces, mixed pickles, etc. When dried and ground, it is called Cayenne Pepper (which see).

Capucine (Fr.)

Indian cress or nasturtium. (See Nasturtium.)

Carafe (Fr.)

A glass water bottle or decanter.

Carafon

A small carafe or decanter, containing ordinarily about $\frac{1}{2}$ pint.

Carambola

A fragrant Asiatic fruit ranging from the size of a hen's egg to that of a large orange. It has a smooth thin skin. Its flavour varies from acid to sweetish, eaten both raw and cooked.

Caramel

Liquid burnt sugar, used for colouring and flavouring.

Carapace (Fr.)

Shell.

Caraway (Cumin, Fr.)

Highly aromatic fruit or " seeds ", deep brown in colour, of a plant which grows wild in Holland and northern Germany. They have a spicy flavour. In Germany they are especially popular for flavouring bread and in Holland for cheese, while in England they are principally used in confectionery called seed cakes.

Carbohydrate

A class of organic compounds as sugars, gums, pectin, starches and cellulose, so called because in them the hydrogen and oxygen are in the same ratio as they are in water. Glucose and sucrose are typical carbohydrates. With the exception of cellulose, their function is to supply energy and heat to the body.

Carbonade (Carbonnade, Fr.)

Braised or stewed meats.

The term originally meant half burned or grilled. Now applied to entrées usually consisting of braised loin of mutton or pork.

Carbonated Beverages (Soda Water)

Beverages rendered sparkling by impregnating them with carbon dioxide (" carbonic acid gas ") under pressure. The carbon dioxide is produced preferably from bicarbonate of sodium.

Many spring waters, carbonated by nature, have important medicinal properties. Carbonated water is always cooler as a beverage than plain water held at the same temperature, as the escaping gas carries off part of the heat stored in the water. (See also, Aerated Water and Mineral Waters.)

Carcase, Carcass (Carcasse, Fr.)
The dead body of an animal ; the framework or skeleton of a bird.

Cardamom (Cardamome, Fr.)
The fruit of a reed-like plant native to the mountains of the Malabar coast of India. Used in making curries and confectionery. Their flavour merits a more general use. (See also, Grains of Paradise.)

Carde
The edible portion of the cardoon. (See Cardoon.)

Cardinal
Denoting scarlet, as coral or lobster sauce dusted with cayenne pepper.

Cardoon (Cardon, Fr.)
A plant similar to the common artichoke, of which the stalk leaves are eaten as a vegetable. Some varieties attain a height of 8 to 10 feet, with leaves often 3 feet or more in length. The stalks of the inner leaves, bleached till white, are crisp and tender.

Carelet
See Flounder and Witch.

Carême, A.
Chef to King George IV, and after with M. Rothschild, an author of many culinary works. Many dishes are named after this famous chef.
When Carême returned to France, George IV offered to double his salary if he would come back to his services. He declined, for while in England he was greatly discouraged. He took back to France the art of skinning a sole which he admitted he learned while in England.

Caret (Fr.)
The green turtle.

Carmelite
À la Carmelite—Carmelite style. In England, Carmelites are called White Friars, being one of the four mendicant orders. There are in all some 2,000 Carmelite friars, and the nuns are much more numerous. À la Carmelite is applied to fish dishes. It would be a great mistake to apply it to any meat dishes.

Carmine (Carmin, Fr.)
A rich crimson-red pigment prepared from the cochineal fly, used for colouring confectionery. (See Cochineal.)

Carnivorous
Flesh-eating.

Carolina Tea
See Yaupon.

Carotin
A substance found in the colouring matter of butter and carrots. A precursor of vitamin A in the animal body.

Carp (Carpe, Carpeau, Fr.)
A young carp is called in French " carpeau ", and a very young one " carpillon ". Carp spend much of their time on muddy bottoms and banks, and an unpleasantly muddy flavour is

often noticeable in pond fish taken in the summer months. This can be eradicated by keeping the live fish in fresh water for a few days. Where this is not practicable, the result can be obtained almost equally as well by skinning and then soaking in mildly salt water for 3 to 4 hours, as a great part of the muddy flavour lies in the skin and the fat immediately beneath. Only the smaller fish should be fried.

Carp roe is consumed as a cheap grade of caviare. Its pink or red tint distinguishes it from true caviare.

There exists a species of carp, almost devoid of scales, known as leather carp, because of its thick skin.

Large specimens weigh from 15 to 18 lbs., and may live to a great age, when they may weigh 40 lbs. or more.

Carpentras, à la (Fr.)
Carpentras style. Usually this name denotes that truffles are embodied in the dish in some form. Carpentras truffles are just as famous as those from Perigord so that dishes styled à la Perigueux are nearly identical to those styled à la Carpentras.

Carragheen or **Carrageen**
A species of small edible seaweed, also known as Irish Moss. The plants are washed and bleached several times and when marketed the greater part of the supply is employed in the clarifying of malt beverages. It is much used in Ireland for making a kind of milk jelly.

Carré (Fr.)
The neck part of lamb, mutton, pork and veal.

Carrelet (Fr., or Carelet)
See Flounder.

Carrot (Carrotte, Fr.)
A colourful root vegetable with a pleasing bland flavour. One of our most wholesome vegetables. Its food value is greater than its 88% water content. Its sugar content runs from 5 to 10%. It is noteworthy for its vitamin content—a good provider of calcium, phosphorus and iron.

Carte, à la (Fr.)
See À la Carte.

Carte du Jour, la (Fr.)
The day's bill of fare—a priced list of dishes.

Carver
One who cuts meat for, or at, table. A large table knife used for carving.

Cascara
A mild cathartic made from the bark of the California buckthorn. Often given for habitual constipation.

Caseine
One of the most easily digested forms of protein, it being the curd of milk from which cheese is produced. It supplies all the acids necessary for the body tissue.

Casha
A favourite Indian dish, a light flavoured type of cream made from buffalo's milk.

Cashew Apple
A pear-shaped fruit with a bright yellow or scarlet skin, which is easily bruised. It is used for preserves and distilling beverages. The seed, which hangs from the end of the apple, is the familiar cashew nut.

Cashew Nut
A kidney-shaped nut, the fruit of the cashew. Because of the thick caustic acid present, they are always roasted before eating. They are nutritious and their flavour resembles that of almonds. They are excellent salted.

Cassareep
The juice of the bitter cassava, or manioc. It is boiled to the consistency of thick syrup and used as a base for sauces. (See Cassava, also Manioc.)

Cassava
Known in the West Indies as manioc. The roots of this large woody plant, when fully refined, are utilised in many commercial products, including compressed yeast, tapioca, etc. (See also Manioc.)

Casserole
To cook in an earthern, covered dish, in the oven.

Cassia Bark (Cannelle de Chine, Fr.)
See Cinnamon.

Cassia Buds
The dried flower buds of the tree which yields cassia cinnamon. In appearance they somewhat resemble cloves.

Cassis
A liqueur with the flavour of blackcurrant, almost black in colour.

Cassolette (Fr.)
Small casseroles to hold individual portions.

Castillane (Fr.)
Name of a style of garnish consisting of small tomatoes (chats) cooked in oil, placed on the tournedos and surrounded by fried onion rings and croquette potatoes.

Catalo
A cross of the bison, or buffalo, with domestic cattle. It was at one time acclaimed as a means of increasing the meat supply, by producing heavier beef animals.

Catchup
The word comes from the Amoy-Chinese " koechiap " or " kitsiap ", the brine of pickled fish or shellfish. The name is now applied to products having the juice of edible fungi as their base, and a number of different sauces which consist of pulp—boiled, strained, and seasoned—of various fruits, as tomatoes or green walnuts, or of a thick purée of oysters or other shellfish. Catsup, catchup, and ketchup are a few of the several spellings of the word.

Cater
To buy, provide, or procure food, entertainment, etc.

Caterer
One who caters ; one who provides for any want or desire.

Cateress
A woman who caters.

Catfish
A familiar name for a number of fish which are so styled because of some resemblance, real or fancied, to the cat— such as barbels about the mouth, giving the effect of a cat's " whiskers ", or a purring sound when caught. A number of them are excellent food— their flesh being of fine appearance, flavour, and high nutritive quality. Some attain great size, of 100 lbs. and upwards. The biggest of all catfish is the European sheat fish, which reaches a length of 10 feet and a weight of 400 lbs.

Catsup
One of the many spellings of catchup or ketchup. (See Catchup.)

Caudle
A hot oatmeal drink. A kind of gruel.

Caul (Crépine, Fr.)
A pig's membrane, used for wrapping baked minced meats, faggots and sausages.

Cauliflower (Chou-fleur, Fr.)
A cabbage in which the flower-buds and flower-stalks form a compact white mass, or " curd ", this constituting the vegetable proper, instead of the leaves. Its flavour is not so strong as that of most cabbages, it being delicate and highly prized.

Caviare (Caviar, Fr.)
Caviare is the salted roe of various large fishes of the sturgeon genus. Nearly all the world's supply comes from the rivers of the Caspian and Black Seas and the Sea of Azoff. The finest quality is that from the comparatively small seurage and sterlet species.

Beluga Caviare is the largest, but does not keep.
The finest quality of caviare is salted with a proportion of 2 to 6 lbs. to each 100 lbs. of roe, while the coarser, cheaper grades contain up to 10% of salt. The real test of caviare is its flavour, and this is as often found in the small as in the large grain, and in the black as in the other colours, which may be one of various shades of yellow, grey, dark green, and brown. The gold colour is considered the choicest in Russia ; it is the most rare and therefore the most expensive.
Caviare is generally eaten on bread or toast, with oil, lemon juice or vinegar, and various garnishes. It is also occasionally served on ice, as a special course at luncheon and dinner parties. When fresh, the taste is rather like that of oysters.

KETOVAIA CAVIARE is the roe of the dog salmon. The grain is pink and large, but is not as good as real caviare.

MOCK CAVIARE is made by pounding boned anchovies with a clove of garlic, then mixing with the paste lemon juice, salt, cayenne, and a few drops of salad oil. It should be served spread thinly on bread and butter or toast.

CAVIARELLE is a paste of cod roe.

Cavour (Fr.)
Name of a style of garnish consisting of small semolina croquettes, ravioli and thin strips of noodle paste.

Cavy
See Guinea-pig.

Cayenne Pepper
A hot, red, pungent powder, made from the dried and ground seeds of several species of peppers of the capsicum class.

Céleri (Fr.)
See Celery.

Celeriac (Céleri rave, Fr.)
A kind of celery, cultivated chiefly for its large turnip-like root plant. It is cooked chiefly as a vegetable. Also used in soups, stews and salads.

Celery (Céleri, Fr.)
Celery was first used in Europe as a herb. It is better eaten raw and dressed in a salad, than cooked. Cooked, it is served up in various ways as a vegetable and in soups.

Celery Salt
The ground seeds of the celery plant, plain or mixed with stoved salt. Used as a condiment for flavouring.

Célestin (Fr.)
The Célestines were recognised as a branch of the Benedictines, Célestin being a monk so named after Pope Célestin. From the Latin cœlestic (heavenly). À la Célestine, several dishes bear this name. Dishes of exquisite character.

Centigrade
A thermometer divided into 100° between the boiling and freezing points.

Centigramme
A measure of weight; the hundredth part of a gram; 0.15432 gr. troy.

Cerasella
A delicately flavoured Italian cherry liqueur.

Cereals
Agriculturally speaking, cereal grains with the exception of buckwheat belong to the grass family. The dry seeds will keep for years, without deterioration, in a clean dry place. The cereal grains most commonly used for food are wheat, corn, rice, oats, rye and barley. The word cereal is derived from the name of the Roman goddess Ceres (see below).

Ceres
Goddess of the growth of food - plants. Worshipped in ancient times with the god Cerus over a considerable part of Italy.
Ceres was regarded as the patroness of the corn trade.

Cerf (Fr.)
Red Deer. (See Deer.)

Cerfeuil (Fr.)
A herb. (See Chervil.)

Ceriman (or False Bread Fruit)
A fruit with a pleasing, aromatic flavour resembling a combination of banana and pineapple. The greenish-yellow husky skin is tender and easily removed.

Cerise (Fr.)
The cherry (which see).

Cervelles (Fr.)
See Brains.

Chablis
A town of north-central France, which gives its name to the famous white Burgundy wine.

Chafe
To warm by friction.

Chair à Saucisse (Fr.)
Sausagemeat.

Chair Blanche (Fr.)
Chair—flesh. White meat.

Chair Noire (Fr.)
Dark meat.

Chambord, à la (Fr.)
Chambord is a village of central France, standing in the park of Chambord, which gives its name to the method of cooking fish à la Chambord, in court bouillon au vin blanc with mushrooms.

Champagne
The name of a former province of France and the name of the most famous of all sparkling wines, made within a strictly limited area of the said former Champagne province.

Champagne Fine
The name by which some cognac brandy is known.

Champignons (Fr.)
Mushrooms.

Chancelier, à la (Fr.)
Chancellor style. Consommé Chancelier consisting of chicken broth garnished with royale, peas, shredded mushroom, chicken and truffles.

Chantilly, à la (Fr.)
Chantilly, a town of northern France. Chantilly style, usually with cream, as Chantilly is famous for its rich cream.

Chap
The jaw (see Bath Chap).

Chapelure (Fr.)
Brown breadcrumbs.

Chapon (Fr.)
See Capon.

Chaponneau (Fr.)
Young Capon.

Char (Poisson Rouge, Fr.)
All recipes applicable to trout are suitable for this great delicacy. It is peculiar to the lakes of Cumberland, and is seldom offered for sale in the London market. Its name means red, and its belly is red. The flesh is rather like that of a trout. Weight from 1 to 2 lbs. the head being nearly one-sixth of the whole body. The different stages and varieties are known in this country by the names Case Char, Gilt Char, Red Char, Silver Char. The red char are those most frequently caught.

Charcuterie (Fr.)
Cooked cold meats. Usually refers to cooked dressed meats made ready for a buffet or side table.

Chard
A variety of cabbage—a name given to sea-kale.

Charlotte (Fr.)
A cream or fruit mixture in a case of biscuits or crisped slices of bread, as Apple Charlotte, Charlotte Russe, etc. The mould or dish is lined with biscuits or thin slices of buttered bread and filled with cream as a cold sweet, or fruit to be baked. A corruption of the old English word "charlyt", meaning custard.

Charolaise, à la (Fr.)
Charolles style. Charolles is a town of east-central France, the capital of Charolais, noted for being the centre for trade in the famous breed of Charolais cattle. À la Charolaise should, therefore, only be applied to good beef dishes or beef consommé. Never to the fish course, as is so often the case.

Chartreuse (Fr.)
A sweet liqueur originally made in Voirons in France, until the monks were turned out. Now made in Spain. The secret of the recipe is closely guarded. Made in two colours, yellow and green. The name is also applied to fruits, vegetables, poultry or game, shaped in a mould of jelly, with the centre filled with cream.

Chasseur (Fr.)
A chaser, a hunter. With, or of, game. From the famous Chasseurs of light infantry or cavalry regiments who hunted for their food in forest or on mountain heights. Hunters' style. Sauce Chasseur consists of minced shallots and mushrooms sauté, reduced with white wine, enriched with meat extract and parsley.

Chat (Fr.)
The smaller sized tomato used for garnitures.

Châtaigne (Fr.)
See Chestnut.

Châteaubriand
Viscount Francois Auguste Châteaubriand was born at St. Malo on 4 Sept., 1768, died 4 July, 1848. French author and a great gourmand. The favourite dish of a double fillet steak is named after him.

Château Potatoes

Quartered potatoes with all sharp corners rounded off, cooked a few moments in butter in a sauté pan and then roasted in an oven. Used extensively to garnish roast meats.

Châtelaine (Fr.)

Name of a style of garnish consisting of artichoke bottoms and tomatoes with château potatoes and braised celery.

Chauchat (Fr.)

Name of a style of garniture for fish dishes, consisting of a border of sliced potatoes masked with Mornay Sauce.

Chaud (Fr.)

Warm.

Chaudeau (Fr.)

A light sweet sauce.

Chaudfroid (Fr.)

Hot-cold. The name applied to cooked meats, poultry or game, which, when cold, are masked with cold sauce, decorated and glazed with aspic jelly.

Chaudron (Fr.)

Calf chitterlings.

Chaufferette (Fr.)

A chafing dish.

Chauffroiter (Fr.)

To decorate with Chaudfroid Sauce.

Chayote (or Mango-squash)

A pear-shaped vegetable with a single large edible seed, varying in colour from almost white to dark green. The flesh is firm, crisp and delicately flavoured. They can be plain boiled or used in pies, puddings, or as fritters.

Cheddar

A rich fine-flavoured cheese made at Cheddar in Somerset.

Cheese (Fromage, Fr.)

A product made from the casein of milk, together with part (or nearly all) of its fat. The hard kinds are cooked and subjected to high pressure. Those subjected to less pressure have many gas holes or " eyes ". There are more than 400 varieties available, of which only a minor part are in general use. Cheeses are divided into 3 classes, hard, soft and processed. They are made from all types of milk, cow's, sheep's, ass's, goat's, etc.

Cheese may be produced by curdling the milk by souring alone, by souring and rennet, or by rennet alone.

Cheese is one of the most concentrated sources of protein, a superior source of calcium, and phosphorus, and a good source of iron.

Cheesecake

A tartlet made of light puff pastry, filled with a mixture of cheese curds, sugar and butter.

Chef-de-Cuisine (Fr.)

Chef, in French, is a chief or head person—head cook—chief of the kitchen.

Chemise (Fr.)

Lined. With the skin on.

Chemiser (Fr.)

To coat or line a mould with aspic or ice cream, etc.

Cherimoya

A sub-tropical fruit cultivated in South and Central America. It is brownish-yellow on the outside and similar to a custard apple inside, its flesh being white and juicy. It varies in size from 3 to 12 inches in diameter.

Cherry (Cerise, Fr.)

Of all the 300 varieties or more, the black morella is the most favoured for cooking, while for the dessert the white-heart is most esteemed. In vitamin A content, cherries are higher than apples, grapes or pine-apples.

Lucullus is credited with bringing a tree laden with fruit to Italy to mark his triumph over Mithridates, King of Pontus, 68 B.C.

Cherry Brandy

An English liqueur, also made in other countries. There are two kinds, dry and sweet.

Cherry Gin

A liqueur with cherry flavour.

Cherry Whisky

A liqueur, dark red in colour, and strong in alcohol.

Chervil (Cerfeuil, Fr.)

An aromatic herb with a mild flavour, similar to parsley. Only the young leaves should be used for flavouring purposes. Curled chervil has more eye appeal than parsley, but is more perishable.

Cheshire Cheese

One of the oldest types of English cheese. It is a hard cheese, made in two colours, red and white. The red obtains its colour artificially, and sometimes it matures and develops blue veins as in the Stilton. In this stage, the Cheshire Cheese is considered at its best. The white has a much milder flavour than the red.

Chesky

Cherry whisky distilled in France.

Chestnut (Marron Châtaigne, Fr.)

Chestnuts are one of the starchiest nuts (42%) and are preferred in stuffings because they are less fat than other nuts. Originally called " acorns of Sardis " because they were first known in Sardis, Lydia. They contain up to 15% of sugar. They should be well roasted, steamed or boiled, to make them easy of digestion.

Chevalier, à la (Fr.)

Chevalier style. Chevalier of the Legion of Honour, Chevalier of St. George, are but two of the famous Legions that have given their names to the field of culinary terms.

Chevreuil (Fr.)

Roebuck. Also name of a sauce consisting of Sauce Poivrade stewed with venison bones, red wine and herbs. Usually served with venison.

Chevreuse (Fr.)

Name of a style of garniture for tournedos and noisettes con-sisting of artichoke bottoms filled with a purée of mush-rooms and topped with sliced truffle, served with noisette potatoes. Named after a dis-tinguished French statesman.

Chewing Gum

Chicle is now almost universally employed as the chief ingredi-ent, having superseded spruce gum and refined paraffin wax, etc. Chicle, being a gum, is obtained from the latex secreted by the bark of a tree, Achras sapola, the sapodilla tree. Mexico and Central America are the main sources of supply. Chewing gum aids digestion by stimulating the secretion of saliva. (See Sapodilla.)

Chianti

A popular Italian dinner wine.

Chicken

BABY CHICKENS are known in culinary French as " poussins ". Next come SPRING CHICKENS and COCKERELS, known in culin-ary French as " poulets de grain " and " poulets reine ".
FAT FOWLS are known as " poulardes ".
BOILING FOWLS are known as " poules ".
Baby Chickens (poussins) weigh ¾ lb. to 1¼ lbs.; Spring Chickens (poulets), 2½ lbs. to 3 lbs. ; Fat Fowls (poulardes), 3½ lbs. to 4 lbs. ; Boiling Fowls (poules), 4 lbs. and over.

The age can be determined by:
1. The lower tip of the breast bone, which in a young bird should be as flexible as the human ear, becoming brittle at a year or so and hard and tough when older.
2. The feet are soft and smooth in young and hard and rough in old birds.
3. Claws will be short and sharp in young, but larger and blunt in the older bird.

Chicken Halibut

Young, small halibut, under 10 lbs. in weight.

Chicken Turbot

See Turbot.

Chick Pea

Said probably to be the pulse of the ancient Hebrews. The fruit of a pea-like plant, grow-ing one or two in a pod, larger than the common pea, roundish, flattened on two sides. There are a number of varieties—white, black and red. The white are the best.

Chicle

See Chewing Gum.

Chicory (Chicorée, Fr.)

A salad vegetable belonging to the dandelion family. The root is used as a vegetable, and the leaves as a salad. When raw, the root is white and fleshly, but roasted it resembles roasted coffee. It contains no caffeine. Added to coffee in the pro-portion of 1 oz. to the pound, it makes it go farther by adding colour and body.

Chiffonnade (Fr.)
Literally vegetables in rags. Long shreds of vegetables.

Chili
Several types of small fruit capsicum, used ripe or unripe, in pickles. They are largely consumed in hot countries, especially in Mexico, where Chili Con Carne is a highly prized dish.

Chili Con Carne
A popular Mexican dish, whose chief components are beef, beans, chilies, garlic and spices.

Chill
To place food in a refrigerator or in a cold place, but not freezing.

Chilled (Refroidi, Fr.)
Food or drink brought below room temperature but not frozen.

Chine
The 2 undivided loins of pork of a young pig, which correspond to the saddle of mutton. When butchering the larger pig for bacon, the name is given to the spine and the 2 inches of meat attached to either side.

Chinese Mustard
A plant grown for its tufts of succulent root leaves, popular as a Chinese green vegetable.

Chinois (Fr.)
A conical strainer usually made of perforated tinned steel and used for straining soups and sauces when using a tammy cloth.

Chipolata
Originally an Italian ragoût of small sausages. Now applied to small sausages made in sheep casings, used chiefly as cocktail savouries.

Chitterlings
The cleaned and boiled intestine of ox, pig and calf.

Chives (Ciboulettes, Fr.)
Chives are cultivated principally for their leaves, which grow in thick tufts, 6 to 8 inches high. They can be cut freely, for new leaves quickly replace those taken. The entire plant is used for flavouring, as it is much stronger in flavour than green onions.

Chocolate (Chocolat, Fr.)
Made from the seeds of the cacao tree ; the term cocoa is a corruption of " cacao " (a Spanish adaptation of the Mexican " cacauat "). The seeds in the fresh stage are very bitter ; the flavour of the finished paste, cake or powder depends largely upon the roasting process. Too little roasting leaves the beans crude and unflavoured and too much will make them bitter. The cocoa-nibs designated for each blend are filled into heated " grinders " which reduce them to a thick oily liquid. The liquid is cooled to proper temperature, run into moulds and chilled to hard cakes, as the chocolate we know.

Choisi (Fr.)
Choice, excellent.

Choisy (Fr.)
Name of a garnish consisting of braised lettuce and château potatoes.

Chop
As applied to meat, it is a cut from the loin of mutton, lamb or pork.
When applied to Chinese tea, it signifies the grade—first chop.

Chopine (Fr.)
Half bottle—see Bottle, for all sizes.

Chop Suey (Chinese)
A thick stew with varying ingredients. Its main ingredients consist of bean sprouts, bamboo shoots, mushrooms, rice, noodles. These are finished off with chicken, lobster, etc., as—Chicken Chop Suey, Lobster Chop Suey, etc.

Chou (Fr.)
See Cabbage.

Chou-au-lard (Fr.)
Cabbage cooked with bacon. Sautéed in bacon fat, as tossed cabbage.

Choucroute (Fr.)
Pickled cabbage, the sauerkraut originating from Germany. (See Sauerkraut.)

Chou de Bruxelles (Fr.)
See Brussels Sprouts.

Chou de Mer (Fr.)
See Sea Kale.

Chou-fleur (Fr.)
See Cauliflower.

Chou-rave (Fr.)
See Kohl-rabi

Chou Rouge (Fr.)
See Cabbage, Red.

Choux Paste
A rich, boiled paste into which as many eggs as possible are incorporated, for use in the manufacture of cream buns, éclairs and petits choux. The name is so applied because of the cauliflower-like appearance of the paste when baked as for cream buns.

Chow-Chow
A mixture of pickles of various sorts, especially mixed vegetables in mustard, which are seasoned with strongly flavoured aromatic spices. Originally a Chinese sweetmeat consisting of ginger, orange peel, and numerous other articles put up in a thick syrup.

Chowder
Chowders are the most popular of American soups. The word " chowder " was supposedly coined by Chinese navigators, who called the Indian stews " Chow ", so it is said. Obviously, this must have been mistaken for " Chou Chou ", which is a Chinese term for any mixture.

Christmas Pudding (Pouding de Noel, Fr.)
The following formula has gained several gold, silver and bronze medals at important exhibitions, and is given in full as a typical example of culinary art and the science of food as it is approached to-day. Note carefully how each step in its

manufacture is carefully carried out to ensure a perfect combination of ingredients, the exact timing of its cooking and its ultimate use.

Make your Christmas puddings three weeks before Christmas. Black, bitter Christmas puddings make me shudder ! They are unpalatable and a waste of time and materials. The really good plum pudding is a deep chocolate in colour, has a tempting delicate aroma, and is not stodgy in texture.

Many a good pudding is utterly ruined by over-cooking, which causes caramelisation of the fruit sugars, which go black and have a horrid, bitter taste. Ingredients, also, are often bought at random and are sometimes unsuitable for the purpose. Choose fruit of a low iron content for best results. Don't use any old bread, and certainly not too old (a very big mistake). The bread should not be from a batch which has been over-proved, as this has a sour smell when a day or two old. Choose from a batch that has a smooth, silky texture and is not more than two days old. Bread that is too old and dry will absorb all the moisture from the other ingredients just as old dry crumbs will make bread sauce like putty.

Never use candied peel. It is too hard, and, again, will absorb moisture from the other ingredients.

Use flour sparingly when chopping the suet, as too much will cause the pudding to have a close texture. Otherwise flour is unnecessary for good puddings.

MIXED SPICE

As bought mixed spice is often unreliable in composition, try making up your own from the following :

2 oz. ground nutmeg
1 oz. ground ginger
2 oz. ground cinnamon.
$\frac{1}{2}$ oz. ground cloves

Mix very thoroughly and store in an airtight tin.

PUDDING RECIPE

Here is a straightforward recipe, sufficient for six 2-lb. puddings :

1 lb. 8 ozs. chopped suet
2 lb. crystal Demerara sugar
2 lb. medium Vostizza currants
1 lb. 4 oz. stoned muscatel raisins
1 lb. 3 oz. Smyrna sultanas
6 oz. ground sweet almonds
12 oz. cut, mixed, moist peel
$\frac{1}{2}$ oz. mixed spice
2 medium sized lemons (rind and juice)
2 medium sized oranges (rind and juice)
$\frac{1}{4}$ pint milk
2 lb. fresh breadcrumbs
8 oz. brandy or whisky
14 eggs.

Don't use old beer—it is an old wives' tale ! Use spirits and put life into your puddings.

Place the fruit and all dry ingredients, including the spice, into a large bowl and mix well.

Make a bay and add the grated rind and juice of the oranges and lemons. Next add the eggs and milk, draw in part of the ingredients, then add the brandy and complete the mixing. Weigh off into basins that have been greased with melted lard, place a greaseproof paper cover over each and tie over with a cloth.

Hints on Cooking

Steam steadily for 7½ to 8 hours. Do not submerge the puddings in water and boil them, as this only takes the goodness out of them. If using a pressure steamer, set it at 6 lb., and with a water steamer see that the water is steadily on the move before putting the pudding in. Do not steam for more than 1½ hours when reheating.

For a really good, full-flavoured pudding, try this method of forming an emulsion of part of the fruits :

Use exactly the same recipe with 1 lb. extra sultanas. Mince very finely all the raisins, cut peel and the 1 lb. extra sultanas using the finest mincing plate you have. Break this mass down with the fruit juices and brandy. Add the mixture just before the eggs and proceed in the usual way. When you have once tried this method you will never go back to putting all the fruit in whole. Three-pound puddings should be steamed for 9½—10 hours.

After Cooking

When the puddings are cooked, uncover and allow the steam to escape. As soon as the steam is nicely away cover the puddings lightly with sheets of greaseproof paper. Next day recover and tie up with clean cloths and store for no more than 2 to 3 weeks for best results.

Chub (Cheverne, Fr.)

Chub is a common fresh-water fish. It is watery in texture when cooked and is full of bones. If you take the trouble to cook any of this fish, then do so the very day it is caught, making sure to clean the throat from grass and weeds, which are usually in it.

Chufas or Earth Almonds

Chufas mature underground like pea-nuts. They rank high in nutrient qualities and their nutty flavour makes them equally pleasing raw and baked, fresh and dried.

Chulan Blossoms

Flowers used to flavour Pekoe tea (which see).

Chupatty

The staple native bread of upper India, it is an unleavened flat-shaped cake of coarse wheat flour, which is baked on a griddle.

Chutney

A sweet pickle, generally based on mangoes, and highly seasoned. Other kinds have a number of chopped vegetables, with the addition of raisins, ginger, chilies, spices, etc. Chutneys are most suitably served with curries, stews, and sausages.

Ciboulette (Fr.)
See Chives.

Cider (Cidre, Fr.)
The juice of apples, both fermented and unfermented. The flavour and general quality of any and all types of cider depend both on the fruit employed and the skill in preparation. Hard cider is that which has been fermented until the sugars are changed to alcohol.

Cinnamon (Cannelle, Fr.)
The thin inner bark of the cinnamon tree. The bark is dried in quill-like rolls, is pale brown in colour, and has a fine aromatic flavour, making it a popular adjunct in cookery and confectionery. Ceylon cinnamon is of a pale yellowish brown colour, and is cleaner and smoother in appearance than cassia, which is the outer bark and the cheaper type of cinnamon.

Citrange
A fruit produced by crossing the inedible Japanese orange with the common sweet orange. The citrange resembles an orange in general appearance, but is more tart and the skin is bitter. The juice is used in beverages.

Citrange-quat
A fruit produced by crossing the kumquat with the citrange and used extensively in marmalade, because of its bitter skin and acid juice.

Citric Acid
A white, crystalline acid, obtained chiefly from citrus fruits. A gallon of lemon juice contains from 8 to 10 ozs.

Citron
A fruit imported chiefly from Palestine. It is oblong, of a greenish-yellow colour, and very fragrant. The rind is candied or preserved. In glacé or candied form the thick spongy skin is popular in cakes and preserves. The acid juice is expressed and used much as is lime juice.

Citrus Fruits
The fruits characterised by a thick rind or skin, which protects the fruit from injury. All have a high citric acid content and a high percentage of vitamin C. Lemons, limes, oranges, tangerines, grapefruit, etc.

Civit or Civette (Fr.)
A brown stew of game, usually of hare or venison. (See jugged.)

Clam (Clovisse, Fr.)
There are clams, and clams. In America, they are the most common shellfish, eaten fresh in enormous quantities, and also extensively consumed in canned form.

There are certain kinds found on the west coasts of Ireland and Scotland, and some parts of Wales. They are not much used in England, but people living on the sea shore might make several by no means un-interesting dishes from them. Soyer says that they are much superior in flavour to the oyster and if eaten raw should be about the same size ; but, if larger, they should be made into soup or cooked in the same way as the oyster.

Claret
The name by which the red wines of Bordeaux are known among the English-speaking people. The excellence of claret, and the reason why it may rightly claim precedence over all other wines, is that it is the most harmonious and natural of all wines.

Claret Cup
A beverage composed of iced clar-et, a little brandy, lemon, orange and other flavouring ingredients.

Clarification
A process by which clouded liquids are cleared, aspic and sweet jellies being clarified with white of egg or albumen. Soups and stocks are cleared with finely minced raw meat.

Clear Turtle (Tortue Claire, Fr.)
See Turtle for parts used in making Turtle Soup. Full directions for making Clear Turtle Soup are given in " The Master Book of Soups ".

Cloche (Fr.)
Under cover.

Clotted Cream
See Devonshire Cream.

Cloudberry
A soft, reddish berry, resemb-ling the raspberry, common in sub-arctic and arctic regions. It is of high anti-scorbutic value, both fresh and canned.

Clove (Girofle, Fr.)
The dried flower buds of the clove tree. They are reddish when plucked, but this changes to the familiar dark brown in the process of drying. The best come from the Island of Zanzi-bar. The clove tree bears two crops yearly, and may continue to do so until 100 years old.

Clovisse (Fr.)
See Clam.

Coalfish
The Scots have a better name for this fish—Saithe. It is closely related to the pollock, being a member of the codfish family. It is considered in-ferior to the cod, but is largely consumed, both fresh and salted. Big specimens will weigh 25 lbs. and upwards, and show a length of 3 feet or more. For cooking, use any of the recipes for cod.

Cobblers
An American name for long drinks made up of various wines served in tumblers with shaved ice and pounded sugar.

Cob-nut
See Filbert.

E

Cochineal (Cochenille, Fr.)

A natural dyestuff procured by pulverizing the dried female insect known as " coccus ", now obtained from Mexico, Peru, Algiers and southern Spain. The female is wingless and is found in proportion of 150–200 to one of the male. The best crop is the first of the season, which consists of the unimpregnated female.

Cochon-de-Lait (Fr.)

See Sucking Pig.

Cock-a-Leekie

Large quantities of this famous Scottish soup were consumed at the Burns Centenary Festival at the Crystal Palace, Sydenham, 1859.

It is hard to trace the origin of this famous soup. Some say it originates from the days of cock-fighting, the defeated cock being thrown into a pot, with leeks to give added flavour. The soup was then handed round with parts of the bird, to spectators. Another version is that in olden times, when the cock had passed its youth, the last purpose it served was the feast of " the Cock-a-Leakie ". However, it was, and still is, a grand dish if the bird is served in the soup.

Cockles (Coques, Fr.)

Cockles are a small shellfish. They are best roasted in a tin, laid on a stove, and eaten while hot with bread and butter and a little pepper and vinegar.

They may be dressed in all the ways (except frying) practised with oysters and mussels, and make quite good fish sauces in place of oysters and mussels, when these are not available.

Cocks' Combs (Crêtes de Coq, Fr.)

When cooked, cocks' combs are used for garnishing rich stews, ragouts, etc. They can be obtained preserved in glass jars.

Cock's Kernel (Rognon de Coq, Fr.)

See Rognon de Coq.

Cocktail

An appetiser. May be liquid (vegetable or fruit juice or alcoholic beverage), or solid (fruits or shellfish with sauce).

Cocktail Cherries

Generally sold marischino red and yellow and in curaçao or Menthe green.

Cocoa

Chocolate with part of the fat removed and pulverized. The fat being run off as cocoa-butter and the residue dried and milled, which then becomes cocoa in the powder form.

Cocoa-butter

The oil, or fat, extracted from the cocoa bean, used in confectionery and in the making of toilet preparations and cosmetics for theatricals. It will melt at body temperature and is used extensively as grease paint.

Coco-nut

The older spelling, cocoanut, is obsolete. The coco-nut is the fruit of the coco-palm and should not be confused with the bean of the cacao tree, from which cocoa is made. When fully ripe, the coco-nut contains only a small amount of milk, the bulk having coagulated to form the thick flesh, coco-nut meat. This meat contains some 35% of oil. The flesh is dried, when it is then called copra and used extensively in the manufacture of margarine.

Coco-nut Milk

The milk naturally developed in the ripe coco-nut, most of which coagulates to form the thick flesh of the nut. A tropical preparation is made by grating the flesh of the coco-nut and mixing with water and straining through cloth. This milk looks somewhat like cow's milk, and is drunk as a substitute for it in India, in addition to being used in cookery.

Cocotte (Fr.)

A small, individual earthenware fireproof pot, for cooking such dishes as Poulet en Cocotte, Œufs en Cocotte.

Cod (Cabillaud, Fr.)

Cod is one of the most abundant of food fishes found in all Northern seas. The average market weight is less than 10 lbs., but a good-sized specimen, or " steak cod ", will range from 20 to 35 lbs., and a big one up to 100 lbs. or more. This fish is extraordinarily prolific, the roe often containing from 2 to 8 million eggs and sometimes constituting a full half of the weight of the female.

Cod comes into season about the beginning of October, when other large fish are going out. If the weather is cold, it is then very good. It is at its best about Christmas. The best cod are those which are plump and round at the tail, the sides having a rubbed appearance, with yellow spots upon a pure skin. Cod meat can be distinguished from its occasional substitutes, the hake and pollock, by its whiteness and flakiness. The other meats are darker and tougher.

Cod, Salt (Morue Salée, Fr.)

Salt cod of all kinds has been, when possible, cured immediately after catching. The fish are first split from head to tail and then thoroughly cleaned of all traces of blood, by repeated washings in salt water. Part of the backbone is next cut out and the fish, after being drained as nearly dry as practicable, are placed in vats, or similar receptacles, and covered with salt, remaining thus until sufficiently cured. When the process has been completed, they are taken out of the vats, washed and brushed to remove superfluous salt, and placed to dry in the sun, spread out on wooden racks on the beach or elsewhere. They are considered fit for market when they show " bloom "—a whitish appearance on the surface. Salt cod is a most important staple food in all European countries, more particularly in Catholic countries during the Lenten fast and other meatless days, such as Ember days.

De-salted salt cod must never be boiled, as boiling will tend to make it tough and stringy. The water in which salt cod is cooked should merely " simmer ".

Codfish

Cod and codfish are all one and the same, but many people prefer the word codfish to just cod.

Codling (Petite Morue, Fr.)

Codling are small codfish and should not be referred to, or be confused with, whiting (which see).

Cod Liver Oil

Oil extracted from the liver of cod. One of the best sources of vitamins A and D.

Cod Sounds or Swim Bladders (Nau de Morue, Fr.)

These are popular delicacies. They are dried, salted and pickled, in addition to being eaten fresh. Usually cooked in milk like tripe. The pickled or salted sounds are well soaked before cooking.

Coffee (Café, Fr.)

The seed or berry of an evergreen tree. Every variety has a characteristic flavour and nearly all roasted coffee on the market is a mixture of 2 or more varieties which have been blended to improve flavour, or body, or both. Every blend of coffee can be treated in 9 different ways. It can be roasted high, medium or low ; each one of these roasts can be ground coarse, medium or fine. Thus, 10 blends of coffee can be treated in 90 different ways. There are at least 12 different ways of brewing coffee. No wonder we in England have difficulty in obtaining a uniform good coffee.

Cognac

The name of the brandy distilled from wine made in the Cognac district of France.

Cohune Nut

Containing up to 50% edible oil, used extensively in the manufacture of margarine. Oval in shape, up to $2\frac{1}{2}$ inches in length and $1\frac{1}{2}$ inches in diameter. The fruit of a Central American palm with an exceedingly thick shell.

Coing (Fr.)

See Quince.

Cointreau

The trebly distilled, colourless orange liqueur.

Cola-nut

One of the many spellings of Kola-nut (which see).

Colbert

Two famous dishes—Sole à la Colbert and Consommé à la Colbert—are in constant demand. The sole is named after Charles Colbert de Croissy, famous French diplomat, while the delicious soup is named after Jean-Baptiste Colbert, statesman of France in the reign of Louis XIV. Jean-Baptiste was the elder of the two brothers, born 1619, his brother Charles being born 1625. Charles died in 1696, nine years after his brother. The consommé is distinguished by being garnished with small poached eggs, while the sole is noted for its stuffing of maître d'hôtel butter placed inside just before being sent to table.

Colcannon

Originally a Scottish dish, it being a corruption of Kailcannon. Similar in character to bubble and squeak. Composed of potato and cabbage, chopped together, mixed with seasonings, shaped into round flat cakes, and baked in mutton fat.

Cole Slaw

Never to be pronounced cold slaw. Cole is a general type of brassica. Slaw has developed from the Danish word for salad. It is made from the raw heart of the cabbage, cut into long shreds and eaten with vinegar and seasonings, either cooked or raw, but most frequently eaten in the raw state.

Colewort

From the wild colewort all the cultivated varieties of cabbage have sprung. A variety of cultivated cabbage bears this name.

Colin (Fr.)

The Pollock (which see).

Collared

Meat, fish, poultry or game, pickled or fresh, tightly rolled into a pan like a large cake tin, boiled with suitable herbs and spices, pressed in the mould and served cold—as Collared Eels.

Collops (Escalopes, Fr.)

Thin, boneless pieces of meat, usually brushed with egg, dipped in breadcrumbs and cooked in a sauté pan, in clarified butter or fat, as Escalopes of Veal.

Comestibles

A term borrowed from the French, used in Continental Europe and England to embrace every class of edible goods.

Comfits

The original comfit was a grain or small piece of spice covered by successive coats of sugar. To-day, the term is applied to such sweetmeats as sugar-coated almonds, or distinctive centres coated in similar fashion.

Commissariat

A highly organised system for providing food for large numbers of people in groups or scattered places.

Commodore (Fr.)

Name of a style of garnish for fish dishes consisting of cray-fish tails, mussels and quenelles of fish.

Compôte (Fr.)

A " stew " of fruits, usually applied to fruits cooked slowly in syrup, which have retained their natural shape. Should not be applied to stewed or boiled fruits, which have split or burst and gone mushy.

Compressed Yeast

Was first introduced from Germany about 1862 and is the most powerful of all fermenting agents used in domestic life. Thousands of tons are used annually in this country, in the manufacture of bread. (See also Yeast).

Concasser (Fr.)

To chop roughly. A coarse mince.

Concombre (Fr.)

See Cucumber.

Condé

Name of some 20 villages in France, also of an old French family, Prince Louis de Condé (1530—1569), Prince Louis de Condé II (1621—1686). Many soup and sweet dishes are styled à la Condé, most of which have rice in some form as an ingredient—such as Pear Condé.

Condensed Milk

Both Switzerland and America make claim to have invented the first commercially success-ful process of condensing milk. Using the vacuum process, the milk is evaporated at a tempera-ture so low that there is com-paratively little change in chemical composition or flav-our. All the same, the C vitamins are largely destroyed in its preparation. So large is the industry, that in America alone there are some 450 fac-tories employed in its manu-facture.

Condiments

Condiments taken in modera-tion stimulate both appetite and digestion. Their excessive use tends to injure the stomach. Articles such as salt, pepper, mustard, vinegar, and all spices fall under the heading of condi-ments, taken with food to season or improve its flavour. Appetising and seasoning in-gredients added to food.

Confectionery

A word applied to sugar, candied fruits, and flour con-fectionery. A combination of sweet edibles, including pastry.

Conger Eel (Congre, Fr.)

The conger eel is a sea fish reaching a length of 7 to 8 feet. It is entirely scaleless, greyish or dusky brown in upper colour-ing and silvery below—the true sea serpent. The smaller con-ger eels are best, and while plentiful along the south coast of England, are not sufficiently appreciated. The flesh is wholesome and nourishing, and by no means unpalatable. When caught, it is usually wasted, an unreasonable prejudice existing against it. It can be cooked in several ways and in fact all recipes which are given for cod may be used for it. The head and tail are best for soup. (See also Eels and Elvers.)

Connoisseur
A critical judge of any art or matter of taste.

Conserve
To the working confectioner the term " conserves " means sugar and added ingredients cooked rapidly and carefully and without producing a grainy effect, such as in jam, fruit jellies, and the like.

Consommé (Fr.)
A rich, clear soup that has been boiled down. Made usually from a combination of meats.

Conti (Fr.)
Name of a style of garnish for joints consisting of a purée of lentils with diamond-shaped pieces of cooked bacon.

Contre-filet (Fr.)
Slices of tenderloin beef.

Cookery
Foods are cooked to sterilize them and to soften the tissues, thus making them more palatable and more easily digested. The fundamental principles of cookery may for general consideration be divided under the headings of baking. boiling, broiling, frying, parboiling, roasting, sauté, steaming, stewing (which see).
Proper methods of cooking retain a maximum of the nutrients, natural flavour, and appearance of foods. Improper methods reduce the nutritive value. Too high temperature toughens protein and causes decomposition of liquid fats. Too long cooking, or too much water in cooking green vegetables, dissolves out certain mineral salts and vitamins and makes the vegetables soft or mushy.

Coot (Fouique Morelle, Fr.)
The coot is a water bird, about 18 inches in length, sometimes weighing over 2 lbs. It is not much valued as food to-day, but before the age of canning (which widened our bill of fare) the coot was much sought after, costing at one time from 1/6 to 2/- each. It has a sooty-black plumage, and a characteristic of the adult bird is a bare white patch or callosity on the forehead. The toes are fringed by a lobed membrane. It should be skinned, not plucked, as soon as killed.

Copra
The dried meat of the coconut (which see).

Coq (Fr.)
The cock bird. Principally applied in culinary terms to Coq Noir—black cock.

Coq de Bruyère (Fr.)
See Black Cock.

Coques (Fr.)
See Cockles.

Coquilles
Coquilles—French for shells; the name of the filling follows that of coquille, such as Coquilles of Cod. Usually the deep scallop shell is used, filled with any and every sort of fish.

Coquilles Saint-Jacques
See Scallops.

Coral
The unimpregnated eggs or ovaries in the hen lobster, which when cooked turn red and are used in the making of sauces served with lobster.

Corbeau (Fr.)
See Rook.

Cordon Bleu (Blue Ribbon)
A term applied to an especially competent woman cook. The award, consisting of a medal suspended on a blue ribbon, cordon (cord), bleu (blue), originally represented the highest French order of knighthood, and was first conferred upon a female cook by King Louis XV (himself a great gourmet) at the suggestion of Madame du Barry.

Cordon Rouge
Originally the ribbon of the French order of St. Louis. Now a culinary distinction granted by an English society to clever cooks of both sexes and to others prominent in the invention of articles of food and drink, also to authors of culinary and gastronomic arts.

Core
To remove the heart, as in coring an apple or pear.

Coriander (Coriandre, Fr.)
Smooth, small, straw-coloured, seed-like fruit, the size of mustard seeds. They have a pleasant taste and smell, reminiscent of orange. They are used to flavour soups, curries, pastries and liqueurs.

Corlieu (Fr.)
See Curlew.

Cormorant (Cormoran, Fr.)
The adult bird is quite uneatable, having a dark rank flesh. The younger birds are much esteemed by the northern islanders. The cormorant squabs taste rather like hare when roasted, and are delicious when added to a game pie.
The Master of the Cormorants was one of the officers of the Royal Household. The practice of using cormorants for fishing is nearly obsolete in Europe.

Corn

The title " corn " is used in a general way to designate all the principal grains—as wheat and rye, also Indian corn, maize. In culinary terms, Corn on the Cob is always applied to Indian corn.

The seed of the Indian corn is one of the most beautiful and luxuriant of all grains and the most abundant in product. It has a high energy value, the endosperm is high in starch content, low in fat, while the germ is rich in fat and low in starch, having more fat than any other cereal except oatmeal.

Corncrake (Roi des Cailles, Fr.)

Like the coot, the corncrake was at one time held in high esteem, and in the 14th and 15th centuries it cost as much as a brace of partridges would fetch to-day. Its plumage is of various shades of brown on head and back, and of yellow-ish-white below. It was considered in season from the middle of August to mid-September, but to-day it is protected by law. It is cooked in the same manner as grouse.

Corned

The word " corned " originally signified meat preserved by dry salting, by being embedded in corns of salt (i.e. coarse salt) instead of being preserved by brining. Then, one spoke of a " corn " of sugar or sand, as well as a corn of salt.

Corned Beef

Beef that has been corned, or salted. The process of softening the fibres by first soaking in a solution of salt, sodium nitrate, sugar and spices, then boiling and canning.

Cornflour or Corn Starch

A refined starch prepared from Indian corn. It has a distinct flavour and has many commercial uses. It is one of the most readily and most easily digested of starch foods. In the process of manufacture it is freed from all fibre, dried in cakes, and then pulverized to the fine silky powder we know.

Cornichon (Fr.)

Gherkin. Sauce aux Cornichons is a purée of cucumbers blended with Béchamel sauce. (See Gherkin.)

Cornish Pasty

A torpedo - shaped pastry pinched high along its entire length and filled with meat, onions, bacon, parsley, etc. The true Cornish pasty has mutton as its base.

Cornmeal

A flour lacking in gluten, used extensively in South America and Mexico in cornmeal mush, corn pones and hoe cakes.

Corn Oil

Oil made from the germs of the grain. When pure, it is golden yellow and marked by a pleasing taste and aroma, somewhat suggestive of freshly ground grain.

Corn on the Cob
See Corn.

Corn Starch
The American term for corn-flour (which see).

Corn Sugar
Commercial dextrose or solid glucose (see Glucose).

Corn Syrup
See Glucose.

Cos Lettuce or Romaine
The tall, long-leafed variety of lettuce. If tied during the latter stages of growth, it is tender, crisp, and of fine flavour.

Costmary
See Alecost.

Côte (Fr.)
Meaning a piece of meat with a portion of the rib attached.

Côtelettes (Fr.)
Cutlets. Small slices of meat cut from the neck.

Côtes de Bœuf (Fr.)
Ribs of Beef.

Cotton Seed Oil
A 100 lbs. of cotton seed produces some 16 lbs. of crude oil. The refined oil is an excellent and inexpensive substitute for olive oil, and is used in packing sardines, as a salad oil, and for frying. " Choice " oil is of a light lemon colour and mild and neutral in flavour. Prime oil is slightly darker and is sweet in flavour.

Coulibac, Koulibiak
A type of fish cake cooked in a pastry case, much esteemed in Russia.

Coupe (Fr.)
A goblet or cup. A goblet or cup of fruit and ice cream is termed a Coupe St. Jacques.

Courgeon (Fr.)
See Vegetable Marrow.

Court Bouillon (Fr.)
The prepared stock for cooking fish, consisting of white wine, water and herbs, with onion and root vegetables added if desired.

Cow Heel
Cow heels are extremely nutritious, as, of course, are those of the ox, but when dressed for sale all are referred to as cow heels. They are excellent for making broths and stews for invalid cookery.

Crab (Crabe, Fr.)
A shellfish found in both fresh and salt water and obtainable all the year round. They are at their best from May to August.
Crabs multiply very rapidly—a female may produce as many as 3 million eggs. The meat principally eaten is that from the inner top of the back and the claws—less easily obtained than that of the lobster and in smaller quantity, but a good deal sweeter and more delicate. The centre of the body is filled mostly with the liver, a soft yellow substance which is not generally consumed, though connoisseurs consider it a delicacy, especially when mixed with the eggs, or " coral ".

SOFT-SHELLED CRABS are those which have just cast off their old shells in favour of the new ; the new shells, unlike the old, being markedly blue on top. One has to travel to America to enjoy soft-shelled crabs at their best.

" BUSTER ", or " SHEDDER " CRABS, are those in which the old shells are loose but have not yet come off. This is considered the choicest stage by many epicures.

Crabs have a high percentage of iodine and phosphorus.

Choose a crab of medium size and heavy ; the light crabs are watery. The male (cock crab) is the best for the table, and may be distinguished by its larger claws. When selecting a crab which has been cooked, it should be held by its claws and well shaken from side to side. If it is found to rattle, as if it contains water, the crab is of inferior quality. Preference should be given to those which have a rough shell and claws. The joints of the claws should be stiff, the shell bright red, and the eyes bright and firm.

Crab-apple (Pomme Sauvage, Fr.)
Crab apples vary from very small, up to an average of 1 inch in diameter. Their harsh, acid taste renders them almost inedible when raw, but they make delicious preserves, jellies and spiced pickles, Crab Apple Jelly being a great favourite when served with pork, duck or goose.

Crabe (Fr.)
See Crab.

Crackers
Crisp biscuits, sweetened and unsweetened. In America, the term is applied to all classes of biscuits. Thin, dry, brittle crackers are an outgrowth of Hardtack, which was in its day the only cracker.

Cracklings
The crisp remains after rendering fat. The skin of pork or goose after it has been roasted and made crisp.

Cracknels
Biscuits twice cooked, the paste being boiled before it is baked.

Cranberry (Airelle Rouge or Canneberge, Fr.)
A small, red, acid fruit, largely used for making sauces, jellies and tarts. Taken in too large a quantity, they can affect the kidneys. Sugar added in cooking gives them energy value. They contain a high percentage of citric acid and have a high value as an anti-scorbutic.

Crane (Grue, Fr.)
This bird at one time realised a higher price than a fat capon. To-day, it is no longer sought after, such are the changing fancies of English fare. In Saxon times, roast crane was a royal dish.

It is best from November to February, and should be hung at least a fortnight, to mature. It is a wading bird, resembling the heron.

Crapaudine (Fr.)
A word applied to birds split spread-eagle fashion, a mode of cooking small poultry or game birds when split down the back and grilled or fried. (See also, Spatchcock for fuller description).

Crawfish (Langouste, Fr.)
One of the best shellfish, usually caught on the south-west coast of England. It is not generally appreciated like the lobster, because of its lack of claws, but the meat of the body is very tender and there is more of it than in the lobster. All the same, it has not the flavour of a good fresh lobster.
All recipes for lobster are suitable for crawfish.

Crayfish (Ecrevisse, Fr.)
A small, fresh-water, lobster style crustacean, found in rivers, and in season from September to April. The flesh from its tail is served in many entrées and salads. The average market length is 3 to 4 inches. Of a dull green or brownish colour above, and paler brown or yellowish below. They dig themselves in banks by day and come out at night to feed on insects, snails and frogs. They are used very extensively in French cookery. Care must be taken in their preparation. The crayfish must be washed well and gutted. This operation involves the removal of the intestinal tube

with the point of a knife. The intestinal tube is found in the opening under the middle phalanx of the tail. Care must be exercised in pulling it out, so as not to break it. Any portion not removed would cause an unpleasant bitterness when cooked.

Cream (Crème, Fr.)
The fat of milk which, suspended in small globules, will rise to the top when the fluid is allowed to stand, and form a layer of cream.

Cream, Double (Crème Double, Fr.)
Usually the rich cream from Friesian cattle, which has been allowed to settle on the milk longer than the usual 12 hours for single cream. Nowadays this is controlled by the screw adjustment on the cream separator, which controls the density of the cream.

Cream, to
In all cases where reference is made to creaming butter and flour for thickening sauces, the butter and flour are brought to room temperature (65°F.). By gentle amalgamation the two ingredients are blended, and by continuous beating they are creamed together until practically white, to ensure a perfect white finished sauce. This preparation is known as Roux (which see).

Cream of
The best part of a food, as in soups—Cream of Asparagus.

Cream of Tartar

A substance found in the juice of grapes and obtained in wine-making after fermentation, being the " grounds " or lees at the bottom of the cask or barrel, which is refined to give us one of the main ingredients of baking powder.

Cream, Whipped (Crème Fouettée, F.)

Cream into which air has been incorporated to give it bulk. Cream will whip best when 48 hours old, and give greatest bulk when whipped at 50°F. If chilled too much, bulk will be lost, just in the same way as when whipped at over 65°F.

Crécy Soup

This French soup is claimed by England because it was served to the soldiers on the battle-field of Crécy on 26 August, 1346, when the Black Prince defeated the French. The soup must have been splendid because it was made of the famous golden carrots of Crécy. Other titles are—Potage à la Crécy, Purée à la Crécy, Crème à la Crécy. Crécy à la Chantilly is a purée of carrots and lentils. Consommé à la Crécy is consommé with a garnish of carrots cut julienne style.

Crème (Fr.)

Cream. A term also applied to certain soups. (See Cream, Cream of, Cream, to.)

Crème, à la (Fr.)

Cooked in, or served with, cream or cream sauce.

Crème de Menthe

A very popular liqueur possessing valuable digestive properties. When it leaves the still it is quite colourless, but as a rule it is coloured green. The original Crème de Menthe is compounded by Cusemier and marketed under the name of Freezomint.

Crème de Moka (Fr.)

A French liqueur, light brown in colour, and with a coffee flavour.

Crème de Prunelles (Fr.)

A liqueur, sweet and green in colour.

Crème de Riz (Fr.)

A white soup made of rice flour. Finely ground rice.

Crème de Thé (Fr.)

A colourless liqueur, with the flavour of tea.

Crème d'Orge (Fr.)

A white soup, made of barley flour. Finely ground barley.

Crème Fausse (Fr.)

Mock cream.

Crème Fouettée (Fr.)

Whipped cream.

Crémeux (Fr.)

Creamy—as, creamy rice pudding.

Créole (Fr.)

A name applied to many dishes of which rice forms a large part, as in pear, peach, apricot créole. Sometimes applied to sweet dishes with a covering of chocolate.

Crêpes (Fr.)

Pancakes.

Crêpes Suzette (Fr.)
Pancakes spread with a rich mixture of butter and sugar flavoured with liqueur, always finished at the table and usually flamed.

Crépine (Fr.)
Pig's caul.

Crépinette (Fr.)
Thin slice of veal udder. (See Udder.)

Crescents (Croissants, Fr.)
Rolls of Vienna bread dough in crescent shape.

Cress (Cresson, Fr.)
One of a number of pungent flavoured plants of the mustard family, used as a condiment, for garnishing, and in salads. The most widely used are watercress and garden cress. Watercress is dealt with under its heading. It is a good source of vitamins A, B, C and D.

Cress, Indian
See Nasturtium.

Cresson de Fontaine (Fr.)
See Watercress.

Crêtes de Coq (Fr.)
Cocks' combs.

Crevette (Fr.)
See Shrimp.

Crimped, Crimping
To make crisp or brittle. In crimping fish, deep cuts are made in perfectly fresh fish, which is laid in water and vinegar for an hour or two. Crimping renders the flesh firmer and makes it better to cook.

Croissants (Fr.)
See Crescents.

Cromesquis, Kromeskis (Rus.)
Minced chicken, meat, fish or game, made into shapes as for croquettes, dipped in batter and fried in deep fat.

Croquant (Fr.)
Having a crisp, crackling skin or shell.

Croquettes or Rissoles
A preparation of mince, with a breadcrumb coating. These words both signify something crisp.

Croustades (Fr.)
Fried shapes of bread used for forming a base or foundation for serving delicate cooked meats.

Croustadines (Fr.)
Flat bouchées of different shapes, made with puff paste.

Croûte (Fr.)
A slice of fried or toasted bread, usually cut in fancy shapes, on which are served savoury meats or fish. (See also En Croûte.)

Croûte-au-pot (Fr.)
A favourite type of French beef broth.

Croûtons (Fr.)
Slices of bread, plain or spread with savoury mixtures, cut into cubes and fried, for serving with soups.

Crumpet or Pikelet
A kind of cake, pitted with holes, it being ideal for toasting and buttering because its many holes readily absorb the butter.

Crustaceans
A large division of aquatic animals, which includes lobsters, crabs, crayfish, shrimps and prawns.

Cubat, Pierre
A most successful chef to Emperor Alexander II of Russia. He was paid so much per head for preparing all of the Emperor's meals, no matter how large the attendance.

Cucumber (Concombre, Fr.)
One of the most popular of salad vegetables. A long, slender member of the gourd family, dark green in colour. They are crisp and refreshing, but have very little nutritive value. May be eaten without evil consequences if dressed with vinegar.

Cuisine (Fr.)
Kitchen—cookery.

Cuisinier (Fr.)
A cook. One who prepares food.

Cuisse (Fr.)
The leg.

Cuissot (Fr.)
The haunch.

Cuit (Fr.)
Cooked.

Culinaire (Fr.)
Applied to anything or anyone in connection with the art of cooking.

Cullis (Coulis, Fr.)
A concentrated, rich liquid, for the making of soups, sauces and stews. In earlier times as much as 1 cwt. of beef or ham was used to make 5 or 6 gallons of cullis or concentrated stock for a sauce.

Culotte (Fr.)
See Aitchbone.

Cumberland
An English duke, who gave his name to Cumberland sauces, one served with game, the other a rich sweet sauce.

Cumin (Fr.)
See Caraway.

Cumquat
Another spelling for the Kumquat (which see).

Curaçao
A sweet digestive liqueur made of wine or grain spirit, sugar and orange peel. Colours are red, white, blue, green and orange.

Curcuma (Fr.)
See Turmeric.

Curd
The coagulated part of milk obtained by natural souring, or with the acid of rennet, and used in cheese-making.

Cure
The salting and preserving of foods, often with the aid of smoking.

Curlew (Corlieu (Fr.)
The curlew is of the snipe family, and was held in high esteem during the 15th and 16th centuries, when prices ranged from 1/6 to 7/6 per

bird. To-day, a curlew would not fetch 1 /–.

The colour is drab above, mottled with dark brown and white beneath. Its beak is long, like that of the snipe, measuring up to 6 inches in length. The body of the bird is slender and graceful, measuring 20 to 24 inches when full grown.

Currant

Two fruits entirely different except in their size, are known as currants—one used fresh and the other dried. The colours of the fresh are red, white and black. The red and white are more delicate in flavour. The black has a most distinctive and pleasing flavour. The dried currant extensively used in flour confectionery is a small, seedless raisin, the most famous of which are the Patras and Vostizza.

Curry (Currie or Kari, Fr.)

A mixture of powdered spices. Some curry powders contain up to 16 different ground spices. Curry was at one time an epicurean rite of English army circles in India, officers priding themselves on the special combination of spices they had invented.

Cushion

The leg cut, nearest to the udder, in either beef or mutton.

Cusparia

See Angostura.

Cussy, Baron de

A great gourmet who served with Napoleon. Many dishes bear his name—as Filet Mignon à la Cussy. As a garnish it consists of grilled mushrooms filled with a chestnut purée, cocks' kernels and truffles cooked in Sauce Madère.

Custard

A combination of milk, eggs and sugar, flavoured and boiled, baked or steamed. In recent years custard powders containing no eggs have come to be used when the custard is to be served as a sauce, but they are useless for steamed or baked custards.

Custard Apple (Pomme Cannell, Fr.)

A heart-shaped, tropical fruit with a diameter of 3 to 5 inches. It has a smooth, reddish or reddish-brown skin, marked by impressed lines into hexagons. Sweet, but insipid in flavour.

Cutlets (Côtelettes, Fr.)

Small pieces of meat, as of veal, cut from the ribs or leg, for boiling or frying ; or a mince of left-over fish, fowl, game or meat, mixed with a sauce to bind it, shaped as a cutlet, egged, crumbed and fried.

Cuttlefish

Another name for the Squid (which see).

Cygne (Fr.)

See Swan.

Cygnet (Fr.)

Young swan.

D

Dab (Limande, Fr.)

The dab is a species of flat fish, it being distinguishable from plaice and flounder by the distinct arch in the lateral line at the anterior end. It is of a brown, or ashen grey colour, with irregular dark markings and close set scales, the length attained being 12 inches. The species sand dab, or rusty dab, is found on the coasts of North America. In England, the Thames furnishes a particularly good kind, which when fried or dressed in buttered paper, is very delicate.

Dabs are at their best the latter part of autumn. If soaked in salt and water before cooking, they will be much improved in flavour.

Dabchick

A small moor hen or water fowl.

Dace, Dare or Dart (Vandoise, Fr.)

Dace is closely related to the chub, but has a smaller head and smaller mouth, and is silvery in coloration ; it rarely reaches a length of more than 12 inches. It is a fresh-water fish, and is often referred to as a Dart, probably so-called from its swiftness. In some respects it resembles the roach. Like many other fish of its class, it scarcely pays for its cooking. It is best fried or boiled, and is at its best from midsummer to December.

Dace is much enjoyed by those who angle for amusement's sake, and is usually served with a lemon sauce. Cook as trout (which see), with plenty of herbs and seasonings.

Daim (Fr.)

Fallow deer (see Deer).

Dainty (Délicieux, Fr.)

Delicate and pleasant to the palate. A delicacy, dressed in artistic manner.

Daiquiri

A cuban rum of very high quality and very pleasing flavour.

Dairy

A place for the cooling and storage of milk, and where butter and cheese are made.

Damascene

An inferior variety of damson, smaller in size and rounder. (See Damson.)

Damson

A rather small, oval variety of the common plum. The orchard damson is oval, blue or black in colour, with a firm, juicy, amber flesh. It is excellent cooked or in pies, but is generally too astringent to be eaten raw. The name is shortened from Damascene—Damascus.

F

Damson Cheese
A preserve similar to apple butter. The fruit is boiled to a pulp and freed from skin and stones. The pulp is then boiled with its own weight of sugar, like jam, to form a preserve of a cheese-like consistency.

Damson Gin
English gin flavoured with damson.

Dandelion (Dent-de-lion, Fr.)
The French name means " Lion Tooth," from the shape of the leaves.
A common edible weed, which is cultivated in many foreign countries and is certainly entitled to a much higher place than it holds in general estimation here at present. Cooked as spinach it is excellent. If the young leaves are gathered before the plants have flowered, they make excellent salad greens. After the plant has flowered, a bitter taste develops. It is especially rich in iron. Dandelion coffee and dandelion chocolate are made from the roasted and ground root.

Danish Blue Cheese
This cheese is of the Gorgonzola–Roquefort family, but a little less pungent than either. When ripe, it can be spread like butter.

Danoise (Fr.)
Danish. As a sauce it consists of white wine sauce flavoured with grated cheese and lobster butter.

Dare
See Dace.

Dariole
A small cup-shaped mould, holding a mince ; a pâté. Moulds of dariole size and shape are also used for jellies and creams. Originally a custard tartlet called daryal, and of very old English origin.

Darne (Fr.)
A middle cutlet of fish, usually applied to the centre cuts of salmon.

Dart
See Dace.

Dartois (Fr.)
As a garniture for meat and poultry, comprises fancy mould shapes of duchesse potato, filled with peas, accompanied with Sauce Madère. Also a term applied to very light French confections made of puff pastry, used also for croûtes as savouries.

Darwen Salmon
A name given to dogfish by Lancashire folk. The name originates from Darwen, Lancashire. (See Dogfish.)

Date Plum
See Persimmon.

Dates (Dattes, Fr.)
The fruit of the date palm. In cultivated form, one male tree serves from 40 to 100 females. There are hundreds of varieties which are classified

as sweet, mild sweet and dry. The mild sweet are eaten fresh, the dry or camel date is pressed whole or ground into flour, and forms a staple diet of the Arabs. The sweet is the only type known outside the home of the date palm. They are high in energy value and are a good source of vitamin A.

Daube (Fr.)

A style of braised meat, poultry or game—as Ox Heart en Daube —being larded ox heart steeped in a marinade from 6 to 8 hours and braised with vegetables.

Daumont

As a fish sauce, it comprises Hollandaise Sauce including oysters, mushrooms and truffles, made sharp with lemon juice.

Dauphiné (Fr.)

A particular style of garnish used chiefly for poultry or game, consisting of nests made of straw potatoes to hold the food. Dauphiné was one of the old provinces of pre-Revolutionary France, and Dauphin was the name given to the eldest son of the King of France from 1349 to 1830.

Decant

To pour off liquid carefully, so that the sediment remains in the bottom of the vessel.

Decanter

An ornamental bottle into which wine is decanted.

Deer, Fallow, Red and Roe

(Daim, Cerf, Chevreuil, Fr.)
In English and Scottish kitchens all deer are prepared under the name of Venison. The liver of the deer is exceptionally good eating, but one must travel to the Scottish Highlands to enjoy this delicacy, for it does not travel well. In maturing deer meat, a lot depends upon when and how the deer are killed. If stalked and shot on very high ground late in the day, it is not always easy to get the carcases away the same day, and they are left to collect by mule the following morning. Such meat will be clammy when skinned. Deer shot and skinned the same day are best, for the meat is firm and dry to the touch and will mature well. Young deer should be refused, as it is a waste of time to cook.

The haunch and saddle are the only parts worth roasting. All parts of the forequarters (except the cutlets) should be stewed or made into pies.

The red deer produce the Scotch venison, almost invariably known as stag and hind venison. There is no legal close season, stag shooting normally begins in August and ends 30 September, although in a late mating season stalking may continue until about 10 October, when hinds begin to be shot, and their season closes, usually, at the end of January. (See also Venison.)

Dehydration

The extraction by special processes of evaporation, of sufficient of the water content of various foods to guard against moulding or fermentation. There is, of course, the additional advantage in the great reduction of bulk for transportation.

Dates, figs, prunes, sultanas and currants, etc. are dehydrated by sun-drying processes in the open air. Other fruits and vegetables are first sliced or shredded, very slightly cooked or brined, and then evaporated by special dehydrating machinery. If properly performed, the dehydrated food can be almost completely restored to its original colour and flavour, by soaking in water.

Déjeuner (Fr.)

The first meal of the day; the breaking of the fast; breakfast. The Continental breakfast consisting of hot rolls and coffee.

Déjeuner à la Fourchette (Fr.)

Late breakfast, usually consisting of meat like the English breakfast.

Déjeuner de Noce (Fr.)

Wedding breakfast.

Delicatessen

A German word signifying " delicious food ". A delicatessen store implies foods prepared ready to eat, or a place where these foods are sold.

Délicieux (Fr.)

See Dainty.

Demi-deuil (Fr.)

As a sauce, comprises rich Velouté, with finely chopped truffles.

Demidoff (Fr.)

Sauces and garnishings bearing this name usually embody truffles and madeira wine; Frenchmen say, the name of a distinguished Russian nobleman, but it should be noted that it was Prince Anatoli Demidov (not Demidoff) who married Princess Mathilde, daughter of Jérome Bonaparte. Thus it would be more correct to say, à la Demidov, than Demidoff.

Demi-glace (Fr.)

Rich brown gravy, reduced by rapid boiling to a consistency slightly thinner than the average sauce. It is not thickened.

Demi-glace Tomate (Fr.)

As above with tomato purée added.

Demi-john

A bottle with a large body and narrow neck, enclosed in wicker work.

Demi-tasse (Fr.)

A small cup holding not more than 4 ozs. fluid capacity. A half cup.

Denatured Alcohol

Ethyl alcohol to which are added various minerals or dyes to render it displeasing for beverage purposes, but not for industrial purposes—such as methylated spirit—which is a mixture of 9 parts of alcohol with 1 of pyroxylic or wood spirit.

Dent-de-lion (Fr.)
See Dandelion.

Deodorise
Deodorised oils or fats are those which have passed through certain processing methods, to remove all unpleasant smell.

Dépecer (Fr.)
To slice or carve.

Dés (Fr.)
Dice—cut into cubes.

Desiccation
The process of drying up, as in desiccated coco-nut, being coco-nut with most of the moisture removed, to prevent mould forming, or fermentation.

D'Eslignac (Fr.)
Name given to a clear soup, garnished with custard royale, celery and truffles, in honour of a French nobleman.

Désossé (Fr.)
Boned or filleted (a slice or fillet).

Dessécher (Fr.)
The cooking of pastes, purées, etc. over heat, requiring constant stirring with a spatula until they no longer cling to the sides of the pan.

Dessert
A sweet course to prolong the end of a meal. Generally indicating fruits, petits-fours, friandises, and the like. A custom of the ancient Greeks and Romans, to prolong one feast into another, when they feasted for 3 or 4 days on end. The period when unfaithful guests desert their host.

Devilled (Diablé, Fr.)
To prepare with hot seasoning or sauce. Sauce Diablé, minced and browned shallot reduced in white wine and vinegar, blended with demi-glace and highly seasoned.

Devonshire Cream
Clotted cream. The cream is allowed to rise on the milk, then milk and cream are scalded and set aside to permit the layer of scalded cream to harden. It is high in energy value, but not so easily digested as ordinary cream.

Dewberry
A large variety of blackberry, but of different flavour. It is distinguished from the blackberry by its trailing habits, and fewer and more scattered fruits.

Dextrin
Starch altered by the action of acids, diastase, or heat, till it loses its gelatinous character. It is formed from starch by heat, as in bread when toast is made. In digestion it is soluble or gummy matter into which starch is converted by diastase and is the result of the first chemical action in the digestion of starch. So called because when viewed through polarised light it turns the plane of polarisation to the right.

Dextrose
Glucose or grape sugar.

Dhall
An Indian split pea or lentil, used extensively in kedgeree by the Indian working classes, who cannot afford rice and better quality grains in their kedgeree.

Diablé (Fr.)
See Devilled.

Diable, à la (Fr.)
Applied to dishes with hot seasonings, or sauces which contain mustard, Tabasco, paprika, but not curry.

Diane (Fr.)
As a sauce, comprises a highly seasoned Espagnole sauce, richly spiced and enriched with cream. Diana was the Roman goddess of the moon and of the chase.

Diastase
An enzyme, or ferment, which occurs in germinating seeds and other plants, capable of converting starch and glycogen into maltose and dextrin.

Dibs
An Arabian syrupy wine, of exquisite flavour.

Dice (Dés, Fr.)
To cut into small cubes.

Dieppoise Sauce
A rich fish sauce, containing mussels, mushrooms and shrimps. À la Dieppoise—sea food style.

Diet (Diète, Fr.)
Food taken according to rule. An adequate diet consists of all food elements, carbohydrates, fats, protein, vitamins, mineral salts, water and bulk, in sufficient quantity and correct proportion to maintain health.

Digby Chickens
Small smoked herrings from Digby, Nova Scotia. Smoked sprats named after Digby, a seaport in Nova Scotia.

Digester
A heavy type of cast-iron cooking pot, fitted with a lid that securely slots into grooves, which forms a complete seal. It is fitted with a valve through which steam can escape. Used extensively in the 18th and 19th centuries, for the making of broths and especially beef tea. It has been superseded by the pressure cooker.

Digestible
Foods capable of being digested. In a healthy digestive tract practically all food materials are digestible, except cellulose. Some foods leave the digestive tract in from 1 to 2 hours; others take from 5 to 6 hours. Light, plain foods (milk, eggs, etc.) are more easily digested than rich foods, such as pork, duck or goose.

Dill (Aneth, Fr.)
An annual herb resembling fennel in leaf and flower. Little used in England, except in the manufacture of gin, but extensively used in soups and sauces in France. It goes very well with fish. Dill vinegar is made by soaking the seeds in vinegar.

Dinde, Dindon, Dindonneau (Fr.)
See Turkey.

Dinde Farcie (Fr.)
Stuffed turkey.

Dinde Rôtie (Fr.)
Roast turkey.

Dinner (Dîner, Fr.)
From the time of the Normans it has indicated the main meal of the day, which at one time was mid-morning, but has gradually been made later by the modern mode of living. Now recognised as the main meal of the day which is usually served in the evening, between 7 and 10 p.m. Those who state they are having dinner at noonday, are quite correct, if it is their main meal of the day.

Diplomate (Fr.)
As a sauce, comprises creamy Béchamel, flavoured with anchovy and enriched with lobster butter and essence of mushrooms.

Distillation
The vaporising of a liquid by heat and then conducting the vapour into a cooled vessel where, due to the action of the intense cold on the vapour or steam, it condenses into a liquid.
Alcohol vaporises at a much lower temperature than water, so it is quite a simple matter to separate one from the other by the action of distilling—which is the action which takes place when distilling spirits. (See also, Still, Spirit and Alcohol.)

Distilled Water
Water purified by boiling. It has a flat taste, due to lack of dissolved gases and mineral matter, which are removed by distillation. It must be kept bottled, otherwise it will pick up impurities very quickly. (See Distillation.)

Ditali Lisci (It.)
Small, elbow-shaped pieces of macaroni.

Ditali Rigati (It.)
Small, grooved, elbow-shaped pieces of macaroni.

Dogfish or Flake (Rousette or Chien de Mer, Fr.)
A destructive shark-like fish, usually sold without head and fins, seldom sold as dogfish, but generally under the name of " flake ". They are eaten both fresh and salted. Fishermen hate them, because they injure the nets.

Doily or Lace Paper (Papier Dentillé, Fr.)
A fancy-cut paper mat, laid on or under a dish. From Doyley, a famous haberdasher.

D.O.M.
See Benedictine.

Dop
A brandy made from grape skins.

Doré (Fr.)
Glazed with beaten whole, or yolk of, egg, as for pie-crust.

Doria
As a garniture, comprises small balls of cucumber cooked in butter, with noisette potatoes.

Dorure (Fr.)
Egg-wash, or the beaten yolks of eggs, used for glazing pie-crusts and pastries.

Dory
See John Dory.

Dough
Same as batter, only thicker—usually thick enough to handle. (One speaks of biscuit dough.) A stiff paste, dry enough to mould with the hands.

Doughnut
A fried cake of rich leavened dough. Usually spiced, and rolled into castor sugar after drying. They are made into a variety of shapes, but of recent years the ring-shaped variety has gained in favour.

Doux, Douce (Fr.)
Sweet.

Dove (Colombe, Fr.)
The dove is a small species of pigeon. Only the wild dove is eaten for food. In England, tame doves, being pets, are usually given a special corner of the garden when their cooing ceases, and the soil is moistened with a few tears.
All recipes given for preparing pigeons are suitable for doves.

Drachona
A delicious Russian sweet, consisting of butter, milk, eggs, flour and sugar.

Dragées (Fr.)
Little balls of spiced or scented sweetmeats, used extensively at one time to sweeten the breath. Special boxes, called drageoirs, like snuff boxes, were used to contain the dragées.

Drambuie
A Scotch liqueur with the flavour of whisky and honey.

Drawn Butter
Melted, clarified butter.

Dredge
To sprinkle or coat with flour or seasoning. Usually applied to foods which require coating to prevent their sticking together.

Dregs
The impurities in liquor which settle to the bottom when allowed to stand for a long while.

Dress, to
The act of trimming, cleaning and dishing foods in artistic style. Where a recipe instructs one to dress the food on a dish, it means trim, garnish and present artistically.

Dressé or Garni (Fr.)
Dressed (see above).

Dripping
The fat of foods which comes away during the process of roasting or baking. Beef dripping—fat which has come away from a joint of beef during the cooking process.

Drizzle
The name by which small ling are known on the Yorkshire coast.

Drupe Fruits
Fruits belonging to the rose family—apricot, peach, plum, date, cherry, and all fleshy fruits with a hard seed or stone.

Du Barry, Marie Jeanne
Favourite of Louis XV who decorated her cook with the Cordon Bleu.

The Countess du Barry gave her name to many French dishes, principal of which is the well-known cream of cauliflower—Crème du Barry. As a garnish the name denotes cauliflower in some form.

Dublin Bay Prawns (Langoustines, Fr.)
These are the largest and best of all prawns and are often seen in shops but understood by few. They can be prepared in the same way as crayfish and the larger ones in the same way as lobster.

Dubois, Urbain
Name of a famous French chef who gave his name to numerous French fish dishes, such as Merlus à la Dubois (fried hake with horseradish sauce), Soles à la Dubois (boned, stuffed with tomatoes, and served with tomato sauce).

Dubonnet
A French medicated wine with a bitter quinine taste.

Duchesse (Fr.)
Duchess. The name principally applied to creamed potato, prepared in fancy shapes, baked, or egged, crumbed and fried. Also to dishes with a rich, creamed mashed potato topping, such as Cottage Pie Duchesse.

As a sauce, comprises Béchamel with tongue and mushrooms, enriched with butter.

Duck (Canard, Fr.)
This universal favourite requires no praise, if only you will choose young farmyard ducks fattened at liberty but cleansed by being shut up for 2 or 3 days before killing and fed only on barley meal and water.

Of all the ducks available to us in this country, there is none to surpass the white Aylesbury, which are at perfection from December to March. The general tests for age and condition, given under the heading of Chicken, apply to buying ducks. An additional test for age is found in the windpipe, which can be easily squeezed and moved in a young duck, but is fixed and stiff in old birds. The best of the imported ducks are the famous Long Island variety. There, duck farming is carried on very extensively, the birds being very carefully tended.

Duck, Wild
See Wild Duck and Mallard.

Ducklings (Canetons, Fr.)

Ducklings are in season from March to September and offer a pleasant variety in our daily fare when the young green peas are ready, although with modern refrigeration excellent frosted peas are available as soon as the ducklings can oblige. There is little on a duckling, but there is nothing to equal the crackling of a young bird, or the tang of the sage and onion stuffing, if made from freshly gathered sage, and used when the ducklings are over 5 months old. If used when the birds are under 5 months, it is too overpowering for their delicate flavour. Two young ducklings make a better dish than a large, handsome hard-fleshed drake, which as a rule is only fit for the casserole.

Duglère (Fr.)

A noted French chef, who gave his name to fish dishes served à la Duglère. The method is composed of richly flavoured tomato Béchamel, blended with butter and chopped green herbs, dressed over poached fillets of sole. Sometimes the sauce is only lightly flavoured with tomato, but extra diced tomato is added later.

Dulse

An edible, purplish-red seaweed, which can be eaten raw or cooked as a vegetable. It needs to be well washed in several waters. In Scotland, it is roasted by twisting it around red-hot tongs.

Dumas, Alexandre

Born 1802, died 1870. A prolific writer and author of the " Dictionnaire de Cuisine ".

Dumplings (Quenelles, Fr.)

Ball shaped food which may be comprised of forcemeat, suet dough, or foods encased in a crust, such as apple dumpling. Finely minced fish, fowl or meat, are mixed with yolks of eggs and bread, and formed into balls no larger than an olive, poached, and used extensively as quenelles in soups or garnishings.

Durian

A greenish, oval fruit, about the size of a large coco-nut, grown in Malaya. Its flesh is cream coloured, and of fine flavour, despite its odour, which is objectionable to those who come in contact with it for the first time.

Dushab

An Arabian drink consisting of a mixture of grape juice and date wine, reduced to a heavy syrup.

Dutch Oven

A half-moon shaped metal shield, fitted with shelves and sometimes hooks, which may be pushed close up to an open fire, for roasting foods by the trapped heat. Some Dutch ovens are clamped on to the bars of the grate, to form a metal cupboard in front of the fire.

Dutch Sauce (Sauce Hollandaise, Fr.)
See Hollandaise.

Duxelles or d'Uxelles (Fr.)
A famous French gastronome who gave his name to sauces and methods of garnishing, of which the principal ingredients are tomato purée and chopped mushrooms or mushroom liquor. The finely chopped mushroom garnish (duxelles) used extensively in fish cookery, is named after this famous gourmet.

E

Earth-nut
See Pea-nut.

Eating Habits
Eating habits should be taken with as much seriousness as the necessity to breathe air or drink water, for it is upon our eating habits that our health depends from the moment we are weaned. Habitual over-eating, or eating too fast, overburdens the digestive organs and in time results in some disorder. Eat regularly, slowly, and in moderation, choosing a well-balanced diet. Chew your food well, for the action of the saliva on foods is of great importance to the digestion.

Hoteliers and restaurateurs should create dining rooms with a pleasant atmosphere, to enable the diners to relax completely while eating, for if the nerves are strained the foods will not be so easily digested. (See also Diet.)

Eau (Fr.)
See Water.

Eau-de-vie (Fr.)
" Water of life " (old brandy). Potable alcohol or spirit not necessarily distilled from wine. If distilled from wine, it is called eau-de-vie-de-vin.

Eau-de-vie de Grain (Fr.)
See Whisky.

Eccles Cakes
Small, round, pastry cakes, filled with spiced vine fruits.

Échalote (Fr.)
See Shallot.

Échauder (Fr.)
The scalding of birds to facilitate plucking, or pigs and such animals, to remove the hairs.

Éclair (Fr.)
A confection made from a rich, boiled, egg paste—piped into finger shapes, filled with flavoured cream, and finished with a top coating of fondant.

Éclanche (Fr.)
Shoulder of mutton.

Écossaise, à l' (Fr.)
Scottish style. As a sauce, it comprises rich Béchamel with chopped hard-boiled eggs.

Écrevisse (Fr.)
See Crayfish.

Écureuil (Fr.)
See Squirrel.

Écuyer (Fr.)
See Equerry.

Edam Cheese
We read in the Bible of Esau's mess of edom (red) pottage. Hence the name edam (red) cheese. This is a Dutch cheese, ball-shaped, weighing about 5 lbs., bright red outside and yellow inside. It gets its shape by being pressed into round moulds at very high pressure. Of mild and pleasing flavour.

Edible Frog (Grenouille, Fr.)
See Frog.

Edible Snail (Escargot, Fr.)
See Snail.

Eel (Anguille, Fr.)
A fish of strong individuality of appearance. There are four kinds of eels—the broad-nosed and the sharp-nosed, the grig and the snig. The sharp-nosed are the brightest of colour and best of flavour. The flesh of the eel is tender and very oily. The oil content is reduced by removing the skin before broiling or frying.
Smoked eel is delicious, and considered by epicures far superior to smoked salmon.
Eels were formerly a regular dish on the tables of rich and poor alike. They were the gentlemen who paid the rent in many of the weald and marsh-lands of Kent and Sussex. So many roods of land were paid for by providing the manor house with so many rods of eel. Always choose the smallest for boiling. Remove gut, heads and skin, wash well, and simmer in a little salt and water with chopped parsley. As eels when brought into the kitchen are frequently alive, it is first necessary to kill them. Because of their tenacity of life, this is found by some not too easy to accomplish. It is, however, merely necessary to insert the point of a sharp knife into the spine at the back of the head to a depth of an inch (if a large one) and the eel will become perfectly motionless. (See also Conger Eels and Elvers.)

Eel-pout
Another name for the lote.

Effervesce
To boil, bubble or froth. To form bubbles on the surface of a liquid, usually in mineral or table waters by the addition of foam essence.

Egg Nog
A most nutritious drink, consisting of new milk, eggs, sugar and sometimes flavouring. Easy of digestion and invaluable for persons suffering from mal-nutrition. It forms a popular drink when brandy, whisky or rum is added.

Egg Plant (Aubergine, Fr.)
A perennial of the nightshade family, closely allied to the potato. This delicious vegetable is egg-shaped, 3 to 5 inches in diameter and 12 inches in length. Its colour is from light purple to almost black. It can be sliced, or cubed, fried, baked, or boiled. It is also excellent when stuffed. Brinjaul or Bangou is the name of the West Indian egg plant.

Eggs (Œufs, Fr.)
The eggs of almost all birds or fish are relatively rich in all elements required for growth. The yolk of the hen's egg is of more importance from a nutritive standpoint than the white, as it contains all the fat and almost all the vitamin and ash constituents.

Eggs are sold wholesale by weight, and will vary from 10 lbs. per long hundred (120) up to 18 lbs. per long hundred. Yet most recipes say—" take 2 eggs "—or whatever number is considered necessary. It is owing to the variation in size of hens' eggs that we get the greatest variation in our culinary endeavours. Hens' eggs should be cooked at a temperature just below boiling point, to avoid toughening.

Fish roes (eggs) are also an excellent form of food, especially those from the herring.

Eggs, Dried
Emulsified eggs from which the moisture has been extracted by spraying the emulsified liquid egg through warm cylinders or drums, the moisture being driven off into a vapour and the powder falling to the bottom of the cylinder.

Eggs, Frozen
Shelled and emulsified eggs frozen in block form, which is given preference by bakers and confectioners because it saves time and labour costs. Most of our supply comes from China and Canada.

Egyptienne (Fr.)
Egyptian style. Usually denotes lentils in some form.

Eland
The largest of the South African antelopes used as food.

Elderberry (Sureau, Fr.)
The dark, black berry of the elder tree, which usually grows wild in this country. Excellent when used in pies, puddings and elderberry wine. There is a certain superstition against the elder, it being supposed that it was on an elder tree that Judas hanged himself.

Elmassia
A rich, gelatinous, Turkish stew of calves' feet.

Elvers (Alevins, Fr.)

Young eels are known as "elvers". The transparent larvae, which have needle-shaped teeth, live near the surface of the ocean, and as they spread out across the Atlantic, grow from about 5 inches to 35 inches long in about 2½ years. The full-grown larvae occur off the Atlantic coast of Europe and in the western Mediterranean during the early summer; then cease feeding, lose their larval teeth, shrink in length and depth, and change into elvers, or little eels, which enter our rivers in large numbers. They are caught in very large quantities, at a stage when they are transparent, pale amber in colour and very thin, in the Severn and other rivers. These little fellows are delicious if cooked in the same way as whitebait.

Émincé (Fr.)

Cut in thin slices or fine shreds.

Emmer

A species of wheat or coarse grain, used for stock feeding.

Émonder (Fr.)

To blanch, as pistachio, almond or other nuts, by steeping them in boiling water to facilitate the removal of the skins.

Emulsification

The breaking down of fats with liquids, as is performed in artificial cream or ice cream manufacture. The ingredients to be emulsified are usually raised to a uniform temperature and subjected to violent agitation by centrifugal force to break down the globules of fat to smaller proportions, so that the resultant mix is smooth and creamy.

Emulsion

A mixture of two or more liquids brought about by emulsification (see above). Fats may be emulsified with liquids, by first melting the fat and heating the liquid to the same temperature.

En (Fr.)

In, as en casserole, en caisses.

Enchilada

A Mexican dish, consisting of cornmeal, pumpkin, rice, meat and garlic.

En Croûte (Fr.)

Encased in paste or crust, as in the preparation of dry game in a paste or dough prior to cooking.

Endive (Fr.)

The salad leaves of the chicory plant. The mature root roasted and ground produces the chicory used to adulterate coffee. The leaves are usually creamy white and unless well blanched and crisp, are bitter.

En Papillote (Fr.)
Paper-bag cookery. Small fish, birds or meats, wrapped in oiled paper in which they are grilled or baked, to preserve the flavour. It is usual to send such foods to the table in the paper in which they are cooked. Mullet lends itself particularly to this mode of cooking.

En Tasse (Fr.)
Served in individual cups—as Consommé en Tasse.

Entrecôte (Fr.)
The middle cut of sirloin steak. Sometimes, when this cut is in short supply, the rib of beef is used and given the same name.

Entrée (Fr.)
A conventional term for side-dishes. Chiefly applied to dishes which immediately follow the fish course and are served with a sauce. A made dish.

Entremets (Fr.)
Second course side dishes, consisting of dressed vegetables, sweet dishes and savouries. Between dishes.

Enzyme
Substances produced by animals and plants, found particularly in the digestive juices. Their great activity is carried on at a temperature approximating that of the body ; their effect is retarded by low temperatures and destroyed at higher temperatures than that of the body. Yeast used in bread-making can be given as an example of its destruction by heat and its retardment by low temperature, for yeast is an Enzyme.

Epanada
The Spanish cook's term for panada, or soaked bread used in stuffings.

Épaule (Fr.)
Shoulder. Épaule de veau—shoulder of veal.

Épergne (Fr.)
An ornamental stand for holding a large dish as a centre-piece for the table.

Éperlan (Fr.)
See Smelt.

Épice (Fr.)
Spice or savoury seasoning. (See Spice.)

Epicure
After Epicurus, a Greek philosopher who indulged in the luxuries of the table. One given to the luxuries of the table.

Epicurienne
As applied to sauce, comprises rich mayonnaise mixed with gherkins, chutney and cucumber purée (essentially cold). As applied to consommé, denotes a garnish of shredded almonds and chervil leaves.

Epigrammes
A culinary term for small cuts or fillets of poultry, game or meats. Usually applied to boned and rolled breast or loin of lamb or small mutton.

Épinard (Fr.)
See Spinach.

Epsom Salts
Chemically the salt is lepta-hydrated magnesium sulphate, and can be found in sea water and mineral waters, especially those at Epsom, from which place it takes its name. Used medicinally as a purgative.

Equerry (Écuyer, Fr.)
Originally a title given to the man in charge of the horses' food (the stable man); later, it was applied to cooks or persons in charge of food, and recently applied to officers of the Royal Household.

Érable à Sucre (Fr.)
Sugar-maple tree (see Maple Sugar).

Erdapfelknödeln
Name of a German dish consisting of very rich and highly spiced cheese and potato dumplings. Usually served in a rich beef gravy.

Ersatz (Ger.)
Substitute.

Erwtensoep
Name of a Dutch pea soup.

Esau's Mess of Pottage
In reading Genesis, Chapter 25, Verses 29 to 34, carefully, we are able to discover the colour was edom—red, and the main ingredient lentils. Thus we find red lentil soup is the earliest soup known. Incidentally, the Dutch Edam cheese obviously denotes red cheese.

Escabecia
A favourite Spanish dish, consisting of partridges in a very highly seasoned sauce.

Escalloped or Scalloped
Food baked in a dish with breadcrumbs, butter and seasoning.

Escargots (Fr.)
See Snails.

Escarole (Fr.)
The broad-leaved endive or chicory plant. The leaves are wavy instead of curled as in the common endive, and the midrib is thicker.

Escoffier, A.
A noted French chef and author, who invented the ever-popular Pêche Melba.

Escollope (Fr.)
Thin slices of meat, usually egged, crumbed and fried in shallow fat.

Espadon (Fr.)
See Swordfish.

Espagnole (Fr.)
Name of a rich brown sauce, originating from Spain, being one of the four mother sauces from which almost all other sauces are made. It is made with brown roux and rich brown stock, tomatoes, mushrooms, ham and herbs. The four mother sauces are—Espagnole, Béchamel, Velouté and Allemande. (See Introduction to Sauces, " Master Book of Poultry and Game ".)

Essence
The concentrated goodness extracted from any edible substance. An extract used for flavouring.

Essential Oils
Chiefly the oils of plants and spices which possess the characteristic odour of the plant or its seed. Used extensively in perfumery and medical practice, also for the flavouring of foods.

Estouffade (Fr.)
A form of casserole cooking which requires very little liquid, as braised foods cooked under cover. Estouffade generally conveys finished in rich brown sauce.

Estragon (Fr.)
See Tarragon.

Esturgeon (Fr.)
See Sturgeon.

Etamine (Fr.)
Tammy-cloth—a cloth for straining soups or sauces.

Ethyl Alcohol
See Denatured Alcohol.

Étourneau (Fr.)
See Starling.

Etretat (Fr.)
Name of a French sauce, comprises Sauce Allemande flavoured with fish essence and tomato purée.

Ewe
A female sheep.

Ewe Cheese
Cheeses made from the milk of ewes, some of which are—Roquefort, Brousses, Brossons, Cachat, Brocchio de Corse.

Excelsior
As a garnish, conveys braised lettuce and fondant potatoes.

Extractives
Substances extracted from various animal tissues ; although not food principles, they give flavour to meat.

Extra-fin (Fr.)
Of extra or finest quality.

F

Faarikal
Name of a Scandinavian dish consisting of braised lamb and cabbage to which sour cream is added just before serving.

Faggot of Parsley
A handful of parsley, 6 young spring onions, 1 bay leaf, 1 sprig of thyme, tied together with string to facilitate its easy removal from the pot or pan when cooking is completed.

Faggot of Thyme
Reverse the quantities given for parsley and thyme under Faggot of Parsley.

Faggots
Small, square, savoury cakes of forcemeat, prepared from pigs' offal, herbs, onion and soaked bread, wrapped with caul and baked.

G

Fagot (Fr.)
See Faggot of Parsley and Thyme.

Faisan (Fr.)
See Pheasant.

Fallow Deer (Daim, Fr.)
See Deer.

Fanchonnettes (Fr.)
Varieties of small, puff pastries, usually filled with custard, cream or jam, and covered with meringue.

Farce, Farci (Fr.)
A coarse kind of forcemeat used for raised pies or stuffings. It may consist of fish, poultry, game, or almost any kind of meat. Stuffed with forcemeat.

Farina
The flour of any grain or root. A fine flour or meal made from cereal grains or dried roots of plants.

Farinaceous
Starchy—mealy. Pertaining to flour.

Farina Dolce
An Italian flour made from dehydrated ground chestnuts, slightly sweet.

Farine (Fr.)
Flour.

Fariné (Fr.)
Powdered.

Farle
A quarter of a Scotch bannock. Just as a round of scones is divided in four before being baked, so the Scotch bannock was usually divided. Each quarter was called a farle.

Fascine (Fr.)
Bundle, as bundle of rhubarb, asparagus, or leeks.

Faséole (Fr.)
Kidney bean.

Fat (Graisse, Fr.)
Fat is a compound with a melting point so high that it remains solid at ordinary room temperature. The fatty part of animals. Fats do not build tissues—they are energy producers.

Faubonne (Fr.)
As a soup, comprises a purée of haricot beans, garnished with a julienne of vegetables.

Fausse (Fr.)
Mock.

Favorite (Fr.)
Name of a garniture for meats consisting of sliced truffles, foie-gras and asparagus tips.

Fécule de Marante (Fr.)
See Arrowroot.

Fécule de Marron (Fr.)
Chestnut flour.

Fécule de Pommes de Terre
Potato flour.

Fécule de Riz
Rice flour.

Fedelini
Italian paste, finer than ordinary vermicelli. Not to be confused with Fidelini (which see).

Feints
The tops and bottoms of the spirits from a pot-still. The poorer qualities.

Fennel (Fenouil, Fr.)
A perennial herb of the cow-parsley family. Well-known for its distinctive scent, which tradition has joined to mackerel. Much used for fish dishes and sauces.

Fenugreek (Fenugrec, Fr.)
The seeds of this herb are ground and used in curries. It has a celery-like flavour and derives its curious name from Fœnum Græcum (Greek hay). In Oriental countries it is eaten by women to promote fleshiness.

Fermentation
Fermentation is the chemical change produced in certain liquids during which process the sugar is converted into alcohol. Bacteria and yeast are important factors in fermentation. To cause a ferment, heat, air and moisture must be present. All intoxicants and vinegar are classed as fermented products, wine vinegar being the exhausted products of fermentation.

Fermenty
See Furmenty.

Fermière, à la (Fr.)
Farmhouse style. Fresh and simply prepared. As a garnish, it comprises young carrots, turnips, onion and celery hearts.

Fettuccelle
See Fidelini.

Feuillage (Fr.)
Leaves.

Feuillé (Fr.)
Decorated or garnished with leaves.

Feuilletage (Fr.)
Light puff pastry ; flaky pastry.

Fèves (Fr.)
Beans.

Fèves d'Espagne (Fr.)
Runner or scarlet beans.

Fèves de Marais (Fr.)
Broad beans.

Fidelini, or Fettuccelle
A kind of flat Italian paste, not unlike noodle strips.

Fig (Figue, **Fr.**)
There are several hundred varieties of fig, covering a wide range of colour and differing considerably in appearance—from round to pear-shaped and from nearly white to purplish-black. As ripe figs are very fragile, most of those which reach this country are in a dried condition, the sugar content of which is as high as 75%. The sweet, seedy pulp has laxative properties. The finest are imported from Smyrna. Fresh figs are highly esteemed for dessert.

Fig, Barberry or Indian
See Prickly Pear.

Figaro (Fr.)
Name of a pink-coloured sauce, consisting of ordinary mayonnaise mixed with concentrated tomato purée, used extensively for masking cold fillets of fish and poultry.

Fig-bird, Fig-eater, Fig-pecker (Bec-Figue, Fr.)
Brillat-Savarin put the fig-pecker first among small birds, for it has always moved gastronomes to rhapsody. They are seldom seen in England or Scotland to-day, for they prefer the southern climates, where they feed on figs and grapes. Occasionally, they are imported in small quantities, when they are soon snapped up.
All recipes you have for ortolans or plovers are suitable for preparing this little morsel, which is best wrapped in a vine leaf before roasting to hold its delicate flavour.

Figue (Fr.)
See Fig.

Filbert (Aveline, Fr.)
The filbert is usually confused with the hazel-nut or cob-nut. Filberts are those with fringed husks extending beyond the nut ; hazel-nuts are those with husks shorter than the nut. When deprived of the husks, it takes an expert to classify them. Then the nuts can be detected as being longer, the hazel-nut smaller and roundish. The cob-nut so much cultivated in Kent is large, roundish and angular.

Filé (Fr.)
Spun in fine cobweb threads, as spun sugar, sucre filé.

Filet de Bœuf
Fillet of beef cut from the tenderloin.

Filet de Veau
Fillet of veal.

Filet Mignon
Very small fillet of beef.

Fillet (Filet, Fr.)
In animals, it always refers to the cut from the tenderloin or undercut from the loin. In poultry and game birds, it is applied to the meat cut from the breast. In fish, the boned sides are called fillets. When tenderloins are in short supply, slices from the leg of veal, mutton and pork are erroneously called fillets.

Filtering
The straining of consommé, jelly or aspic, through fine flannel, or several thicknesses of cheesecloth, after the process of clarification.

Financière (Fr.)
As a sauce, it consists of rich brown Sauce Madère with mushroom liquor and shredded truffle. When applied to garnishings, it consists of cocks' combs, cocks' kernels, truffles and ox tongue served in rich Espagnole sauce.

Findon Haddock—Flamande, à la   95

Findon Haddock, Finnan Haddie
Findon haddock is the original title given to the haddock cured around Findon, a fishing village about 6 miles south of Aberdeen. It is best known now as " finnan haddie ". Somehow, the word finnan slips out more easily than Findon, which is probably the reason so many people have never heard of the little village which has made the smoked haddie world famous.

When next in Aberdeen, slip down to Findon and experience the delights of a really fresh smoked haddock.

Fine Herbs (Fines-herbes, Fr.)
A mixture of finely chopped fresh garden herbs, used as Omelette Fines-herbes, Sauce Fines-herbes, Filet de Sole Fines-herbes, etc., etc.

Finger Rolls
Italian bread made in stick form, measuring from 6 to 18 inches in length.

Finings
Egg white, isinglass, gelatine or patent powders, added to wines or beers to remove the mucilage or sediment held in suspension to establish a clear, bright liquor.

Firkin
The fourth part (9 gallons) of a barrel of beer, or 56 lbs. of butter.

Firmity
See Furmenty.

Fish (Poisson, Fr.)
All shellfish have a high percentage of iodine, oysters being greatly esteemed because they are eaten raw and lose none of their valuable properties through cooking. Most fish are best just before spawning. As a food, fish is very similar to lean beef in its composition. In fat content it is lacking—except herring, salmon, trout, tunny, and most canned varieties of fish. Full description and methods of cooking almost every available fish in these Isles is contained in the " Master Book of Fish ", containing over 1,000 recipes.

Fish Stew
See Matelote.

Fizz
Term applied to any effervescent beverage, but more particularly to Champagne.

Flageolet (Fr.)
A variety of green kidney bean.

Flake
See Dogfish.

Flaki
A Polish dish of tripe.

Flamande, à la (Fr.)
Flemish style. As a sauce, it is applied to a rich mustard-flavoured sauce. As a garnish, small braised vegetables (carrots, turnips, peas, potatoes) are mixed with tiny pork sausages and served in a demi-glace sauce.

Flamber (Fr.)
To remove hairs from poultry and game birds by singeing.

Flan (Fr.)
Varieties of open custard, cheesecake, or fruit tarts. Of more recent years the fruit flan has gained great prominence, being a pastry case filled with fruits and set in jelly.

Flanchet (Fr.)
Flank (which see).

Flank
The side of the animal from the rib to the thigh ; the belly. It forms a cheap roast when boned and stuffed, but is best braised or stewed.

Flapjack (Tôt-fait, Fr.)
A broad, flat pancake, of rather crude preparation, also known as Slapjack.

Flavour
That quality in food which gratifies the palate and is remembered long after the meal is eaten. Of the five senses, it has been said that flavour is the most difficult to define. If the character of flavour could be described as well as that of colour, then the science of feeding would become a simple matter.

Flavouring
A majority of natural flavourings are obtained by extracting the aromatic essential oil from the blossoms, fruits, roots or fruit rinds, by expression, absorption, distillation or maceration. Other concentrated flavours are produced by synthetic combinations of compound ethers, together with special oils or the extractive matter of the true food. Seasonings, spices, herbs, all contribute to impart taste and flavour to food, in order to render it of a pleasing nature.

Fleischsalat (Ger.)
Name of a German meat salad consisting of thin slices of cooked meat mixed with shredded celery, pickled cucumbers, cooked potatoes, apples and onions, mixed with seasoning herbs and dressing.

Flensjes
A Dutch dish consisting of very thin pancakes spread with jam.

Flesh
The soft tissues of all animal and plant life.

Flet (Fr.)
See Flounder.

Flétan (Fr.)
See Halibut.

Fleuriste (Fr.)
As a sauce, it consists of rich Velouté, with a julienne of chicken breast. As a garnish, it consists of tomatoes scooped out and filled with young spring vegetables with château potatoes.

Fleurons (Fr.)
Crescent shapes of baked flaky pastry, used for garnishing.

Flip
A type of egg nog (which see), consisting of eggs, sugar, milk and alcoholic liquor, served hot in cold weather. Sometimes the milk is omitted, if a potent drink is desired.

Flitch of Bacon
A side of hog, minus the ham, salted and cured.

Florence Oil
A title applied to high-grade olive oil.

Florentine
As a garniture for fish or sweetbreads, it always comprises spinach in some form. When applied to consommé, it denotes a garniture of gaily coloured royale.

Florian (Fr.)
Name of a style of garnish consisting of browned button onions, braised lettuce, shaped carrots and fondant potatoes.

Flounder (Carrelet or Flet, Fr.)
Flounders are at their best from February to September. They are flat sea fish with a row of sharp little spines on their upper side. They often enter fresh water, and ascend rivers to a great distance from the sea ; the Avon, for example, to within 3 miles of Bath, and the Thames to Teddington and Sunbury. Their partiality to a mud bottom has procured for them the name of mud-flounders in Scotland.

The body of this fish is more elongated than that of the plaice and the greatest width of the dorsal and anal fins is a little behind the middle, while in the plaice it is just about the middle. The flesh is inferior to that of most other flat fish.

Flour (Farine, Fr.)
Grain or dried root of any kind, ground to fine powder. In general use, the term usually signifies wheat flour. White flour will always keep much longer than brown or wholewheat flours. The true wholemeal flour contains all of the grain. The average analyses of wheat flour show from 9% to 12% water, 8% to 15% protein, 1% to 3% fat, and 60% to 80% carbohydrates.

Flour should be sifted so that the particles may be thoroughly disintegrated before use, and for all baking purposes should be warmed to average room temperature for best results. Good flour will improve in flavour and character up to about 6 months, and in proper conditions will retain its qualities for a considerable time afterwards. (See also Wheat.)

Flour, Self-raising
Flour to which have been added all the substances used in baking powder, in the proportion of ½ oz. to 1 oz. of ingredients to 1 lb. of flour, depending on the strength and

lightening agency of the ingredients added. Salt is sometimes added as well as lightening ingredients. The resultant flour proves a time-saver to the busy housewife, but seldom finds favour in commercial kitchens or bakeries.

Fluke
See Witch.

Flummery or Frumenty
A thick hasty cold sweet, made of oatmeal or rice flavoured with milk and ground almonds, and set in a mould. It originally signified wheat or oatmeal that had been steeped in water and allowed to ferment a little before boiling. The title is also applied to a variety of fancy custards flavoured with spices. (See also Furmenty.)

Foie (Fr.)
See Liver.

Foie de Veau (Fr.)
Calves' liver.

Foie-gras (Fr.)
Fat goose liver. Usually imported, preserved in earthenware pots, from France.

Fond (Fr.)
Concentrated broth of meat.

Fondant (Fr.)
Melting. Also name of a soft white icing, made by boiling sugar to the " ball ", allowing it to cool and working it till it stiffens to a white, creamy mass. It is used for icing cakes, chocolate centres and bonbons.

Fond Blanc (Fr.)
White stock.

Fond Brun (Fr.)
Brown stock.

Fond de Gibier (Fr.)
Brown game stock.

Fondu (Fr.)
Melted. Beurre fondu—melted butter.

Fondue (Fr.)
Toasted or melted cheese, used as a savoury.

Fontainebleau (Fr.)
Name of a style of garnish consisting of potato nests made of duchess potatoes filled with diced vegetables.

Fontina d'Aosta
A fatty Italian cheese with holes like gruyere.

Food
Any substance capable of being used by the body for growth, repair or the maintenance of vital processes. Nutritive materials which, when taken into the body, are converted in the digestive organs into substances which make blood, bone, muscle, nerves and brain. Most important of these materials are—water, protein, certain additional chemical elements (or minerals) and the all-important vitamins, of which so much has been learned in recent years. Without these neither growth nor replacement, nor even life, is possible.

Fool
See Gooseberry Fool.

Forati
Italian paste five times as thick as ordinary vermicelli.

Foratini
Italian paste four times as thick as ordinary vermicelli.

Forbidden Fruit
Another name for the shaddock (which see). Also the name of an American liqueur.

Forcemeat
All types of stuffing come under this heading, which is also applied to finely minced or pounded meats used for such stuffings. Such preparations can be made out of fish, meat, poultry or game birds.

Forequarter (Quartier de Devant, Fr.)
The neck, shoulder and breast of the animal, unseparated.

Forestière (Fr.)
Name of a style of garnish consisting of mushrooms, diced ham and noisette potatoes.

Fork (Fourchette, Fr.)
This instrument, which was originally made with only two prongs, was first introduced to England in 1608. Original specimens were heavy and clumsy and were at first scorned and ridiculed. It is now used as the principal instrument for conveying food to the mouth at table, in all civilized countries.

Fouetté (Fr.)
Whipped.

Foulque Morelle (Fr.)
See Coot.

Four (Fr.)
See Oven.

Fourchette (Fr.
See Fork.

Fowl (Volaille, Fr.)
A large, edible bird.

Fraise (Fr.)
See Strawberry.

Fraisia
A French liqueur, red in colour, and flavoured with strawberries.

Framboise (Fr.)
See Raspberry.

Française, à la (Fr.)
The term applied to a number of French dishes cooked and prepared in a simple manner, and chiefly denotes a particular style or finish of the district of France in which the chef or cook originally lived. When applied to sauces, it usually denotes rich Béarnaise mixed with tomato purée and flavoured with concentrated fish essence. When applied to garnishings, it comprises all types of young fresh vegetables, served in rich demi-glace or Sauce Madère.

Francatelli

Name of an eminent English chef, who was employed at the Reform Club, and later as chef to Queen Victoria. During the year 1846 he wrote " Francatelli's Modern Cook ", which was dedicated to the great admirer of his work, The Right Hon. The Earl of Errol.

François

As a sauce, denotes tomato sauce reduced with white wine, and sliced mushrooms added.

Frangipane or Franzipane

Originally applied to a perfume from the flower of the red jasmine. Subsequently, a dessert sweet of almond cream, flavoured with this perfume, became the rage. In later years, various cheap substitutes have appeared, which consist chiefly of butter, sugar, eggs, almonds, and a liberal amount of cake crumbs. It is used as a topping for various tarts, until now it is more universally recognised under the title of Frangipane Tarts.

Frankfurters

(1) Smoked pork sausages, flavoured with garlic.
(2) The filling for the " Hot Dog ".
(3) The nationalised American sausage.

Frappé (Fr.)

Diluted, sweetened fruit juice, frozen to a mushy consistency, and served in glasses. Iced fruit drinks. Iced, as for wines.

Freezomint

See Crème de Menthe.

French Beans

Green or string beans, grown for their delicate soft pods, which are gathered before the seeds have properly formed, when 6 to 8 inches long.

French Dressing

A mixture of 4 parts virgin olive oil and 1 part wine vinegar or lemon juice, with the addition of finely minced chives, sweet herbs and seasoning. Used for dressing salads at the very last moment.

French Fry

A term applied in English-speaking countries to foods cooked in hot fat deep enough to float the food.

French Rolls

French rolls differ in character from Vienna rolls, due to the addition of milk and butter to the dough from which they are made. They are made into various shapes, some of which are a yard long. They have a delicious, crisp, nutty-flavoured crust.

French Sauce (Sauce Française, Fr.)

Béarnaise sauce with tomato purée and reduced fish stock.

French Vinegar (Vin-aigre, Fr.)

Literally, sour wine. Made from French sour wine, unlike the English vinegar, in which malt forms the chief substance. Also known as White Vinegar. (See also Vinegar.)

riand (Fr.)
Dainty in character.

riandines (Fr.)
Very small, savoury patties.

riandises (Fr.)
Term applied to a variety of very small, sweet confections, which include glazed whole, or portions of, fresh fruit, petits-fours, etc.

riar's Omelette
A baked round apple omelette, consisting of a bottom layer of creamed eggs, the centre filled with apple purée, with a top layer of creamed eggs, baked more like a sandwich than an omelette.

Fricandeau (Fr.)
The prime parts of veal, smoothly trimmed and larded, and brightly glazed with a concentration of their own liquor. Invented by Jean de Carême, direct ancestor of the famous Carême and cook to Pope Leo X.

Fricandelles (Fr.)
Small thin cakes of minced meat, braised or fried, or, as the Americans will have it, a Hamburger.

Fricassée (Fr.)
To cook by braising. Food cut in pieces and prepared in sauce or gravy. At one time only applied to a white stew of chicken, veal or rabbit. To-day, we have the white or brown fricassée.

Fried (Frit or Frite, Fr.)
Food cooked in a pan with hot fat.

FRYING IN DEEP FAT
Fat does not boil, but can be raised to as high as 390°F. and not burn, if of good quality. Lard, clarified dripping, or pure vegetable oils, are the only fats suitable for deep frying, being free from water content. Butter or margarine is useless.

Sufficient fat should be placed in the fryer to cover the food to be cooked completely, gradually raised to a temperature of 360°F. to 380°F. according to the thickness of the food to be cooked, for if it be thick then it will take longer to cook, and should the fat be too hot, the food will be browned too much on the outside before it is cooked through. For spring chicken or poussin, the fat can be raised to 375°F. provided, of course, the fat or oil is of good quality and will stand being brought up to this heat without burning. (Poor quality fats or oils will burn before reaching that degree.)

It is most essential to have plenty of fat available for the deep frying process, because the more fat you have, once you have raised it to the correct temperature, the more likely it is to hold its heat when the pieces of food are submerged in it. This is a most important point, for if too many pieces of food are submerged in too little fat, the temperature of the fat will fall rapidly and the food will be soggy and greasy instead of emerging a nice crisp golden brown.

The fat should never smoke, as advised in some cookery books. When fat smokes, you are burning it, and that means you will not be able to use it over and over again. Besides, the flavour of the burnt fat will have an effect on the flavour of delicate food. Instead, raise the temperature of the fat steadily till you see what is termed the "blue haze", which is like the shimmering haze seen on a hot day, or the heat haze being emitted from a hot engine. An engine can emit a shimmering heat haze, but if you saw smoke rising, you would detect danger. So it is with frying fat.

All food to be deep fried should first be well dried, as beads of moisture dropped into hot fat can be extremely dangerous to the unwary. Season the pieces of food, dredge lightly with flour, brush over with well-beaten egg, and roll into bread-crumbs (brown or white). Press the pieces lightly to ensure that the crumbs adhere well, lay the pieces on a wire tray to fit the pan, and gently lower them into the hot fat. No pieces should overlap each other. They will not need turning, as they are being evenly cooked on all sides. Take up the pieces, allow all surplus fat to drain away, and dress on a platter with a paper doily placed upon it.

After you have finished with the fat, it should be carefully strained through fine muslin to remove all stray bread-crumbs, and stored in a cool place. Crumbs left in the fat from time to time will appear as objectionable black specks on your next batch of food to be cooked, and in time the burnt black crumbs will stain the cooking fat or oil a dirty colour, which in turn will be noticed by the dull colour of the fried pieces of food.

A word of warning regarding deep frying. Always see that the pan used is deep enough to allow for expansion by volume when the pieces of food are lowered into the fat. Also, when food is added to hot fat, some of the surface moisture will boil rapidly, as the fat will be between 360°F. to 375°F., and the moisture on the food boils at 212°F. This may cause the fat to foam and boil over, thus causing a great deal of mess, and sometimes fire has been caused, with disastrous results.

Frying in Shallow Fat

Unlike deep frying, clarified butter or margarine may be used in this process, as very little fat is used, it being usual to have a shallow heavy frying or sauté pan for this mode of cooking. It is only suitable for fillets of fish or thin slices of food. Large birds or thick slices of food cannot be cooked successfully by this method. If unclarified butter or margarine is used, because of its salt and water content, it will splutter a little, but not violently, as in deep frying.

Dry the pieces of food to be fried, season with salt and pepper, and dredge with flour where described in the recipe ; otherwise, leave plain. Heat enough fat to cover the bottom of the pan, or to come one-third way up the food. Fry the fillets or slices until golden brown on one side, turn carefully, and brown the other side. Should the fillets or slices be thick, like chops or cutlets, and require some time to cook through, the heat must be lowered after the food is nicely browned, then continue cooking slowly until tender.

Frikadeller

Swedish meat balls or croquettes.

Frisé (Fr.)

Curled. Curly kale—chou frisé.

Frit or Frite (Fr.)

Fried. (See Frying in Deep Fat, Frying in Shallow Fat, under Fried.)

Fritter (Beignet, Fr.)

Foods dipped in batter, or egged and crumbed, and fried in deep fat. Beignets de Fromage—cheese fritters.

Frog (Grenouille, Fr.)

Frogs are not meat, and are consumed in considerable quantities in some countries during Lent. The hind legs of several species of frogs are enjoyed to a limited extent in both Europe and the United States, as a delicate food much resembling chicken. The large frogs are the more convenient, both for general use and for market purposes. The smaller are, as a rule, more delicate in flavour.

Frog farming has never succeeded in England, but the wild creatures are sometimes used. Some very good edible bullfrogs abound on Hampstead Heath, their croak being heard 400 to 500 yards away. They are in season in spring, chiefly Lent.

Froid (Fr.)

Cold.

Fromage (Fr.)

See Cheese.

Fromage de Cochon (Fr.)

Hogshead cheese or brawn.

Fromage de Porc (Fr.)

Pork cheese or pork brawn.

Frosting

A term applied to dishes which are covered with meringue and sprinkled with sugar. When baked, the sugar sparkles like frost. In America, the term is applied to almost all sweet cake toppings, which we would call fondant or royal icing.

Frothing

A very old practice of dredging meats or poultry with flour just before taking up, and by applying fierce heat the surface of the joint or bird takes on a froth-like, crisp appearance.

Fructose, Levulose

Fruit sugar, such as corn syrup, honey, etc.

Fruit

Modern refrigeration and science now bring to us almost every type of fruit all the year round, so that the enjoyment of early strawberries for instance, is quickly losing its distinction as a mark on the calendar. In recent years, we have learnt much about the health-giving properties of most fruits, the leader in this field being the blackcurrant. With very few exceptions, most fruits are best when eaten raw, as when cooked some of the valuable vitamins are lost.

It is a mistaken idea always to force certain fruits on to invalids, to tempt the appetite, for many forms of indisposition are accentuated by its consumption. All fruits, including berries (unless really fresh and clean) should be washed before eating, as all forms of insect life abound on fruit, field and orchard.

Fruit Butters

These comprise preserves of fruit less sweet than jam, generally spiced to aid their keeping qualities, and of the spreading consistency of butter

Fruit Juices

Commercial bottled or canned juices are essentially the expressed juices of ripe fruits, pasteurised and hermetically sealed before fermentation has commenced. If the fruits are quite sound, and the process of manufacture carefully controlled, no preservative need be employed. In all bottled or canned juices, some of the all-important vitamin C is lost.

Fruit Sugar

See Fructose.

Fry (Frire, Fr.)

To cook in shallow or deep fat. See Fried, for particulars of application.

Frying

For full particulars of application, see Fried.

Fudge

A type of small grained sugar candy or sweetmeat made in a variety of colours and flavours. The sugar is boiled to the soft ball stage, butter and flavouring are then added and the whole beaten until creamy. It is easy to chew and does not stick to the palate like hard-boiled caramels.

Fumé (Fr.)

Smoked.   Saumon   fumé— smoked salmon.

'umet (Fr.)
The concentrated broth of game, fish or vegetables.

'umet de Poisson (Fr.)
Fish stock.

'ungus
Vegetation which obtains its foods from organic substances —animal or vegetable matter, alive or decaying. Mushrooms, truffles, yeast, bacteria and moulds, belong to this group.

'urmenty (Fermenty, Flummery, Firmity, Frumenty)
In olden times, when potatoes, tomatoes, tea, canned goods, etc., were unknown, the diet of the British Isles was of a very simple, but ingenious nature. Fermenty, as the original name implies, was a product of grain from the harvest fields, consisting of new wheat steeped in water and left upon a very slow fire from 1 to 2 days, when a form of maltose was formed. The grain was then treated with milk, sugar and spices, and eaten with honey. In certain parts of the country, the composition has gradually changed, and its original received name many twists. Milk custard sweetened with honey, oatmeal moulds flavoured with honey, all claim one of these titles, and many counties claim its origin. A Scottish name for this dish is Sowens.

G

Gage
A slang term for the greengage (which see) and other varieties of plum.

Galatine (Fr.)
A moulded roll or shape of meat, poultry or game, stuffed with forcemeat, usually of an elaborate nature and coated with savoury or aspic jelly.

Galette (Fr.)
A very light, French breakfast roll.

Gall Bladder
The small, pear-shaped reservoir attached to the liver of animals or birds, which contains the extremely bitter bile, and which, if fractured, will taint all parts of the flesh with which it comes in contact.

Gallino Rennet
Rennet produced from the rough skin which lines the gizzards of poultry. The skin is carefully removed, washed and dried. A little is then soaked in boiling water, producing a rennet more delicate than that made from calf's rennet.

Gallon
A measure equal to 10 lbs. of distilled water, which is equivalent to 277.274 cubic inches. It is divided into 4 quarts or 8 pints.

Galuska

Name of cork-shaped Hungarian type of dumplings, which may be eaten with meat, or with honey as a sweet course.

Gambit [Café]

Many English cafés bear this title, which indicates that they were at one time used for the playing of chess or as a chess club. Gambit being a mode of opening a game of chess.

Game (Gibier, Fr.)

Under this term are included all wild animals which are used for human consumption ; and in nothing is the skill and knowledge of the chef or cook so much displayed as in its management. The " Master Book of Poultry and Game," containing 1,000 recipes, will assist all in general hints on its preparation. (See also Pies.)

Game Sauce (Sauce Gibier, Fr.)

Espagnole sauce flavoured with game.

Gammon

The thigh and hind leg of a hog when cured with the side. When cut from the carcase and separately cured, it is termed the ham. A square-cut ham. The lower part of a side of pork.

Gantry

The shelf for barrels which, as home brewing died out, was used for salting the sides of bacon.

Gaper or Spoonshell (Brelin, Fr.)

Gapers live buried in mud or sand, in an upright position. Holiday-makers at Ramsgate or Broadstairs are often intrigued, watching the men dig the gapers up with a long skewer and slipping them off into a shallow basket, to be used as bait.

They are found chiefly at the mouths of rivers and estuaries, near low-water mark. The shell is permanently open at the posterior end. In Devonshire, they are better known as Spoonshell.

Garbure (Fr.)

Originally a soup of salt pork and cabbage. Now more generally recognised as a kind of maigre broth made with vegetables and bread crusts. Best described as something between a soup, a stew, and a bake.

Garçon (Fr.)

Waiter.

Garçon de Salle (Fr.)

Restaurant waiter.

Garçon Premier (Fr.)

Head waiter.

Garde Manger (Fr.)

The larder cook. One who looks after the larder.

Garden Balm

See Balm, Garden.

Gardon (Fr.)

See Roach.

Garfish or Needlefish (Orphie, Fr.)

Garfish are often caught off Hayling Island and on Brighton beach, and are a capital fish. The fact that their bones are bright green alarms the timorous, but it is not a danger sign, and should not prevent investigation of their many good qualities.

The garfish is elongated, slender and spear-mouthed. It might be likened to a cross between a mackerel and an eel. The flesh is wholesome and pleasing.

Garibaldi

The name applied to sauce signifies Espagnole Sauce flavoured with curry, mustard, anchovy paste and capers.

Garlic (Ail, Fr.)

A vegetable similar to a small onion, but with a white-skinned bulb, divided into 10 or 12 sections known as " cloves " (clove of garlic).

Garni (Fr.)

To garnish, fill or stuff. (See Garnish.)

Garnish

To decorate. Something set around or on a dish as an embellishment, or added for flavour or relish.

Garum

A highly seasoned and very salty relish, made from fish gills and blood when in a state of fermentation.

Gasterea

The goddess of gastronomy. When the term is applied to the menu it conveys light, easy of digestion, stimulating, promoting vim and vigour.

Gastronome (Fr.)

A person who pays great attention to his diet, an epicure, being the art or science of good eating, love of good eating, gastronomically speaking.

Gastronomy (Gastronomie, Fr.)

It has been said that " gastronomy is not merely an art, but the only art which is perfect ". To perfect the art of good living, one needs a long apprenticeship to all its laws, its formulae, and its fixed processes. Gastronomy is the art of good living, or the science of life, wherein one discovers the use not only of the foods immediately at hand but those gathered from all corners of the earth, and uses them to the best effect upon individual or nation.

Gâteau (Fr.)

At one time a French country cake for high days and holidays. Now the term is applied to a rich, fancy-shaped cake, generally split and filled with flavoured cream and tastefully decorated. See also Genoise.

Gâteau de Noce (Fr.)

See Wedding Cake.

Gaufre (Fr.)

A light, spongy sort of wafer biscuit. The waffle (which see).

H

Gelatine (Fr.)
An animal protein manufactured from the hooves, skin and other tissues. A good quality gelatine is odourless, tasteless, and is practically transparent in sheet or leaf form. The powdered varieties are generally not quite so refined, and have a yellowish tinge. It is useful in the diet, as it is capable of carrying other foods in attractive form, in sweet or aspic jellies. (See also Agar-Agar.)

Gelée (Fr.)
See Jelly.

Gelinotte (Fr.)
See Hazel Hen.

Genevoise (Fr.)
Geneva style. As a sauce, it signifies a brown fish sauce, flavoured with madeira wine, garlic and anchovy essence.

Genièvre (Fr.)
See Juniper Berry.

Genipap
An orange-shaped fruit with a greenish-white skin, subacid and juice of purplish tinge. A fruit of a tropical American tree, used in certain preserves and a type of marmalade.

Génoise (Fr.)
Genoese style. Chiefly applied to foods rich in butter and eggs, as Génoise fancies. Génoise as applied to flour confectionery always denotes a rich flat cake, which forms the foundation for most afternoon fancies, or is cut into fancy shapes to make layer cakes or gâteaux.

Gerome
A fermented and refined French cheese, best served in winter months.

Gervais (Fr.)
A French cream cheese, slightly sweet in taste.

Getmesost
A soft, sweet, Swedish cheese, made from goat's milk.

Ghee
Butter as clarified in India, the best from the milk of cows and an inferior quality from that of buffaloes. It is one of the most common articles of diet in India, and is used extensively in all forms of cooking, a favourite dish being semolina cooked in ghee.

Gherkin (Cornichon, Fr.)
A small, prickly cucumber, used chiefly for pickle. It is light green, from 1 to 3 inches in length, about half as thick as it is long.

Gibelotte (Fr.)
A stew consisting of rabbit.

Gibier (Fr.)
See Game.

Giblets (Abatis, Fr.)
Poultry or game-bird offal, comprising all the trimmings (neck, heart, liver, gizzard, feet). The internal edible parts of a fowl.

Gigot d'Agneau (Fr.)
Leg of lamb.

Gigot de Mouton (Fr.)
Leg of mutton.

Gigue (Fr.)
Leg of roebuck.

Gill

A measure equal to ¼ pint.

Gin

The term " gin " is an abbreviation of Geneva, a corruption of " Genièvre ", being the French for juniper berry. Gin is a spirituous liquor, which derives its characteristic flavour from the juniper berry and other aromatic substances, which each manufacturer tries to keep a closely guarded secret. Angelica gives gin a pleasing flavour, as also coriander.

LEMON GIN is gin with the flavour of lemon, slightly yellow in colour.

PASSION GIN is gin flavoured with passion fruit.

Ginger (Gingembre, Fr.)

The powdered ginger that we know so well is obtained from the root of a plant that grows throughout the tropics. The roots are gathered when the leaves of the plant have withered, then washed and dried in the sun. For the best ginger, the roots are scraped after washing. They are then ground and sifted for the powdered ginger. Preserved or Canton ginger consists of green roots boiled in a heavy syrup and put up in fancy jars or packed in casks. Crystallised ginger is also made from the young roots. The best is that imported from China, and an inferior grade comes to us from Africa.

Ginger Ale

A carbonated, non-excisable beverage, generally manufactured from artificial ginger flavour or extract, sugar, citric acid, caramel, foam essence and water.

Ginger Beer

A brewed, non-excisable beverage, generally manufactured from bruised ginger, licorice, hops, cloves, sugar, yeast, citric acid and water. Foam essence is employed in cheap brands.

Ginger Brandy

A brandy cordial, flavoured with ginger.

Gingerbread (Pain d'Épice, Fr.)

Gingerbread is one of the Christmas festival breads and is connected with English fairs to the present time. Gingerbreads of honour were offered to the royal family at the time Peter the Great was born. They were baked in special moulds, one bearing the arms of the city of Moscow, and another had a double-headed eagle moulded upon it. Certain gingerbreads were so elaborately decorated and gilded for presents in olden times, that the gold leaf had to be specially protected during transit. It is from this mode of decorating the Christmas festival breads, that first arose the familiar saying—taking the gilt off the gingerbread.

Ginger Snaps
Very brittle cylindrical flour confections, at one time filled with brandy-flavoured cream. Now sold without cream or brandy, principally at country fairs.

Gingko-nut
A thin-shelled, greenish nut, of the maiden-hair tree. It is actually the seed of the fruit which resembles a small persimmon. The fruit itself is rather offensive in odour, but the nut is sweet and agreeable to the palate. They are generally eaten roasted.

Gin Sling
An American drink consisting of gin, sugar, lemon, ice and a flick of nutmeg.

Gipsy Cake
See Tipsy Cake.

Girdle Cakes
See Griddle Cakes.

Girofle (Fr.)
See Clove.

Gitana, à la (Fr.)
Gipsy style. Usually cooked in embers or finished with field mushrooms. In salad garnishings, dandelion leaves are employed.

Glace (Fr.)
Ice.

Glacé (Fr.)
Glazed, frozen, iced. Candied fruits or nuts. When dishes are glazed with concentrated stock, the term is sometimes applied to convey a smooth, glossy surface.

Glace de Viande (Fr.)
Better known as Glaze, being the reduction of meat extracts, stock or gravies by rapid boiling to drive off all superfluous moisture, to produce a thick jelly-like liquid for the glazing of hot or cold cooked meats, or for enriching of special soups or sauces.

Glace Royale (Glace de Sucre, Fr.)
A combination of pulverised sugar with white of egg, which is beaten to a smooth velvety texture for the icing of wedding and other celebration cakes. It dries quite hard and acts as a preservative when keeping heavy fruited cakes over a long period.

Glacière (Fr.)
Refrigerator or cooling cabinet.

Glai (Fr.)
See Jay.

Gliadin
A protein which is most noticeable in wheat, which gives elasticity to bread dough and enables it to expand as the leavening agent gives lightness to the dough. (See also Gluten.)

Globe Artichoke
See Artichoke ; also Jerusalem Artichoke, for information on the tuber variety.

Glucide (Saccharin)

A white, crystalline powder, 500 times sweeter than cane sugar. Used as a sugar substitute in mineral waters and tablet jellies. It is a coal tar derivative, with no food value.

Glucose, Dextrose or Grape Sugar

A heavy, colourless, syrupy substance, of the consistency of ordinary golden syrup, not so sweet as cane sugar, but in fuel value it is equal to any sugar. As it is an uncrystallisable sugar, it is much valued for toffee and sweet manufacture.

Gluten

Vegetable albumen. The nitrogenous part of flour, whether of wheat or other grains, insoluble in water. It is a sticky, elastic mass, formed by a combination of gliadin and glutenin when wet. Gluten bread is made from flour with much of the starch removed, hence the low energy value.

Glutenin

The toughness or elasticity in gluten that gives to bread doughs the power to hold together as it expands with fermentation.

Gloucester

Name of an English sauce consisting of mayonnaise, flavoured with Worcestershire Sauce, and diluted with sour cream.

Glycerine

A colourless, odourless liquid, with an insipid sweet taste.

Glycerine was first discovered in olive oil in 1779. The largest source of supply is obtained from fatty oils. In periods of war, when such fatty oils are in short supply, it can be obtained by fermentation of molasses or other cheap sugar materials, which can be made to yield up to 25% of their weight in glycerine.

There is the Industrial Glycerine, pale yellow in colour (sometimes referred to as dynamite glycerine) and Chemically Pure (C.P.) Glycerine, which is the colourless and odourless liquid used as a preservative against fermentation, and extensively in cheap grades of flour confectionery, such as slab cakes.

Glycogen

Animal starch, a whitish powder which can be prepared from animal liver and muscle. It is stored in the body for future conversion into sugar. First discovered by Claude Bernard. It is formed from sugar and a part of the fat and protein in the blood. When pure, a white, amorphous, tasteless powder, insoluble in alcohol.

Gnocchi di Latte

A dish of Italian milk dumplings, served with Parmesan cheese. To be at their best, they must come to the table spluttering in their creamy sauce.

Goat

The flesh of the goat or kid is consumed in considerable quantities in many European countries, and if not too old is as succulent as lamb. World War II gave many English people the opportunity to sample goat flesh which, if cooked slowly and treated in any manner as described for lamb, is a very good dish.

Goat's Milk

Goat's milk is higher in fat content than cow's milk, and due to the fact that the globules of fat are relatively small, it is more easily digested, and is preferred by some physicians for infant feeding.

Godard

A very rich garnish for chicken, containing truffles, sweet-breads, mushrooms, etc., and Madeira Sauce. Named after Benjamin Godard, a French composer, born 1849, died 1895. His death was considered a real loss to French art.

Godiveau (Fr.)

A French forcemeat prepared with veal and beef suet. The French veal stuffing.

Gofla

The staple food of the Canary Isles, being corn meal or ground maize. Usually cooked with milk, or sometimes just stirred in cold milk.

Golden Buck

See Buck Rarebit.

Golden Plover

See Plover.

Golden Syrup

The better quality of treacle, containing up to 62 per cent. of total sugars, obtained during the refining process of sugar. (See also Molasses.)

Goldwasser (Ger.)

A colourless, sweet liqueur, with flakes of gold. Flavoured with aniseed and orange.

Gombo

See Gumbo.

Goose (Oie, Fr.)

The male bird, when adult, is a gander, but in the kitchen male and female birds are both called a goose when over 6 months old. Goslings, or green geese, are birds not exceeding 6 months; the term " green geese " is hardly used nowadays. Goslings are best from May to the end of August, and their delicate flavour should not be spoilt with sage and onion stuffing. Fresh goose-berry sauce or a tart orange salad should be their only accompaniment, other than a fresh, crisp green salad. Geese are at their best from September to February.

It is said that Queen Elizabeth was the originator of the Michaelmas goose. She had one on the table before her when the news arrived of the defeat of the Spanish Armada, and she commanded the same dish to be served every succeeding Michaelmas.

Geese can live to a great age, but are not much use for the table when more than one year old. By " goose " and " geese " one means, of course, both male and female birds— ganders and geese—for as a food bird the gander long ago saw his title submerged by that of his mate.

Goose-fat is highly regarded by many races. In Germany, it is largely eaten in place of butter. Some people avoid goose meat, fearing it to be too greasy and not easy of digestion. This prejudice finds its chief basis in poor cookery.

Gooseberry (Groseille, Fr.)

A universal favourite of these Isles. The principal varieties are the green and red. It is an exceedingly refreshing fruit and many dishes may be made with it. The red is the more acid of the two, the hairy type being much superior in flavour to the smooth-skinned variety.

First introduced to this country in the 16th century, and now to to be found in almost every provincial garden and orchard.

Gooseberry Fool

Gooseberry purée mixed with cream, sugar, and iced. A term originating from the French " foule ", signifying pulped. Almost any type of fruit may be treated in this manner.

Gorganzola (Green, White or Pannerone, It.)

An Italian cheese, originating from the town of Gorganzola in the Province of Milan.

The green type is of soft, buttery consistency. White gorganzola, or Pannerone, is made more especially in Lower Lombardy. It is sweeter and not so hot as the green, and is not treated with mould (penicilium glaucum) which gives the other gorganzola its green vein.

Gormandises

Small types of petits-fours, that can be hastily eaten. Not a mouthful.

Gosling (Oison, Fr.)

See Goose.

Goujon (Fr.)

See Gudgeon.

Goulash

A thick Hungarian stew, made from beef or veal, flavoured with vegetables and paprika.

Goumi

A berry which grows wild in China and Japan and is much esteemed for use in many culinary preparations. It is orange-red in colour and of very acid flavour. Cooked in pies, preserves, tarts and sauces, it is excellent fare.

Gourds

The large fleshy group of vegetables of the pumpkin family.

Gourmand (Fr.)
One given to gluttony.

Gourmet (Fr.)
An epicure (which see) originally one with a delicate taste for food or wine.

Goût (Fr.)
The sense of the palate. Of good taste or flavour.

Goûter (Fr.)
High tea of a savoury nature. A meat tea.

Graham Cakes
Small, round cakes, made from wholemeal flour and milk. The name originating from Graham, name of a miller of whole-wheat flour.

Grain
The seed of all grass plants, including all types of corn. A single small corn seed weighs one-seven-thousandth of 1 lb.

Grains of Paradise
This alligator or Melequeta pepper is frequently mentioned in very old recipe books under the title of Grains of Paradise. They are the seeds of a West African plant of the ginger family, exceedingly pungent and extensively used as a spice in Africa. In the reign of George III an act was passed forbidding brewers to have any Grains of Paradise used in their beers, under a penalty of a £200 fine. (See Cardamom.)

Granadilla
A large, egg-shaped fruit of a vine belonging to the passion flower family. It has a slightly acid pulp, enclosing a number of small, flat, marrow-like seeds. In its green state it is cooked as a vegetable. When fully ripe, it can be eaten raw or made into a type of marmalade.

Grand-Duc (Fr.)
Name of a style of garnish for fish or poultry which consists of asparagus tips, sliced truffle and when with fish crayfish tails are added.

Grande Champagne (Fr.)
The finest cognac brandy.

Grande Liqueur (Fr.)
A liqueur made in France, similar to Chartreuse.

Grande Marnier (Fr.)
A golden - brown brandy liqueur, with the flavour of orange.

Grand Veneur (Fr.)
Name of a sauce served with game consisting of Sauce Poivrade with well-reduced venison stock added, flavoured with red-currant jelly.

Granite (Fr.)
A sorbet, or soft water ice, of light texture.

Grape (Raisin, Fr.)

The fruit of the vine, which is now available to all classes of the community. One need not be so old to remember when this succulent fruit was a rarity, save at banquets and balls. They are mildly laxative and an aid in preventing anaemia. It is the combination of the volatile substances of grapes during fermentation which produces the bouquet of wines. The sugar content will vary from 12% to 26% and has a deciding factor in the manufacture of all wines. Hebrew writings disclose that wine was made in Egypt 5,000 years ago. For dessert at dinner, the Alicante or Gros Colmar are considered very fine. (See also Raisin.)

Grapefruit or Shaddock (Pamplemousse, Fr.)

As this fruit often grows in bunches, it has now taken over the more familiar name of grapefruit, as against its early name, shaddock or pamplemousse. It is closely related to the orange and lemon, the fruit growing from 4 to 6 inches in diameter. The rind is yellow and the pulp resembles that of a lemon in appearance, with a slightly bitter flavour which makes it excellent as an appetiser.

The best grades are those from Florida, California being a close second. Smaller fruit come from the West Indies and South Africa. The best are those which are heavy for their size, with few seeds, and very juicy. (See also Shaddock.)

Grape Sugar

See Glucose.

Gras (Fr.)

Fattened—as foie-gras (fattened liver).

Gras, au (Fr.)

Cooked in rich gravy or meat sauce.

Gratin, au (Fr.)

Applied to dishes covered with breadcrumbs or grated cheese, etc. and browned under a grill or in the oven.

Graves

Red and white wines produced from one of the most important wine producing districts of the Gironde, the red being of higher quality than the white.

Gravy (Jus, Fr.)

The natural juices which flow from meat in the cooking, often spoilt by the additions of unnatural flavours and thickeners to the natural juices after the cooking process has been completed.

Gravy Salt

Stoved salt coloured with caramel.

Grayling (Ombre, Fr.)

Grayling are distinguished by rather large scales, a small mouth with feeble teeth, and a long dorsal fin. They are handsome fishes, afford good sport to anglers, and are excellent for the table.

The grayling is later in spawning than its cousin the trout, and normally comes into condition about September, and is perhaps at its best in November. The small grayling do not spawn during their first season of maturity, and these are in condition in the summer. These small grayling, up to ¾ lb., are best, and while Continental species are much larger, in England grayling rarely weigh more than 4 lbs.

Grayling and river trout, salmon and sea-trout, all belong to a royal family of unquestioned greatness, who reign over every feast of distinction where connoisseurs gather.

Grecque (Fr.)
As applied to garnitures for poultry, signifies savoury rice and tomato sauce.

Greengage (Reine Claude, Fr.)
The greengage is considered the sweetest and best of all dessert plums if allowed to ripen fully on the tree, for it is the last 2 or 3 weeks of ripening which give this plum its full, characteristic flavour. The original variety derives its name from Claude, Queen of Francis I, the name " gage " being added by one Sir William Gage, a clergyman, who brought the first cuttings to England. It is a very fleshy, greenish-yellow plum, with a small stone.

Green Goose
A gosling, or young goose.

Green Peas
See Peas.

Green Plover (Vanneau, Fr.)
See Lapwing.

Grenade (Fr.)
See Pomegranate.

Grenadine (Fr.)
A sweet, red syrup, made from the pomegranate.

Grenadins (Fr.)
Small, neatly trimmed slices of veal, usually braised.

Grenouille (Fr.)
See Frog.

Grey Mullet (Mulet, Muge, Fr.)
See Mullet, Grey.

Grey Plover (Pluvier, Fr.)
See Plover.

Grianneau (Fr.)
A young grouse.

Griddle
A flat, smooth, metal plate, for baking cakes and scones.

Griddle or Girdle Cakes
Rich type of scone baked on top of a griddle or girdle stove. A type of Scotch scone.

Gridiron
A light metal grating for placing over or before a fire, for broiling fish or flesh. Usually made in two parts working on a hinge, so that the food to be cooked can be placed between the metal grills and turned easily during the cooking process.

Grille or Grill (Gril, Fr.)

Originally applied to the iron bars of an open fireplace, arranged before or over the fire, the food then being cooked over the heat. Of recent years, with the introduction of the gas and electric grill, the food is generally cooked under the heat. As heat rises, it is a wonder that some means of generating the heat from the bottom of the grill has not been perfected. (See Gridiron.)

Grilled (Grillade, Fr.)

Grilling is suitable for small fillets, steaks or cutlets of food. It is important to see that the grill is pre-heated and the grid or grill rack is rubbed over with mutton or similar fat, to ensure the pieces do not stick to the bars and thus cause breaking when cooked.
Sprinkle the food with salt and pepper, place it under the grill ; when the one side is cooked, turn carefully and cook the other side. Food other than fat types will need to be brushed over with good oil or melted butter before grilling ; otherwise, it will cook dry.

Grilse (Saumonneau, Fr.)

Grilse is the name given to young salmon, on its first leaving the sea to go up-stream. These young fish, on their first return from the sea, generally precede the more mature individuals.

Griskin

The spine or chine of a hog, usually left unsalted when preparing sides of bacon. The term is considered of Irish origin.

Grissini

The name given to the Italian finger rolls 6 to 18 inches in length. Italian stick bread.

Grits

Coarsely ground groats.

Grive (Fr.)

See Thrush.

Groats

Oats or other grain, which have been deprived of the husks.

Grocer

At first applied to one who sold by the gross, a dealer or wholesaler. Of recent years, applied to one dealing in general food supplies by retail.

Grog

Originally a mixture of spirits and cold water. Later improved, as the water was added hot and it was sweetened with sugar.

Grondin (Fr.)

See Gurnet.

Groseille (Fr.)

See Gooseberry.

Grosse-pièce (Fr.)

A large joint of meat, or poultry such as a turkey.

Ground-nut
See Pea-nut.

Grouse
All attempts to introduce grouse to France and elsewhere have failed, hence there is no name for this bird in any other language. The title " grouse " is applied to a large family of American game-birds, but in the British Isles it refers to the red grouse.

A young grouse for table is one shot from 12 August to the end of December of the year when bred. Those shot mid-August to mid-October of the year when bred are considered the best of all game birds. As grouse are usually delivered to the kitchen unplucked (or should be), the young can be recognised by the soft downy plumes on the breast and under the wings, also by the pointed wings and rounded soft spur knob. All other birds should be braised or cooked in casserole. The apprentice or unwary should note, when judging grouse for age, that grouse have no spurs. The spur knob becomes scaly and hard in the older birds.

Young grouse need no additions like most other young game. If cooked to the exact degree of done-ness, it will always be proclaimed a feast for the gods, whether eaten hot or cold.

GROUSE, MOUNTAIN, see Ptarmigan.

Gruau (Fr.)
See Gruel.

Gruau d'Avoine (Fr.)
See Oatmeal.

Grue (Fr.)
See Crane.

Gruel (Gruau, Fr.)
The liquor obtained by boiling oatmeal in water.

Gruyère (Fr.)
A hard, pale yellow, cooked Swiss cheese, its chief characteristic being the gas holes caused by the rapid fermentation of the curd. Like many other cheeses, very little of that made at the village of its birth is exported. The chief supplies come from the surrounding neighbourhood, being the commercial imitation of the true product.

Guarana
A Brazilian beverage, similar in appearance to our cocoa, but having a bitter, astringent flavour, which smells like freshly roasted coffee. It is made from the ground seeds of a native plant, which are moistened and formed into small rolls and then baked. The baked roll is then grated into hot water and sweetened.

Guava

A really delicious fruit when made into jam or jelly, but when canned whole its many hard seeds make it quite objectionable. In size it varies from 1 to 4 inches in diameter. It has a yellow to purplish, thin skin, with an aromatic pulp, sweet or slightly acid. Owing to its very thin skin and soft pulp, it is not exported from the tropical countries in its fresh state.

Guegnolet (Fr.)

A cherry brandy liqueur.

Gudgeon (Goujon, Fr.)

The gudgeon is a small but nicely flavoured fresh-water fish, belonging to the carp family. The upper part of the body is olive-brown spotted with black, gill covers greenish-white, with the under surface white. Their colours, however, vary considerably according to their age and locality. The usual size is from 5 to 6 inches, weighing up to ½ lb.

Guinea Fowl (Pintarde, Fr.)

A domestic fowl with purplish-grey plumage evenly dotted with white. Some have beautiful shades of blue in their feathers, but in appearance the sexes are alike.

The guinea fowl was raised as a table bird by the ancient Greeks and Romans. Later, it was apparently overlooked, not coming into vogue again for centuries. The old French name for it was "guinette", and in England in country districts it is still called "gleeny" from the Latin " gallina ", a fowl—a name be- queathed to us from the Roman occupation.

Its popularity is due to the excellence of its flesh, which has a slight game flavour. It serves as an excellent substitute for game when that is unobtainable or out of season, it being available from February to June. When well kept, it is not unlike the pheasant in taste and appearance.

Guinea fowl are sold like game birds, unplucked. As their feather coats are very thick, this method of selling makes them appear larger in body than they really are.

A squab guinea should weigh ¾ lb. to 1¼ lbs.

A guinea chick should weigh 1½ lbs. to 2¼ lbs.

A guinea fowl should weigh 2¾ lbs. to 3¾ lbs.

Anything beyond that size will be useless for roasting.

Wild guinea fowl are generally useless for table.

The guinea fowl has the real right to the name of turkey. Our domesticated turkey flouts its name under false colours.

Guinea-pig

Guinea-pig as a food is most pleasant, if baked the same as the gipsies serve the hedgehog. It is a small, South American rodent, somewhat resembling a small pig, weighing up to 4 lbs.

Guisada

A popular Spanish dish, consisting of stew of meat and potatoes.

Gull (Mouette, Fr.)

To-day, the gull's eggs are more esteemed than the bird for food, this being a far cry from the time when gulls were fattened as domestic birds. In those days, the price per bird was higher than a pound of fillet steak, such was the desire to break away from beef, mutton or pork.

One may be sure that all fishiness was lost by netting the birds and feeding them on sour milk or buttermilk. They certainly knew a thing or two in olden times, which we may even yet be pleased to copy. In brief, the gull when taken from its natural quarters has an unpleasant fishy flavour, but if kept in captivity and fed on other foods, it soon becomes palatable and good eating.

Gulmauve (Fr.)

See Marshmallow.

Gum Arabic

Gum of the acacia (which see).

Gumbo

See Okra.

Gum Tragacanth (Adragant, Fr.)

A gum derived from a low spiny shrub found in western Asia, which forms the principal ingredient used for gum paste ornaments decorating wedding and other festive cakes.

Gurnet or Gurnard (Grondin, Fr.)

The fins of this fish are beautifully coloured, especially in the young.

When taken out of the water, gurnards emit a grunting noise produced by the vibrations of a perforated diaphragm across the cavity of the air-bladder. Their flesh is white, firm and wholesome. Gurnards are coast fishes ; they are caught chiefly by trawl. The lovely colour of their fins, and the petulant protest on their faces, is enough to make one hesitate to use them. But, sentiment apart, they are to be commended to all fish eaters who do not like fishy fish. They are in season from July to April.

Gurnards are not expensive to buy, but they are not economical, as the head generally weighs one-third of the total weight of the fish.

H

Haché (Fr.)

Minced, chopped, or finely sliced meats.

Hachis (Fr.)

See Hash.

Haddie

See Finnan or Findon Haddock.

Haddock (Aiglefin, Fr.)

Haddock is distinguished from cod by its smaller mouth, and is a dark silvery-grey fish from 1½ to 7 lbs. in weight as generally seen in the market—though often reaching double the latter size. It is allied to the cod and very plentiful in the North Atlantic. Its flesh is of first quality—white, flaky and tender.

Haddock is best from October until the beginning of January, February and March being the spawning time. Those who suppose the thumb mark (or dark spot) is peculiar only to the haddock, should read the notes on the John Dory.

Hafergrutzensuppe mit Äpfeln

A German oat and apple soup, spiced, and garnished with currants.

Haggis

The dish immortalised in a poem by Robert Burns, and now looked upon as the national dish of Scotland. A kind of meat pudding composed of minced sheep's offal, mixed with oatmeal, herbs and spices, encased in a sheep's paunch tied up into convenient sizes and boiled. The case being tripe, the whole pudding is edible. Always a traditional dish in English-speaking countries on Burns Night.

Hake (Merluche, Fr.)

A fish of the cod type, but of a different family. Large specimens attain a length of 4 feet. Hake is the safest fish for invalids and infants, because the backbone is more easily detachable than that of any other fish, and because it is the most free from bones. In recent years, the price of hake has increased considerably, because of its growing popularity. It is a slender fish, with long acute snout, large and seminal mouth and sharp teeth, and is of a voracious nature. The flesh is soft, and considered infinitely finer than cod. Carefully poached, fried as cutlets, or nicely baked in the oven, it is quite acceptable.

Halaszie

A spicy, Hungarian mixed fish stew.

Half om Half

A sweet, brown-red, Dutch liqueur Hollandaise.

Halibut (Flétan, Fr.)

A huge flat fish, brown and scaly above and white underneath—one of the largest edible fishes. The male seldom weighs more than 60 pounds, but the female has been known to exceed 700 lbs., and to attain a size 10 feet in length and 5 in width. A fat female of 70 to 80 lbs. is considered to be the most savoury. For domestic use, the market favours the chicken halibut, averaging 3 to 8 lbs.

Halibut is often substituted for turbot, because of its cheapness, but it can readily be distinguished in the whole fish, as the turbot has spots on the back and the halibut has not. The turbot is also much wider for its length than the halibut. The young undeveloped fish have eyes either side of the head, but as they develop the eyes come together on the right side and the mouth becomes large. It is a valued food fish, with very firm white flesh.

Ham (Jambon, Fr.)

The thigh and hind leg of the pig when separated from the carcase and cured. In England, The York or Cumberland hams are most sought after. In Germany, the Brandenberg is most esteemed ; whilst in America the Virginia peach-fed is considered the best.

Hamburger Aalsuppe

A pleasant German eel soup.

Hanche (Fr.)

See Haunch.

Hand of Pork, or Hamkins

The shoulder or fore-leg of pork, salted, cured and served hot with broad beans or cold with relish.

Hard Tack

Term given by sailors in early days to the ship's biscuits or bread.

Hare (Lièvre, Fr.)

The hare lip is a good indication of age, for in the young hare it is but faintly marked, becoming more pronounced with age. This animal has longer ears and hind legs than the rabbit.

One author of culinary works was accused of saying—" first catch your hare ". This, of course, was the ignorance of the reviewer of the work, who read " catch " for " case ", for in earlier times to " case " a hare meant to skin it. Hares, like pork, should always be cooked right through. Never eat hare if still red.

We have two distinct types of hare, the more common brown hare, and those which principally come to us from Scotland, being the blue or mountain hare, which changes to white in winter. The Belgian hare is a much larger variety than those usually caught in these Isles. The young hare (up to 6 months) is called a leveret and is more esteemed than the adult, which becomes very tough with age. The points given for the selection of rabbit apply equally to hares.

Hareng (Fr.)

See Herring.

Hareng Fumé (Fr.)

See Kipper.

Hareng Marine (Fr.)

See Herring, Roll Mops.

Hareng Salé (Fr.)
See Herring, Salted.

Hareng Saur (Fr.)
See Herring, Red.

Haricot (Fr.)
Originally a bean stew, now applied to mutton stew with almost any vegetables, as in Haricot Mutton, which is a mutton stew with a few haricot beans usually tossed in as an afterthought.

Haricot Bean
A cheap and very nourishing vegetable, easily cooked and not used as well as it deserves to be. In the U.S.A. it is usually referred to as the Boston or Navy bean, and is the type used in the manufacture of the baked beans in tomato sauce.
They are the ripe seeds of the various kinds of dwarf or climbing beans, which all come within the terms of haricot or kidney beans.

Haricots Verts (Fr.)
French beans.

Harslet
A misspelling for Haslet (which see).

Hasenkuchen
A German pâté of hare.

Hash (Hachis, Fr.)
All types of salmi or reheated meats in sauce come under the heading of hash. Re-cooked meats in sauce.

Haslet, Pig's
The edible entrails of the pig, chopped, mixed with herbs and spices, and baked in individual cakes, often covered with caul before cooking.

Hassenpfeffer
Name of a very rich German hare stew. A particularly fine recipe for this dish is given in the " Master Book of Poultry and Game ".

Hasty Pudding
A thin type of sweetened porridge made from fine oatmeal.

Hâtelet (Fr.)
An ornamental silver skewer, used for decorating the cold table, or for serving the ever-popular savoury, Angels on Horseback, or maybe those delicious morsels served en brochette.

Hâtereau (Fr.)
Tiny pieces of pig's liver wrapped in caul and cooked en brochette (which see).

Haunch (Hanche, Fr.)
Actually, the hindquarter, being the leg and loin not cut asunder. The term is usually applied to mutton and venison.

Hazel Hen (Gelinotte, Fr.)

Seldom seen in England alive. When it does make its appearance, it is in a frozen state, being imported chiefly from Europe. It is very good eating, being tender and of fine flavour. Its flesh is creamy white. The young birds should be cooked in the same way as described for grouse. The older birds make quite good pies. Steak and Hazel Hen Pie is delicious.

Hazel-nut

The fruit of the hazel tree, which grows in clusters and has a length of from ½ to ¾ inch. It is extensively cultivated in Kent, and is readily distinguished from cob-nuts by its ample involucre and greater length.

Hélène

A name used quite often in French fish dishes, to signify dressed on noodles and masked with Mornay Sauce.

Herbs

The following herbs will be found fully described under their respective headings :
Alecost, angelica, aniseed, balm, basil, bay leaf, bergamot, borage, burnet, caraway, chervil, coriander, cumin, dill, fennel, fenugreek, hyssop, lovage, marjoram, mint, parsley, penny-royal, purslane, sage, sorrel, tansy, tarragon, thyme, woodruff. (See also Sweet Herbs.)

Heron (Héron, Fr.)

The common heron is one of th few large birds now inhabitin; England. They destroy a con siderable number of youn; salmon in Scotland and ar hated by the keepers, who han; them up as a warning to othe birds when they chance t shoot any. At one time, the; were featured at many ban quets, sometimes costing a; much as a chicken does to-day the chief dish being Hero; Pudding and Heron and Oyste Pudding.

Herring (Hareng, Fr.)

Herrings are consumed in man; forms. First, let us clear u; the many sub-titles.

(1) BLOATERS are half cured whole herring.

(2) BISMARK HERRING is th whole fish put up in pickle flavoured with spices.

(3) KIPPERED HERRING is the fish split, salted, dried and smoked.

(4) MILCHER HERRING is the pickled soft roe fish, the roe being converted into a sauce.

(5) RED HERRING is a whole herring salted and smoked. The title is given to distinguish it from the WHITE HERRING, preserved by salting only.

(6) ROLL MOPS. Pickled rolled fillets.

(7) Salted Herring is credited with dietetic properties by some physicians—perhaps because of the free quaffing of water (or other liquids) which follows its consumption.

(8) Soused Herring is another title for a pickled herring.

When fresh caught and promptly cooked by broiling, herrings are both a wholesome and agreeable food. The yearly harvest amounts to hundreds of millions. This great quantity of food is of vital importance to a large proportion of the population of northern Europe.

Herrings are in season all the year round, but at their best from June to December. For nutritive value, the herring overtops any of our native fish, and the history of the trade is part of the history of England itself. The total value of herrings landed in this country is 33% of the total yield of the North Sea Fisheries. The young of the herring keep close to the coast, where they appear as delicious whitebait in their first year.

On the scales of the herring, there are concentric annual rings (like those on trees), from which age can be determined. As a matter of interest to the ladies, the irridescent substance, guanin, from their scales, is used in the manufacture of artificial pearls.

Highball
Whisky and soda with ice which floats on the top. Usually served in an 8 or 10 oz. glass with a stirring stick.

Hindquarter (Quartier de Derrière, Fr.)
The loin and leg of the animal before being cut apart.

Hirondelle (Fr.)
See Swift.

Hock
The term applied to German wines from the Rhine district. Name derived from Hockheim, a village on the right bank of the Main, close to where it flows into the Rhine.

Hodge-podge
See Hotch-potch

Hog
A castrated boar. A general term for swine.

Hog Pudding (Andouille, Fr.)
Black sausage pudding made of pig's blood and fat pork.

Hogshead
A cask for holding liquor or other commodities. As a measure for cider or beer, it equals 54 gallons. A hogshead of wine holds 63 old wine gallons, or 52½ imperial gallons.

Hollandaise (Fr.)
Dutch style. One of the most important sauces. Its composition includes butter, egg

yolks, vinegar and spices. It is yellow in colour and is especially suitable for serving with fish, cauliflower, asparagus, etc.

Hollands
A spirit distilled in Holland, flavoured with juniper. Known the world over as Hollands Gin.

Homard (Fr.)
See Lobster.

Hominy
An Indian corn porridge consisting of maize hulled and crushed, boiled with water. It is very nourishing and of pleasant flavour.

Honey (Miel, Fr.)
Nectar taken from flowers by bees, modified and condensed by evaporation in the cells of the honeycomb into which it is disgorged as a food store for the community of bees using the hive, or for the housewife if she gets there first. Its colour, flavour and aroma vary with the surroundings. Orange blossom and white clover give the most distinctive flavours. It is very easily digested and can be used in most dessert sweets.

Honeycomb (Rayon de Miel, Fr.)
The store cupboard for the honey, consisting of a mass of waxy cells formed by bees. (Alvéole, Fr. Wax cell of honeycomb.)
See Melon, Honeydew.

Hongroise, à la (Fr.)
Hungarian style. As a garniture, it signifies rich veal gravy flavoured with paprika, small cooked cauliflower and tiny rissole potatoes. As a sauce, it comprises a white or Allemande sauce mixed with sour cream and flavoured with paprika.

Hoppensprossen
A German dish of hop shoots prepared in the same manner as asparagus.

Hops (Houblons, Fr.)
The bitter cones of a plant with a long twining stalk. The young shoots may be eaten and cooked like asparagus, but a knife must be used, as they are not so stiff as asparagus when cooked. Germany takes well to cooked hop shoots, but so long as asparagus is available in this country, hops will be left to the brewer to be employed in the manufacture of beer.

Hors-d'Oeuvre (Fr.)
Appetisers or small side dishes served at the beginning of a meal to stimulate the appetite. From the Russian " zakouska ", meaning foretaste.

Horse-meat
In parts of Europe and especially Belgium, horse-meat is as readily accepted as beef is in England. From the economic and hygienic points of view, there is much in its favour, but until the mechanical age is further advanced, the idea of eating horse-meat will continue

to be repulsive to the general sentiment of the population of these Isles.

Horseradish (Raifort, Fr.)
A white, fibrous, perennial, pungent root. When scraped and grated, it is used extensively in sauces, salads and for Horseradish Vinegar.

Hostel
From the French " hôtel " denoting a humbler or lower type of inn. In ancient times, the lodgings occupied by students of a university.

Hotch-potch or Hodge-podge
A Scottish soup. The pot-au-feu of Scotland. The common pot of stew—a mixture of many things (mutton, barley, vegetables, etc.)

Hotel
The more pretentious public house, affording sleeping accommodation as well as catering facilities.

Hot-Pot
A dish consisting of the cheaper cuts of mutton (breast, scrag, etc.) seasoned and stewed with sliced onions and potatoes, as the typical Lancashire Hot-Pot. In earlier times, usually made in the three-legged iron pot, and when once taken away from the fire, it held its heat for a very long time. This can also be attributed to the pots in those days being of globular shape and having a smaller opening at the top than present-day pots and pans.

Howtowdie
A Scottish dish, consisting of boiled chicken with poached eggs and spinach.

Huckleberry (Airelle Myrtille, Fr.)
Another name for the bilberry or blaeberry (which see).

Huffkin
An old Kentish tea bread lighter than a crumpet. Eaten quite hot, one had to " huff " to cool them a little, to save burning the mouth.

Huile (Fr.)
Oil.

Huile, à l' (Fr.)
Cooked or served in oil.

Huile d'Olive (Fr.)
See Olive Oil.

Huître (Fr.)
See Oyster.

Huîtres en Cheval (Fr.)
See Angels on Horseback.

Hunger
Hunger, as distinguished from appetite, impels one to eat almost any available food, whilst appetite is merely a wish for some special fancy. Appetite can be created, whereas hunger is a definite desire for food, and makes itself known as a dull ache or gnawing pain in the region of the stomach. (See also Appetite.)

Huntsman Sauce (Sauce Chasseur, Fr.)
See Chasseur.

Hûre de Sanglier (Fr.)

Boar's head. The traditional Christmas supper dish in olden times. Boned and stuffed with tongue, truffles, pistachio nuts and forcemeat, cooked with loving care, cooled, glazed, and decorated complete with false tusks and eyes, it was feast for many a king. Occasionally seen at County or Hunt Balls. (See also, Boar's Head and Wild Boar.)

Hussarde (Fr.)

Name of a style of garnish consisting of tomatoes scooped out and filled with onion purée and grated horseradish with duchesse potatoes.

Hyssop

A small, bushy shrub, whose leaves have a strong odour and pungent flavour. Before the flower spikes open, they are cut and dried, subsequently to be used in hyssop tea. The shrubs are usually grown near bee-hives, to give scent and flavour to the honey.

I

Ice (Glace, Fr.)

Water converted to solid state by abstraction of heat until below freezing point.

Ice, Dry

Solidified carbon dioxide, used for transportable refrigeration.

Ice Cream

A name applied to a variety of frozen mixtures, ranging from cheap custards to real cream compounds. Good ice cream compounds contain 10% to 12% fat content, and are made of fresh cow's milk, and as such are a real food for both young and old.

There is no recognised standard in England at present, but see below.

Ices (Glaces, Fr.)

A rich milk product, frozen in a variety of flavours and colours, a good mixture will contain :

10% to 12% butter fat
        12% milk solids

12% to 15% sugar
        5% gelatine or starch.

Modern processing includes pasteurisation, homogenisation, cooling, ageing, freezing and hardening. With all sanitation laws enforced, it can be safely consumed as a food by both young and old.

Icing (Glaçure, Fr.)

Denoting a sugar coating. Royale or fondant icing on pastries or flour confectionery.

Imbu

A Brazilian fruit, like a fully ripened, pale yellow greengage in appearance, with a soft, juicy pulp, which tastes like an orange. Can be eaten raw or made into a jelly.

Impériale (Fr.)
Name of a style of garnish for chicken consisting of truffles, foie-gras, mushrooms and chicken quenelles.

Indian Corn
See Maize.

Indian Cress
See Nasturtium.

Indian Fig
See Prickly Pear.

Indienne, à l' (Fr.)
Indian style. Generally signifies the use or accompaniment of curry or chutney or both. Also highly seasoned foods served with rice.

Invert Sugar
A combination of glucose and levulose or fructose. In natural form, the most familiar is in honey, which contains 60% to 80%. The intestinal juices will change ordinary sugar into invert sugar.

Irish Moss
See Carrageen.

Irish Stew
Considered the national dish of Ireland, consisting of mutton, potatoes and onions, cooked as a baked stew in the oven.

Irlandaise, à l' (Fr.)
Irish style. In all cases where this term is used, it implies sliced potatoes embodied in the dish in some form, either cooked with the food or merely as a garnish.

Isinglass
Isinglass is fish gelatine, which is gradually going out of favour for animal gelatine. It is a hard, translucent substance, prepared from certain parts of the sturgeon and cod, principally used in refining liquors and in the manufacture of jellies and similar dessert sweets.

Italian Meringue
Meringue mixture made with whipped whites of egg and boiled sugar added in syrup form.

Italian Paste
A term applied to macaroni, spaghetti, vermicelli and similar pastes, but not to noodles.

Italienne, à l' (Fr.)
Italian style. As a sauce, the term implies Espagnole Sauce blended with tomato and containing chopped mushrooms, shallots and garlic. When used as a garnish, it usually signifies that macaroni or Italian pastes, grated Parmesan cheese, spinach or tomato, have been incorporated into the dish. As, for example, Consommé à l'Italienne is garnished with macaroni and cubes of spinach and tomato royale.

Ivoire, à l' (Fr.)
This French term implies a rich ivory finish, consisting of a very smooth sauce, and is usually used in conjunction with poultry. Ivoire Sauce is composed of rich white Velouté and cream.

J

Jackfruit
A very large fruit of an Indian tree, which reaches 45 to 50 lbs. in weight and 2 feet in length. It has a hard, green skin, with pointed projections and a mass of yellow pulp in which are embedded seeds the size of a walnut. It forms a very important food for the natives, but to most white palates is unpleasant in flavour.

Jacobine
The original term applied to fancy shapes of flavoured custards, which we now call Royale. As political favour changed in France, so certain culinary terms were also changed. Nevertheless, a few dishes still retain this name, as, for example, Consommé Jacobine.

Jagger, Jagging Iron
An implement not made of iron but usually of brass. It is made in two forms, one which consists of a brass wheel fastened to a handle with a notching device at the end, the other being two strips of metal fastened together spring fashion, for pinching or notching pies and pastries to form a fancy edge. It also has a wheel for pastry cutting.

Jaggery
Coarse, dark-coloured sugar, made in the East Indies, from sap extracted from the coconut palm.

Jam (Confiture, Fr.)
A rich confection of fruit and sugar, in which the fruit is cooked without regard to the preservation of its shape. Good quality jams contain fruit, refined sugar, and sometimes a little added water. Lower grade jams contain added fruit juices and glucose or corn syrup to give bulk. All good quality jams are high energy foods and the breakfast marmalade should always have a prominent position on the table.

Jamaica Pepper
See Allspice.

Jambon (Fr.)
See Ham.

Jambon Froid (Fr.)
Cold ham.

Jambonneau (Fr.)
A picnic or very small ham.

Japanese Artichoke
See Jerusalem Artichoke.

Japanese Gelatine
See Agar-Agar.

Japonaise (Fr.)
Name of a style of garnish for roast joints consisting of small pastry cases filled with sliced Japanese artichokes sauté wlth croquette potatoes.

Jardinière (Fr.)
Gardener's style. A mixed preparation of vegetables stewed down in their own sauce.

Jarret (Fr.)
See Knuckle.

Jarret de Boeuf (Fr.)
See Shin of Beef.

Jay (Glai, Fr.)
One wonders how the jay has escaped complete elimination, so hated are they by all game-keepers and farmers. It is rather insipid eating and best stewed or cooked in pies or puddings, unless very young, when it may be roasted.

Jelly (Gelée, Fr.)
Gelatinised liquids extracted from fruit or meat. In actual preparation the fruit or meat extracts are diluted with water and soaked and melted gelatine added, which then forms a gelatinous mass.

Jerked Beef
Thin strips of beef dried by hanging it in the sun, with or without having been previously placed in brine.

Jeroboam
A bottle with a capacity four times that of an ordinary bottle (see Bottle).

Jerusalem Artichoke (Topinam-bour, Fr.)
This vegetable is neither an artichoke nor does it come from Jerusalem. It is a tuberous root plant, like a nobbly potato in appearance, with a long stalk bearing a flower similar to that of the sunflower. First intro-duced from Canada in 1617, and known then as Canadian potato and described as a dainty for a queen. It has a pleasing flavour to many, but to others it is known as having a windy quality. Used as a vegetable and in the making of Palestine Soup. (See also Artichoke).

Jigger
An American measure for spirits —1½ fluid ozs. A jigger of whisky—a small whisky.

John Dory or Doree (Poisson de Saint-Pierre, Fr.)
The dory is rare, except at sea-side towns or leading London stores. It is highly esteemed by gastronomes, but snubbed by the housewife because it is so hideous in appearance. The flesh is rather firm and usually cooked in fillets. It can be treated in any of the ways described for fillets of sole.
The side is marked with a prominent dark spot, on ac-count of which the dory shares with the haddock the reputa-tion of being the fish from which Peter took tribute money. So many people are of the firm belief that only the haddock bears the dark thumb mark.
It is an exceedingly ferocious fish, and may attain a weight of 12 lbs. The body is much compressed and nearly oval, while the mouth is large and capable of extensive protrusion. It is in season from Michaelmas to Christmas.

Joint (Relevé, Fr.)

The pièce de résistance of dinner. Usually the fifth course at a banquet—(1) hors d'œuvre, (2) soup, (3) fish, (4) entrée, (5) joint. The guests having been carefully built up to receive this, the main course of a meal.

Joinville, Prince de

François Ferdinand Philippe Louis Marie Joinville. Born 14 August, 1818, died 16 June, 1900, the third son of Louis Philippe duc d'Orleans. Many dishes bear his name, most prominent of which are those of the fish course. As a garnish, this style comprises a shrimp or lobster sauce with sliced truffles and mushrooms added. As a sauce—white wine sauce enriched with egg yolks, lobster coral and butter.

Jordan Almonds

The best cultivated almonds from Spain. Most sought after by chocolate and sweet manufacturers for sugared almonds and for toppings on dipped chocolates. They are the almond best suited for salted almonds. Next in order of merit are the Valencia almonds.

Juane Mange

A type of Dutch flummery or furmenty, made with eggs, isinglass, lemon, sugar and raisin wine.

Judic (Fr.)

Name of a style of garnish for entrées consisting of braised lettuce with château potatoes.

Jugged (Civet, Fr.)

Meats, poultry, or game, cooked in a covered jug, jar, or other earthenware vessel, by stewing steadily in the oven.

The origin is supposed to have been due to a large jug which had lost its handle and was turned into a stew pot or sort of casserole. One of the few forms of cooking which the French cannot claim, proving that the ingenuity of the English cook did exist, and it can be claimed as the forerunner of the casserole as we know it to-day. Certainly the best method of cooking a hare, under close cover.

Julep

A Persian term, signifying rose water. Originally used as a vehicle for medicine. American habits altered all this and used stronger liquor such as whisky or brandy, to which was added mint or other flavours, with the usual lumps of ice.

Jules Verne (Fr.)

A style of garnish consisting of stuffed and braised small turnips and potatoes and sliced mushrooms sauté.

ulienne
Jean Julien was a noted French chef, who first made a clear vegetable soup in 1785, with vegetables cut into match-like strips. The name is now applied to all vegetable garnishes cut in this manner.

The original julienne was cut from wood sorrel. Wood sorrel, when boiled, is cooked away, all save the stems, and this is why the great mark of julienne soup is that the vegetables are cut in strips. As in many instances, this style of presenting vegetables in match-like strips was an accident.

Jumbles
Small, crisp, flour confections, of irregular shapes and sizes. Made with sugar, butter, eggs, flour, and grated rind of any citrus fruit. They are dropped on to hot buttered baking tins, like tiny rock cakes. Made both plain and fruited.

Juniper Berry (Genièvre, Fr.)
The junipers, which are a species of evergreen of which there are some 40 different types, bear the juniper berry, used extensively in the manufacture of gin. The oil of juniper is distilled from the unripe fruit and it is this which gives to gin its characteristic flavour.

Junket
A dessert of milk, coagulated by rennet, sweetened and flavoured.

Jus (Fr.)
The natural juice or gravy as it flows from meats during roasting, seasoned but not thickened.

Jus, au (Fr.)
Served in the natural juice or gravy.

K

Kaffir Bread
A tree reaching up to 20 ft. in height, native of South Africa. From the apex of its stem is procured a farinaceous food-stuff, from whence it derives its name. Many such trees are made a feature in English greenhouses and conservatories.

Kagne (Fr.)
A type of fine Italian paste, like vermicelli.

Kail
See Kale.

Kailcannon
See Colcannon.

Kale, Kail (Chou Frisé, Fr.)
A very tall species of cabbage, which grows to a height of 2 ft. It produces large, thick-set leaves, purplish or light red in colour. Scotch Kale is a term applied to a pot-au-feu of Scotland, which really should bear the title Kale Brose, being a broth of which kale is the chief ingredient.

Kale Brose
See Kale.

Kanten
See Agar-Agar.

Kari (Fr.)
See Curry.

Kartoffelnkuchen
A very light German potato cake, made with potatoes, eggs, lemons, almonds and sugar.

Kava
A very peculiar, intoxicating, but non-alcoholic beverage, consumed in the islands of the South Pacific. Its production consists of chewing the leaves of a certain plant which is then mixed with coco-nut milk. Two small doses can produce intoxication in 20 minutes. It is believed that the intoxication is produced by a poison of alkaloidal nature.

Kavkaski Pilav
A Caucasian pilaf of mutton.

Kebobs
An Indian dish, usually made of mutton or fowl. The slices are dipped in highly seasoned and flavoured eggs, rolled in breadcrumbs and cooked on skewers. (See also, Shashlick.)

Kedgeree
A favourite and universal dish in India, made in two colours— white, made with rice, onions, ghee and seasonings; yellow includes egg and is coloured with turmeric. The poorer classes make a mixture of rice, beans or lentils only. In English cookery, fish is generally introduced into its composition, with a flavouring of fennel.

Kelkel
Fillets of sole salted and dried in the same manner as salt cod.

Ketchup
See Catchup.

Kid (Chevreau, Fr.)
A delicacy much enjoyed before the days of chilled or frozen meat when most families were self-supporting. Roast kid, well basted and served with pork stuffing, forms a most enjoyable meal. (See also Goat.)

Kidney Bean (Faséole, Fr.)
See Bean.

Kidneys (Rognons, Fr.)
The aristocratic English breakfast dish before World War I. In order of merit they are, lamb's, sheep's, veal and pork. The ox kidney generally finds its way into commercially made steak and kidney pies. All are rich in iron, copper and in vitamin G, and they are a good source of vitamins A and B.

Kipper (Hareng Fumé, Fr.)
The kipper is a herring split, gutted, salted and then smoked. Large pilchards are sometimes treated this way, but have not that distinctive flavour. This fish requires no addition during the cooking process other than butter. I deplore the idea of poaching kippers in water, which takes away 50% of the flavour and their natural food value.

Kippered
A mode of splitting and curing salmon, mackerel, herrings, etc. Signifies split, salted, dried and smoked.

Kirsh, Kirschwasser (Ger.)
A potable white spirit distilled from wild cherries, usually run at a strength of about 50% absolute alcohol.

Kisslyia Shchi
A Russian sauerkraut soup.

Klösse
These German dishes are composed of a variety of small light balls or dumplings. Rice, potatoes, breadcrumbs and eggs form the base, with the addition of almost any type of fish, meat, poultry or game.

Knuckle (Jarret, Fr.)
The knee joint, but in mutton, pork, veal and lamb the term is applied to the shank or joint below the knee.

Kohl-rabi (Chou de Siam, Fr.)
A cabbage plant which grows a round deciduous turnip body above the ground. There are three varieties, green, purple and white. The term originates from Germany, meaning cabbage turnip. It is best used before fully grown, and in Italy, where it is much favoured, the hen's egg size is most popular.

Kola-nut
A nut used in the preparation of many American soft drinks. A brown, bitter nut, somewhat like a horse chestnut in size. Because of its high caffein content, it is much esteemed when used in beverages, due to its energising properties.

Kosher
Means fit and proper. In food —slaughtered, prepared and cooked for the Jewish mode.

Koulibiak (Rus.)
See Coulibac.

Koulitch
A Russian Easter currant bread.

Koumiss or Kumiss
Fermented mare's milk. A beverage of very ancient usage among the Tartars, being a very important part of their diet.

Kranzkaye
A Danish ring cake composed of macaroon-like rings, each one smaller than the other, so that the cake forms a cone. Used as a dessert, at most functions, usually decorated on top like a wedding cake.

Krapivnie Shchi
Name of a Russian nettle soup.

Kromeskis or Cromesquis
Kromeskis are croquettes cooked in the Russian manner. They consist of almost any meat, poultry or game, finely minced, shaped into rolls or balls, dipped in batter, or egg and crumbed and fried.

Krupnick
A popular Russian soup, next in favour to the national Shchi.

Kuchen

Name of a very rich type of Danish pastry, which is baked in a variety of shapes and brushed over when baked with thin water icing or hot jam. Very popular in America where it is baked in all manner of shapes and sizes.

Kümmel

A sweet, colourless liqueur, flavoured with cumin and caraway seed. Originally made in Riga, capital of Latvia, and not of German origin, as so often is implied.

Kumquat

A small, orange-coloured citrus fruit about the size and shape of a plum. Its rind is thin, sweet and aromatic, and can be eaten with its slightly acid pulp. At state banquets in China and Japan, specially dwarfed trees, 2 to 3 ft. in height, are placed on the table, for guests to pluck the fruit from their branches. Candied it is excellent.

Kvass or Kwass

One of the national drinks of Russia. A type of light beer of very low alcoholic content. Sometimes added to Russian soups.

Kvorost

A Russian dessert, consisting of dough flavoured with vodka, cut into thin strips, fried in oil and dusted with powdered sugar while hot.

L

Lace Paper (Papier Dentelle Fr.)

See Doily.

Lactic

Pertaining to milk.

Lactic Acid

The acid formed in milk by the action of lactic acid bacteria during its souring.

Lactometer

An instrument for measuring the purity of milk.

Lactose

The scientific title for milk sugar. 4% to 7% is found in the milk of all mammals. Crystalline sugar obtained from evaporation of cow's milk.

Lager Beer (Ger.)

Lager, as applied to beer, means aged or stored. Of recent years, the name has become applied to almost any light beer.

Laguipière (Fr.)

Name of a white wine sauce made of the wine in which the sole or other fish is cooked.

Lait (Fr.)

See Milk.

Lait, au (Fr.)

With, or served in, milk.

Laitance (Fr.)

The soft roe of the male fish. (See Roe, Soft.)

Lait Sucré (Fr.)

Milk sweetened.

Laitue (Fr.)
See Lettuce.

Lamb (Agneau, Fr.)
The meat of sheep under 12 months old. The usual test of a carcase is—if the bone above the ankle " breaks " readily, it is lamb ; if it does not, it is mutton.

Lamb's Fry (Animelles, Fr.)
In earlier times, the Lamb-stones (see below). Now applied to a mixture of sliced lamb's offal, cooked as a rich stew.

Lambs' Sweetbreads (Ris d'-Agneau, Fr.)
The pancreas of the lamb, delicate and nutritious as a food.

Lambstones
The kernels taken from young rams to convert them into wethers. Chiefly cooked like sweetbreads.

Lambs' Wool
An old English mulled ale, of mashed roasted apples, ale, sugar and spices, heated in a large copper or vessel. (See Wassail Bowl.)

Lampern
Lamperns, like lampreys, are almost extinct around the coast and in the rivers of England, but are still much in favour in North America. The lampern is much smaller than the lamprey, and, when available, is popular in the form of a pie or potted. Unfortunately, to-day, they are principally used as a bait for cod and turbot, the fishermen preferring to retain them for this purpose. In season October and November—can be cooked in the same manner as eels.

Lamprey (Lamproie, Fr.)
An eel-like, scaleless fish, averaging 30 inches in length. The lamprey has no jaws, but a circular sucker beset with horny projections simulating teeth. It feeds on fish, rasping away the flesh with its sucker and powerful tongue.
At one time, the lamprey was caught extensively in the Severn. It is in season during April and May, leaving salt water at that time, to ascend rivers to spawn.
The flesh of the lamprey is soft, glutinous and delicate, but most people find it difficult to digest. Both lampreys and lamperns have the reputation of being dangerous as a food, which is no doubt due to the two filaments in the back, which are poisonous and which must be removed before cooking. Hence the popular credence in the legend of the death of King Henry I from eating too many of them, and no doubt there was lack of knowledge in those days of how to prepare them properly.

Lamproie (Fr.)
See Lamprey.

Landrail (Roi des Cailles, Fr.)
See Corncrake.

Langouste (Fr.)
See Crawfish.

Langoustines (Fr.)
See Dublin Bay Prawns.

Langue (Fr.)
See Tongue.

Langue de Chat (Fr.)
A fine wafer of rich sponge mixture of the dessert biscuit character.

Langue de Veau (Fr.)
Calf's tongue.

Languier (Fr.)
Smoked pig's tongue used as a hors d'œuvre.

Lapereau (Fr.)
Young rabbit. (See Rabbit.)

Lapin (Fr.)
Rabbit (which see).

Lapwing, Green Plover (Vanneau, Fr.)
The lapwing or peewit is the common plover in England, where it is protected in most counties by law. Its eggs must not be offered for sale any longer in this country.
The green plover is not considered so fine-flavoured as the golden plover or grey plover. (See also Plover.)

Lard
The refined fat of the pig, separated from the tissue by melting and straining. Also the French word for bacon (which see).

Larder
A room or place where food is kept.

Lard Fumé (Fr.)
Smoked bacon.

Larding
This is a fast dying art, for few households, or chefs for that matter, possess a set of larding needles, which are essential for this operation. One wonders what manufacturer will ever get large enough orders to start the remanufacture of these tools as an aid to the culinary art.
Larding of dry poultry or game is not difficult, but how many appreciate it when done !
To lard a bird, first obtain some fat bacon and cut it in slices about three-sixteenths of an inch thick and then cut the slices in strips three-sixteenths of an inch wide and 3 inches long. These are called lardoons. The lardoons are inserted into the end of special needles, which are split at the one end to enable the lardoons to be threaded, as it were, into the cup-like hole of these needles.
The needles are then drawn through the flesh as in a sewing motion leaving the ends of the lardoon (or strips of fat) projecting where the needle entered and was drawn out.
In looks a properly larded bird or piece of meat will have the appearance of a hedgehog, when all the ends are trimmed to the same length with a pair of scissors.

Meats properly barded and basted will be found just as good as an elaborately larded bird or joint.

No, I do not think we shall see larding needles manufactured again in this country. All the same, it is nice to know how good foods can be prepared.

Lardoon

A strip of bacon used for larding.

Lark (Mauviette, Fr.)

Larks are most popular in France in the lark pie, which has helped to make the reputation of the city of Pithiviers.

At one time they were sent to London market in thousands, but were not considered fit for roasting unless they weighed $1\frac{1}{4}$ ozs. each. Larks in aspic were still a favourite at May Week dances, both at Oxford and Cambridge, up to about 1925, when the labour involved in preparing them was no longer considered worth while. They have quite a distinct flavour all their own.

In 1941, and again in 1942, they made their reappearance on the London markets, but those who hoped to sell them had overlooked the labour involved in their preparation, and most of the consignments were wasted, except for the few which fetched 3/6 to 4/– per dozen, and were made into pies, for who would have the patience to bone a lark to-day?

Lasagne

Name of a ribbon form of Italian paste somewhat resembling noodles.

Laurier, Feuille de (Fr.)

See Bay Leaf.

Lavallière (Fr.)

Name of a garnish suitable for poultry consisting of lambs' sweetbreads threaded with truffles.

Laver

A purplish green weed, growing on sea coasts or rocks. It is cooked in the same manner as spinach, in Scotland and Ireland under the name of " sloak " or " slook ".

Lax

A type of canned Norwegian smoked salmon, packed in oil.

Leaven

Sour dough at one time employed in bread-making to excite fermentation in new dough.

Lebkuchen

A famous group of sweet German honey cakes.

Leek (Poireau, Fr.)

The only member of the onion family with flat leaves, all others having tubular leaves. It is cultivated for the blanched lower parts of the leaves, commonly called the stem, which are served asparagus style. Served always on St. David's Day, as the symbol or badge of the Welsh.

K

Leg (Gigot, Fr.)
The limb by which any animal walks—hind leg, foreleg. The fore leg is chiefly referred to as the shoulder.

Légumes (Fr.)
Vegetables of which we use the fruit or seeds, such as peas, beans, lentils and soya beans.

Lemon (Citron, Fr.)
The lemon is a member of the citrus group, oval in shape, of various shades of yellow, with convex oil-cysts in the rind. All lemons are gathered while still green and placed in storage to colour and mature.

Lemonade (Limonade or Citronade, Fr.)
A beverage made from the lemon, popular both for medicinal purposes and as a means of allaying thirst.

Lemon Balm
See Balm, Garden.

Lemon Barley Water
A mixture of lemon juice and barley water, which is now sold ready made. (See also Barley Water.)

Lemon Curd or Lemon Cheese
A type of preserve made by cooking sugar, eggs, butter and lemon juice together. It must always be cooked in a double boiler and kept well stirred to prevent curdling or burning of the eggs. Cheap types of lemon curd are made with citric acid and do not contain any actual lemons.

Lemon Gin
See Gin, Lemon.

Lemon Sole (Limande, Fr.)
In season from December till March. Its colour is a mixture of orange and light brown, and it is freckled over with numerous small brown spots. It is wider in proportion to the common sole, the greatest breadth being equivalent to half its length. It is sometimes referred to as the French sole. (See also Sole.)

Lentil (Lentille, Fr.)
Considered the most nutritious of all legumes except the soya bean. The short, broad, flat pods containing each two seeds, round like a pea, but flat and thin, and varying in colour from grey or yellow to a deep reddish-brown. The " red pottage " for which Esau sold his birthright consisted largely of the red Egyptian lentil (lentil-lon d'hiver, Fr.) being the kind most esteemed on account of its superior flavour.

Lettuce (Laitue, Fr.)
The chief salad plant of modern times. In order of merit we have (1) cabbage or head lettuce ; (2) bunch lettuce, which does not head ; (3) romaine or cos lettuce, which is distinguished by its long, crisp leaves.

Leveret (Levraut, Fr.)
A young hare.

Levraut (Fr.)
See Hare, Young.

Levulose
Fructose or fruit sugar. One of the three simple sugars. (See Fructose.)

Levure (Fr.)
See Yeast.

Liaison (Fr.)
Thickening. The blending of yolks of egg and cream for thickening and enriching soups and sauces. (See also, Thickening.)

Licorice (Réglisse, Fr.)
The familiar black sticks are the condensed juice of the crushed, boiled roots of the licorice plant, mixed with starch to prevent it melting in warm weather. The extract of the root is known as black sugar or Spanish juice.
The drying of the root takes from 6 months to a year before it is ready for shipment.

Lié (Fr.)
Thickened or bound. Farina lié—thickened with cornflour.

Lièvre (Fr.)
See Hare.

Lights (Mou, Fr.)
The term applied to the lungs of animals, originating in the fact that they always floated in the brine tub, because of the air contained in them.

Lillet
A colourless aperitif of quinine flavour, with a basis of white wine fortified with Armagnac.

Limande (Fr.)
See Lemon Sole and Dab.

Limburger Cheese
A cheese made in Belgium and Germany. It is a fermented, full-flavoured and very strong-smelling, whole milk cheese, semi-hard in consistency. Made from December to May.

Lime (Limon, Fr.)
A small species of lemon, with an exceedingly high acid content, used chiefly for lime cordial and preserves.

Lime Juice
The sterilised juice of the lime.

Limequat
A fruit obtained by crossing the kumquat with the lime.

Limonade (Fr.)
See Lemonade.

Limpet
In some parts limpets are used for food, and though coarse and unattractive, are not unwholesome. They merely require boiling in a little salt and water for a few minutes. Limpets, when raw, are said to be poisonous. Cooked, they could replace oysters for sauces and garnishings.

Ling (Linque, Fr.)

The ling reaches a length of 7 ft., being a large, long-bodied fish, of the cod type, with a terminal mouth and strong canines in the lower jaw. Large quantities of this fish are consumed salted, being sold as salt cod. The name " ling " is also incorrectly applied to various other fishes, as the burbot and hake. It is extremely prolific, and so tenacious of life as to survive injuries which other fish could never withstand.

When ling are less than 26 inches long, they are called drizzles on the Yorkshire coast. It is best baked or fried. Boiled, it is insipid.

Linseed

The seed of the flax plant. The infusion of linseed in boiling water yields a demulcent mucilage, which is used as a domestic medicine for coughs. The seeds should not be boiled in water, but infused like tea.

Liqueur (Fr.)

Liquor. Liquids, flavoured, perfumed and sweetened to make them agreable to the taste. Alcoholic content averaging from 30% to 45%, usually served as small after-dinner drinks. There are, of course, a few exceptions, whose alcoholic content is very high, but this is more the exception than the rule.

Liqueur Brandy

An old and good quality brandy.

Liqueur d'Or

A golden sweet French liqueur with flakes of gold.

Liqueur Jaune

A French yellow liqueur, somewhat similar to Yellow Chartreuse.

Liqueur Verte

A French liqueur somewhat similar to Green Chartreuse.

Liquor

Anything liquid—strong drink.

Liquorice

A widely accepted way of spelling Licorice (which see).

Litchi

A Chinese fruit containing a single seed. It has a delicious aromatic pulp.

Liver (Foie, Fr.)

Liver is most valuable for its vitamin content. Good fresh liver should be clear, bright, and yellowish-red. The order of quality is calf's, beef (when young), lamb's, pig's and sheep's.

Livetine

A protein in egg yolk.

Loach (Loche, Fr.)

There are two types of loach in English waters, the spined loach and the stone loach. The largest specimens are 12 inches in length, being elongated in form, naked, or with very small scales with 3 to 6 pairs of barbels.

Loaf (Miche, Fr.)
A regularly shaped mass of food, such as bread, sugar, meat, etc.
LOAF OF BREAD—Miche de Pain (Fr.)

Lobster (Homard, Fr.)
The most highly rated of all shellfish, and considered by many people to be the most delicate and delicious of all sea-food. The true lobsters are distinguished by having the first three pairs of legs terminating in pincers (a tip to buyers offered spiny or rock lobsters). The shells of live lobsters are variable in colour, but the upper part is generally a bluish- or blackish-green, blotched or spotted, with red touches on the tubercles, tips, and under parts of the pincers. The full characteristic red of the cooked lobster comes with the boiling.
A lobster about to molt is known as a " shedder " or " black lobster ", because of the dull, dark tint of the old shell, and as " soft shell " after the molting process. Shedders and soft shells are undesirable as food, for their flesh is lean and watery.
The average weight of a good lobster is from 2½ lbs.—those of 1 lb. or thereabouts being styled " chicken lobsters "— but specimens of 15 to 20 lbs. have been caught, though such large ones are liable to be leathery. A small lobster, heavy for its size, is the choicest— the most tender and succulent. Lightness for size is a defect, no matter what the size may be.

Loche (Fr.)
See Loach.

Locksoy
A fine drawn rice macaroni, imported from China.

Lodigiano
One of the 18 varieties of Italian parmesan cheese.

Loganberry
A cross between a blackberry and a raspberry, resembling a long blackberry in shape and a raspberry in colour.

Loin (Longe, Fr.)
The back of the animal nearest the leg.

Longe (Fr.)
See Loin.

Long Pepper
A strong spice used extensively in curry powder, similar in character, both in taste and smell, to ordinary pepper.

Loquat
A fruit, round to pear-shape in appearance. The skin is yello to deep orange in colour. The flesh is soft, with a sligh ly acid flavour, suggestive of the cherry. Its chief defect is an excess of the large seeds which fill the centre.

Lorette (Fr.)
Name of a style of garnish suitable for entrées consisting of sliced truffle and asparagus tips.

Lorgnette (Fr.)
Applied where fried onion rings are used as a garnish.

Lote or Burbot (Lotte, Fr.)
The depressed head of this fish, its nearly cylindrical body, and oval, pointed tail, give it rather a peculiar and not very pleasing aspect, while its smooth, slippery and slimy skin does not invest it with any additional attraction. Its ordinary length is from 1 to 2 feet, and the weight about 2 lbs. Its flesh is white and excellent, but the roe is quite uneatable.
The lote is of a hardy nature, and can be kept a long time alive out of water.

Louisiane (Fr.)
Name of a style of garnish suitable for large joints consisting of fried banana, creamed corn, fried slices of sweet potato and small moulds of rice.

Loup de Mer (Fr.)
See Catfish.

Lovage
A relative of the cow-parsley, with medicinal virtues. The stems are candied as angelica.

Love Apple
The old name for the tomato.

Love-in-a-mist
The seeds of this plant have a curious aromatic flavour and were at one time sprinkled on cakes, biscuits and Pommel cheese.

Lucine (Fr.)
See Clam.

Lucines Papillons (Fr.)
Soft Clams.

Lucullus
A famous Roman epicure, who always dined on a lavish scale. The name Lucullus is applied to dishes lavishly prepared and garnished. The garnish comprises truffles scooped out, filled with pounded chicken and poached in madeira wine.

Luncheon
Derived from the old English word lunch, meaning lump, as was the fashion to take a chunk or hunk of bread, bacon or cheese on a bar, thus we get luncheon. A repast between breakfast and dinner.

Lyonnaise, à la (Fr.)
Lyons style. As a garnish, generally containing shredded fried onions or onions stewed in white wine. As a sauce, Béchamel foundation lightly flavoured with tomato purée, with minced brown onion added, and enriched with meat glaze.

M

Macaroni (Maccaroni, It.)

The Chinese are entitled to the credit for first making these pastes, subsequently copied by the Germans and finally made an Italian industry. Macaroni, spaghetti, vermicelli, etc., are all made from the same wheaten semolina, which is scalded with boiling water and forced through plates at very high pressure. (See Noodles and Vermicelli.)

Macaroons

Small biscuit-like cakes, made from egg whites, sugar, almond paste or ground almonds.

Mace (Arille, Fr.)

The covering which envelops the shell enclosing the nutmeg. It is used both in "blade" and ground form, to flavour soups, sauces, etc. (See also Nutmeg.)

Macédoine (Fr.)

A mixture of evenly cut fruits or vegetables, of different types and colours. Applied also to sliced fruits or vegetables set in a mould or jelly.

Macéré (Fr.)

Soused or steeped in pickle or wine.

Mackerel (Maquereau, Fr.)

The mackerel ranges in length up to 17 or 18 inches, the average market size being 12 inches, with a weight from ¾ lb. to 1 lb. It is well known for the beauty and brilliancy of its colours, the elegance of its form, its intrinsic value to man as an article of food, both in reference to quantity and quality.

It is best from March to July. To be eaten in perfection, this fish should be very fresh, as it soon becomes unfit for food. When fresh, it is quite stiff, opalescent, with bright protruding red eyes. Avoid limp mackerel, as they can be quite dangerous. No fish can be more unwholesome when stale.

Macon

Synthetic bacon, made from mutton ; also a town in France known for its Burgundy wine.

Macreuse (Fr.)

See Widgeon.

Mad-apple

Another name for the egg plant.

Madeira (Madère, Fr.)

See Madère.

Madeleine (Fr.)

A small flour confection resembling a queen-cake, coated with preserve and rolled in shredded nuts. The name when applied to garniture denotes artichoke bottoms filled with onion purée and topped with haricot beans.

Madère (Fr.)

Madeira wine, used extensively in cooking, most notably in Sauce Madère, which is Demi-glace sauce and tomato purée flavoured with the wine. Madeira wine can be extremely long lived.

Madras
Chiefly applied to foods flavoured with curry.

Magnum
A bottle capable of holding 53⅓ fluid ozs., or 2 ordinary bottles. (See Bottle.)

Maiale Ubriaco (It.)
An Italian dish meaning intoxicating pork, being pork cooked in red wine with a little oil and garlic.

Maids of Honour
Name of a rich almond confection, made in the form of small, round, almond tartlets, for which the town of Richmond, in Surrey, is famous.

Maigre, au (Fr.)
See Au Maigre.

Maintenon
The Marchioness Maintenon invented many dishes to tempt the appetite of Louis XIV during his failing years, most famous of which is the well-known Côtelettes de Veau à la Maintenon.

Mais (Fr.)
See Maize.

Maitrank (Ger.)
A noted German spiced wine, generally drunk on May Day (May drink).

Maître d'Hôtel, à la (Fr.)
Hotel-steward style. Preparations surnamed Maître d'Hôtel generally include flavouring with chopped parsley. Maître d'Hôtel Sauce consists of a white sauce with parsley added. Maître d'Hôtel Butter consists of butter, lemon juice and parsley, and may be served hot or cold.

Maize (Mais, Fr.)
The seed of the most beautiful and luxuriant of all grain grasses, and the most abundant in product. It is native to tropical America. It produces maize semolina (the best), corn oil, starch and cattle food.

Malaga
Dishes flavoured with port wine. Wine from Malaga, Spain.

Mallard (Canard Sauvage, Fr.)
The most common species of wild duck found in these Isles, and the ancestor of a majority of our domestic ducks. The head and neck of the male are a glossy green and the back brown and grey shading to black, with white and blue markings on the wings. The female is principally dark brown and buff. The average market weight is 6 lbs. per couple, though it often goes higher.

Malmsey
A sweet, madeira wine. The grapes are grown on rocky ground and the fruit is allowed to stay on the vines for a month longer than if required for making dry wines.

Malt
Germinated barley in which is developed a fermentable sugar (maltose). It is used in the fermentation of beer.

Maltaise (Fr.)
Name of a style of sauce consisting of Sauce Hollandaise flavoured with the zest and juice of blood oranges.

Maltose
Malt sugar. Found in malt, its products, and in sprouting seeds.

Mammée
Fruit of a large tree native of the West Indies and tropical America. It is a large, oval fruit, with a coarse skin of a light coffee colour. The flesh is crimson and soft, like a melon.

Mandarin (Mandarine, Fr.)
A small variety of orange ; also a French aperitif with a bitter orange flavour. (See Tangerine.)

Mandarine (Fr.)
See Tangerine.

Mangel Wurzel
A cross between the red and white beetroot, used in distillation, the extraction of sugar, and cattle feeding. In wars and periods of shortages, used in jam manufacture to give bulk.

Mango (Mangue, Fr.)
The fruit forming the basis of most East Indian chutneys. Has an orange-coloured pulp, the texture of a peach and a juicy, spicy flavour. Green mangoes are made into chutney, etc.

Mango-squash
See Chayote.

Mangosteen
This fruit has been awarded the title of " the world's choicest fruit " by many travellers. It is the size of an orange, with a skin like a pomegranate. It has a juicy, rose-tinted pulp, and is divided orange style. It has a sweet flavour, slightly tart, and is said to combine all the flavours of the grape, pineapple, peach and strawberry.

Mangue (Fr.)
See Mango.

Manioc
The roots of this plant furnish us with the product tapioca, Brazilian arrowroot (used in the manufacture of compressed yeast), laundry starch, and a glaze for twine makers. The roots form in clusters and grow up to 4 ft. in length and 30 lbs. in weight.

Manna
A sweetish juice obtained from the Manna-ash, which hardens into flakes ; the best coming from Sicily. Its principal use is as a mild laxative for children. The food supplied to the Israelites in the wilderness of Arabia.

Manzanilla
A light, delicate wine, of a fine straw colour, highly aromatic. Produce of Spain.

Maple Sugar (Sucre d'Érable, Fr.)
A sugar obtained by evaporation and crystallising of the sap of the maple tree. It is prized for its richness and flavour. The syrup is more popular these days for use in soda fountains and ices.

Maquereau (Fr.)
See Mackerel.

Maraîchère (Fr.)
Name of a style of garnish which consists of salsify in cream sauce with Brussels sprouts and château potatoes.

Maraschino
A deliciously flavoured liqueur, white in colour. Distilled from wild cherries grown in Dalmatia.

Marbré (Fr.)
The running of colours into one another, marble style. Marbled.

Marchand de Vin (Fr.)
Wine merchant. The term applied to sauces and garnishings containing claret.

Marchpane (Fr.)
See Marzipan.

Maréchale (Fr.)
Name of a style of garnish consisting of cock's combs and truffles in Sauce Italienne.

Marengo, à la (Fr.)
A term used chiefly in connection with chicken sauté. Its preparation and garnish include mushrooms, tomatoes, olives, oil and wine, such ingredients having been the only supplies which were available to Napoleon's chef when he hurriedly prepared the dish after the battle of Marengo, named Poulet Sauté à la Marengo.

Marennes (Fr.)
A town on the south-western coast of France, noted for its oysters. Marennes style—garnished with oysters.

Margarine
Originally known as butterine, but changed by act of Parliament to prevent fraud. Margarine to-day consists of a combination of animal or vegetable fats churned in specially ripened milk, with salt added. It contains up to 17% water and is fortified with vitamins.

Marguéry (Fr.)
The name given to the dish, Filet de Sole à la Marguéry, by a famous Paris restaurateur. The sole is cooked in Chablis, coated with white wine sauce, and garnished with shrimps and oysters.

Marigold
A herb valued in former days for the making of conserves. Said to cure the trembling heart and make pale cheese yellow.

Marinade (Fr.)
A rich, pickling liquor containing spice or wine, vinegar, etc. for enriching the flavour of meat or fish.

Mariné (Fr.)
Mariner style : pickled. (See also Marinade.)

Marjolaine (Fr.)
See Marjoram.

Marjoram (Marjolaine, Fr.)
A small sage-like plant, little used in England, but extensively used in Italy.

Marmalade (Marmelade, Fr.)
Originally a jam or preserve made from the Portuguese " marmelo " or quince. Now chiefly made from citrus fruits —lemons, oranges, grapefruit, limes, etc.

Marmite (Fr.)
Stock pot ; used originally for pot-au-feu. Petite Marmite— a French soup served in small, earthenware casseroles.

Marquise (Fr.)
Name of a style of garnish consisting of fried beef marrow, asparagus tips and sliced truffle in Sauce Suprême.

Marrons (Fr.)
See Chestnuts.

Marrons Glacés (Fr.)
Chestnuts coated with sugar and candied or packed in syrup.

Marrow, Vegetable
See Vegetable Marrow.

Marrowbone (Os à Moelle, Fr.)
The large tubular bones of animals which hold a soft fatty substance used extensively in cookery—especially for broths.

Marrowfat
A large, rich kind of pea.

Marsala
The wine of Marsala in the Island of Sicily. It resembles sherry in some respects and is obtainable dry or sweet.

Marshmallow (Gulmauve, Fr.)
A tall plant, cousin to the hollyhock. The leaves are cooked as greens and from its roots is obtained a tasteless, colourless gum used in medicine. The confection enjoyed as marshmallow is made from gelatine, gum arabic, glucose, sugar and water. The plant grows freely in marshes near the sea, native to both Europe and Asia.

Martini
An Italian vermouth.

Marzipan (Marchpane, Fr.)
A paste formed by crushing sweet almonds with sugar ; used extensively for cakes, chocolate and sugar confectionery. Said to have been invented during the siege of Paris, almonds and sugar being the only ingredients one particular chef had at his disposal.

Mask (Masquer, Fr.)
To cover completely. Usually with mayonnaise or thick sauce.

Masquer (Fr.)
See Mask.

Massenet (Fr.)

Name of a style of garnish for tournedos and noisettes consisting of artichoke bottoms filled with beef marrow, with French beans and Anna potatoes.

Maté (Fr.)

Paraguay tea. Made from the leaves and young shoots of a species of holly bush, which makes a beverage similar to green tea.

Matelote (Fr.)

Sailor style. With a variety of fish, or sometimes with one kind only—as Matelote of Eels. Fish stew is called matelote.

Matzoth or Motza

A most familiar form of unleavened bread, generally made in the form of large, round or square, thin, brittle biscuits. They are made in large quantities for the Jewish Passover.

Mauviette (Fr.)

See Lark.

Mayonnaise Sauce

A rich dressing made of oil, eggs, lemon juice or vinegar, seasonings and plenty of whisking. The most popular of cold sauces. For origin see Richelieu.

Mazarin

A liqueur of France, with a flavour similar to Benedictine. Also, the name applied to small almond cakes and pastries.

Mead

In bygone days, newly-weds spent their first 28 days drinking mead—a fermented liquor of honey and water. Honeymoon meaning honey for the full period of the moon.

Meal

The act of taking food to satisfy one's hunger. Also applied to ground grain such as cornmeal or oatmeal.

Meat (Viande, Fr.)

The edible part of anything, be it animal, bird, fish, fruit, nut or vegetable. Mistakenly applied only to the flesh of animals by many. In the case of animals, the flesh should be well hung, and always carved across the grain, thus cutting through the fibre tubes and making it more tender.

Meat Extract

The broth of boiled meats, boiled in vacuum kettles, filtered and finally evaporated to a paste.

Médaillon (Fr.)

See Medallion.

Medallion (Médaillon, Fr.)

A small round fillet, or a cut of moulded, enriched minced preparation.

Médicis (Fr.)

Name of a garnish for tournedos and noisettes consisting of artichoke bottoms filled with peas, shaped carrots and turnips with noisette potatoes and Sauce Choron.

Medlar (Nèfle, Fr.)
A small, apple-like fruit in appearance, with a harsh taste and russet skin. Used chiefly for preserves, medlar jam being particularly fine.

Medoc
Wine produced in the district of Médoc, in France.

Megrim (Carrelet, Fr.)
The megrim has as many aliases as there are fishing ports, being offered as a substitute for all types of flat fish, and even masquerading as Dover sole. In Cornwall, it is unkindly known as a whiff. The megrims are thin in body and lacking in flavour. The upper side is a light yellowish, or reddish-brown colour, occasionally a little mottled with dark brown. The length is from 12 to 18 inches. All recipes for sole may be used for the megrim, but it should never be used as a substitute for sole.

Mélange (Fr.)
Mixture.

Mélangeur
A milling or rolling machine used for crushing, as in the manufacture of chocolate, where the beans are rolled and crushed for up to 24 hours to obtain a smooth eating chocolate.

Melba
Name of a famous prima-donna who gave her name to many dishes, most famous of which is the Pêche Melba, originally made in her honour by the famous Escoffier. This dish consists of peaches stoned and filled with cream, set on a layer of ice cream and masked with the now famous Melba sauce, which is a form of sieved raspberry preserve rather on the thin side. Nowadays, almost any fruit set on a bed of ice cream and masked with raspberry sauce is called Strawberry Melba, Pear Melba, etc. Melba Toast is bread sliced $\frac{1}{8}$ inch in thickness and either baked in a sharp oven or toasted under a slow grill.

Melettes (Fr.)
See Sprats.

Melisse Citronelle (Fr.)
See Balm.

Melon (Melon, Fr.)
From a nutritive standpoint melons are chiefly sugar and water, averaging 90% to 93% water and 5% to 6% sugar. They are highly esteemed as a refresher and a dessert fruit.

Melon, Honeydew
Name given to a variety of melon which has a smooth, somewhat warted, creamy white to greyish skin, strong but thin. It has a sweet flesh shading from green to white. Good specimens average 6 inches or more in diameter, 7 to 8 inches in length and 6 to 7 lbs. in weight.

Melon, Sugar

A variety of cantaloup which averages 6 to 8 inches in diameter and weighs from 2 to 4 lbs. It has a silvery-grey ribbed skin and a very sweet flesh.

Melon, Water

There are many sizes and shapes of water melon, which range from 15 to 30 lbs. in weight. It has a thick brittle rind which varies from dark to light green or striped. Its flesh is firm and of dark red or yellow colour. It is most refreshing and attractive but its nutritive value is low.

Melt

The spleen ; a soft, pulpy gland.

Menthe (Fr.)

See Mint.

Menu (Fr.)

From the Latin minutus ; the bill of fare, or the minute details of each course. Menu cards were first used in 1541, as a guide to the host only. The idea was copied and subsequently each guest was provided with the minute details of each course, to allow him to save himself for the best.

Mercédès (Fr.)

Name of a style of garnish consisting of grilled chats, mushrooms, braised lettuce with croquette potatoes.

Méringue (Fr.)

The whites of eggs beaten stiff with sugar and baked as a light soufflé confection. (See also Italian Meringue.)

Merlan (Fr.)

See Whiting.

Merle (Fr.)

See Blackbird.

Merluche (Fr.)

See Haddock.

Merrythought

The forked bone in the breast of birds. Presumably derived from the merry thoughts of persons pulling the bone apart to gain the larger half, for their superstitious wishes to come true.

Mess

A gathering of people to eat together, or a quantity of food served up at one time.

Methuselah

A bottle capable of holding $213\frac{1}{3}$ fluid ozs., or 8 ordinary bottles. (See Bottle.)

Mexicaine, à la (Fr.)

Mexican style. As a garnish it consists of sliced and grilled eggplant, capsicums, chats and mushrooms in a hot pepper sauce.

Miche, Miche de Pain (Fr.)

Loaf, loaf of bread.

Middlings

A by-product of flour, being the coarser, common type, not usually sold for bread or pastry.

Miel (Fr.)

See Honey.

Mignardises (Fr.)
Small, dainty confections.

Mignon (Fr.)
Dainty, delicate. Mignon fillets : small, tender fillets, usually from beef tenderloin.

Mignonette Pepper
Prepared from either white or black pepper, being crushed and broken down, sifted to remove the dust so that the pepper resembles mignonette seed.

Milanaise (Fr.)
Italian style—served with macaroni, grated cheese, or tomato purée.

Milcher Herring
See Herring.

Milcon
A South American preparation, not unlike the Italian pastes, made from potatoes and pumpkin.

Milk (Lait, Fr.)
Almost a perfect food for the very young and of high value for both children and adults of all ages. It is one of the foods for which there is no substitute. Its fat content is one of the best sources of vitamin A. Milk should never be boiled for food purposes. (See also Goat's Milk, Sheep's Milk and Skim Milk.)

Mille-feuille (Fr.)
"A thousand leaves." A gâteau made of layers of very light puff pastry sandwiched together with cream and jam.

Millet
A term loosely applied to a number of small-seeded cereals. In the early days of the world's history, millet held a high place as a food grain, and is still of large importance to parts of India. In England, it is now chiefly imported as bird seed.

Milt (Laitance, Fr.)
The scientific name of the soft (male) roe of fish.

Mincemeat
In bygone days, a mixture of finely minced meat, suet, apples, dried fruits, brandy and spirituous liquor. To-day, the meat and the spirituous liquor are omitted, leaving a mixture of apples, suet, dried fruits, spices and sugar.

Mince Pie
A traditional Christmas pie, made of pastry and filled with mincemeat.

Mineral Waters
Waters obtained from natural springs, containing a percentage of mineral salts, having a saline taste. Table mineral waters have little pronounced flavour and many kinds are made effervescent by their content of carbon dioxide, both natural and added. Well-known natural mineral waters are Apollinaris, Perrier, Carlsbad, Vichy, Johannis-Lithia, Seltzer, Seidlitz, etc.

Minestra
A famous Italian thick vegetable soup.

Minestrone
An Italian soup with consommé as its basis, with vegetables, pork, spaghetti and cheese added.

Minnow (Véron or Vairon, Fr.)
A small fresh-water fish which may be cooked in the same manner as whitebait, and tastes just as good. See " The Master Book of Fish " for recipes.

Mint (Menthe, Fr.)
One of the few flavourings originally attributed to Great Britain. There are quite a number of varieties of this small, aromatic plant ; a few of the best are :
BERGAMOT MINT OR LEMON MINT.
It has a pleasant lemon scent ; used in the liqueur, Chartreuse.
PEPPERMINT Used chiefly in sweets and crème-de-menthe.
ROUND-LEAVED MINT Best for mint sauce. Easily distinguished by its broad, woolly, round, sage-like leaves.
SPEARMINT Used chiefly for distillation and in the manufacture of chewing gum.

Mint Julep
A drink of the Americas.

Minute, à la (Fr.)
Quickly cooked. Grills and short order dishes come under this heading.

Mirabeau (Fr.)
Name of a garnish to many dishes consisting of artichoke bottoms, olives, and anchovy fillets. Named after the son of the Marquis de Mirabeau.

Mirabelle (Fr.)
A small, yellow plum, with a delicious flavour. Also the name of a French liqueur, white in colour, with the flavour of the plum.

Mirepoix (Fr.)
The foundation ingredients of most brown soups, sauces, and the first steps in braising, being the preparation of the fat, vegetables, herbs, etc. to sauté, to gain a brown colour.

Miroton (Fr.)
Sliced, cooked meat, warmed over sautéed onions, etc., and served in rich Espagnole Sauce.

Mixture (Mélange, Fr.)
A compound of different ingredients blended together.

Mocha (Moka, Fr.)
A flavour from coffee infusion, also the name of a first quality coffee berry produced in Mysore.

Mock Turtle (Tortue Fausse, Fr.)
A soup containing diced calf's head, flavoured with various vegetables, herbs and spices. It may be a thick or clear soup.

Mode, à la (Fr.)
After the fashion of.

Moelle de Bœuf (Fr.)
See Beef Marrow and Marrow-bone.

Moka (Fr.)
See Mocha.

Molasses
The syrup that is separated from the crystals or grains of " raw sugar " in the process of manufacture. The best is that from sugar made from the first crops collected before the copious periodical rains. The best grades are of bright amber tint, the lowest grade being " blackstrap ".

Mollet (Fr.)
Soft. As applied to soft-boiled eggs—œufs mollets (Fr.)

Mongol
Mongolian style. Chiefly a garnish containing peas and tomatoes, with vegetables cut julienne style.

Monkey Nut
See Pea-nut.

Montadella (It.)
Name of a type of sausage originally manufactured at Bologna, Italy.

Montglas
Potage Montglas is a thick chicken soup garnished with truffles and mushrooms.

Montgolfier
The brothers Joseph Michel and Jacques Etienne, who made the first balloon, gave their name to many dishes of a puffed or blown-out character. Montgolfier style — light, puffy, balloon fashion.

Montpellier (Fr.)
A French city renowned for its cuisine. Montpellier Butter— a green, savoury butter, made of herbs, scalded and pounded raisins, and a variety of other ingredients. Served cold as a fish sauce.

Moor Hen (Poule d'Eau, Fr.)
The moor hen is sometimes referred to as the female of the red grouse, it being supposedly allied to the moor cock, or moor game, which are local names given to the grouse in Scotland. Actually, it is quite distinct from the grouse, being a water bird about the size of a bantam hen when fully grown. In colouring it is dark olive-brown above, iron-grey below, with a scarlet frontlet. As it swims, its white tail coverts are very conspicuous. It may be seen quite often in and around country ponds or streams.
Once caught and tried, it is left unmolested, as it lacks flavour and is coarse eating. The town dweller, when visiting the countryside, is sometimes amazed to see such game in plenty, with hardly any notice being taken of it.

Morello Cherry
A rich, dark red cherry, used extensively in cherry brandy and all types of cookery where cherries are required as a garnish.

L

Morels (Morille, Fr.)
A delicate type of mushroom, said to have great aphrodisiac qualities.

Mornay
Name of a rich cream sauce flavoured with cheese. À la Mornay—with cheese sauce.

Mortar
A vessel in which substances are pounded with a pestle, usually made from a solid piece of marble with a cavity hollowed out, being of great thickness and strength to allow for heavy pounding.

Morue Salée (Fr.)
See Cod, Salt.

Moscovite (Fr.)
Name of a favourite sauce consisting of Sauce Poivrade reduced with marsala wine.

Moselle
A group of light wines from the district of the river Moselle in France. The best are those of the middle course of the river between Trier and Coblenz.

Mothering Cake
See Simnel Cake.

Motza
See Matzoth.

Mou (Fr.)
See Lights.

Mouette (Fr.)
Sea gull. (See Gull.)

Moule (Fr.)
See Mussel.

Mountain Grouse
See Ptarmigan.

Mountain Tea
See Wintergreen.

Mousse (Fr.)
Froth, foam. Chiefly applied to the soufflé type of light, creamy preparations. Dishes containing whipped white of egg or cream.

Moussec
English sparkling wine, made from imported grape juice. (See Must.)

Mousse Frappée (Fr.)
A frozen, whipped cream dessert.

Mousseline Sauce
Frothy Hollandaise sauce, containing whipped cream or beaten egg white. The term " Mousseline de " is also applied in the same manner as " Mousse de " (see Mousse).

Mout (Fr.)
See Must.

Moutarde (Fr.)
See Mustard.

Mouton (Fr.)
See Mutton.

Mozart
Name of a style of garnish consisting of artichoke bottoms filled with celery purée and Copeaux Potatoes.

Muffins

Small, thick, round, light, fermented cakes, baked in hoops on a solid-top stove till half-cooked, then turned, so that the top is flattened and toasted. They are split while hot and filled with plenty of butter.

Mufle de Bœuf (Fr.)

See Ox Cheek.

Muge (Fr.)

See Mullet, Grey.

Mulberry (Mûre, Fr.)

Very few mulberries are cultivated in England to-day, because of the mess made in gathering the fruit. " Here we go round the mulberry bush " now applies more to the silkworm than to children. The leaves of the tree are the principal food of the silkworm. The fruit is like a large loganberry, black in colour.

Mulled

Term applied to alcoholic beverages heated with spices, sugar, etc. Served at outdoor sports, such as hunting, or as a nightcap.

Mullet, Grey (Muge, Mulet, Fr.)

There are two true mullets, different in family, size and appearance, the small red and the large grey. The grey mullet is less delicate in flavour, but is nevertheless an excellent food fish. Its usual size is about 15 inches, but it sometimes extends to 2 ft. The colour of the back is steel-grey, with bluish and partly yellow reflections ; the abdomen is silvery white, and on the flanks there are 6 or 8 lines of a rosy brown.

The grey mullet is best between August and October.

Mullet, Red (Mulle, Rouget, Fr.)

The red mullet is very red, rarely exceeds 6 inches in length, and is firm to the touch. Its firm, lean and delicious flesh brings high prices. It has been esteemed as one of the epicure's choice luxuries— in ancient Rome it was held in extravagant regard among wealthy patricians, and it is said that on one occasion £234 7s. 6d. was paid for three. Bake or grill red mullet, but never steam or boil them. They are best baked in oiled greaseproof paper, to retain their full flavour.

Mulligatawny

This title is derived from two native words signifying " pepper water ". It is a highly seasoned Indian curry soup, of which curry powder is the essential ingredient.

Mum

An old-fashioned alcoholic brew, taking 2 years to mature. Made of wheat-malt.

Mûre (Fr.)

See Mulberry.

Mûre de Ronce (Fr.)

See Blackberry.

Muscat

A white, sweet, scented grape, grown more for table purposes than for wine-making.

Muscovado

The impure sugar left after evaporating the juice from the sugar cane and draining off the molasses. It is known as un-refined sugar and is moist and dark-coloured. Used quite often in the manufacture of wedding cakes.

Muscovite (Fr.)

Moscow style. Usually denotes caviare.

Mushroom (Champignon, Fr.)

Of the many types of edible mushroom, apart from the common mushroom, there are the edible chanterelle, parasol, morel, edible boletus, masked tricholoma, shaggy mane, fairy ring, common ink cap, beef-steak oyster, and many others numbering nearly 100 kinds.
Their nutritive value is slight, and unless very carefully cooked they are liable to retard the assimilation of other foods. Pliny considered them one of the wonders of nature. Culti-vated and canned mushrooms are always safe.

Mushroom Sauce (Sauce aux Champignons, Fr.)

Reduced Espagnole Sauce gar-nished with small mush-rooms.

Mussel (Moule, Fr.)

The mussel is an almond-shaped shellfish, and is cheap and plentiful. Many connois-seurs consider it as palatable as the oyster, but it has never attained popular favour until the Second World War, when mussels could be obtained in most West End restaurants while oysters were scarce and prohibitive. A fair-sized speci-men is about 2 inches in length. The mussel can be eaten raw, like the oyster, but is generally cooked, and is better that way, as the flesh is tougher than that of the oyster. It also makes a very good substitute in all recipes where clams are re-quired.

Must (Mout, Fr.)

Unfermented grape juice. Used extensively for producing British wines. It is sterilized and as such can be imported as grape juice, thus avoiding heavy duties. Yeast is then added and the grape juice fermented for wine. (See Moussec.)

Mustard (Moutarde, Fr.)

Table mustard has as its basis the blended flours made from the crushed seeds of one or more species of mustard plant. The characteristic flavour is developed only when it is moistened. Vinegar will al-ways bring out more of its pungency than water.

A Mrs. Durham, in England, is credited with being the first person to grind the seed and use it as a seasoning, in 1720. Durham mustard is still referred to in many parts of the country.

Mutton (Mouton, Fr.)
The dressed flesh of the sheep, after the lamb stage. Quality depends on breed and sex : the wether (the castrated male) is the best ; next are the ewes ; rams are coarse in texture and over strong in flavour.

Myrtille (Fr.)
See Bilberry.

N

Nansen
Name of a Norwegian scientist and explorer. Dishes bearing his name are usually iced in some form, as Consommé Nansen, comprising iced consommé garnished with small caviare croûtons.

Nantais, à la (Fr.)
Nantes style. Nantes is a city of western France, and among its industries are rice husking and canning of sardines and vegetables. In dishes bearing this name barley or vegetables are used in some form as a garnish.

Napkin
See Table Napkin.

Napolitaine, à la (Fr. from Napoli, It.)
Naples style. Term applied to dishes of a multi-coloured nature, such as the well-known Napolitaine ice, consisting of layers of different coloured and flavoured ice cream. Also, a garnish consisting of spaghetti, tomato sauce and grated cheese.

Nappe (Fr.)
Tablecloth.

Nappé (Fr.)
A light coating of sauce, jelly or icing.

Nartje
The South African tangerine.

Nasturtium (Capucine, Fr.)
Referred to in many old recipe books as Indian cress. The young leaves and the flowers are sometimes employed in salads. Its seeds, pickled, make a good substitute for capers. The flowers are frequently used to garnish Indian and curry dishes.

Natives
The English term for oysters, spawned and bred in Essex or Kentish beds.

Naturel, au (Fr.)
See Au Naturel.

Nau de Morue (Fr.)
Cod Sounds.

Navarin (Fr.)
A type of stew or haricot mutton. Usually implies that turnips are embodied in the dish in some form.

Navet (Fr.)
See Turnip.

Neats Foot
The ox or calf's foot, used for making jellies and gelatinous soups. Neat's foot soup— calf's foot soup. An old English term for what is now known as cow's heels.

Nectar
The honey of flowers. The fabled drink of the ancient gods. Any very sweet and pleasant drink.

Néctarine (Fr.)
A small, smooth-skinned peach, lacking the fuzz found on peaches. It is richer in flavour and aroma, and has a firmer flesh, of red, yellow or white. The stone of the nectarine and peach are identical.

Needlefish
See Garfish.

Nêfle (Fr.)
See Medlar.

Neige (Fr.)
Snow. Œufs à la Neige are whites of egg beaten to a stiff froth with sugar and poached in milk, oftimes in bird shapes. (See Niverolle.)

Nelson
Name of a British naval hero. Seaboard specialities usually bear his name. As a consommé, it consists of a clear turtle soup garnished with red, white and green custard royale.

Nemoirs
Name of a town of France. Also Duc de Nemoirs, second son of the Duke of Orleans, and a great line of dukes going back to the 12th and 13th centuries. As a garnish, the name indicates mushrooms, duchesse potatoes, and rich grown gravy. As a consommé, carrot and egg yolk royale form the garnish.

Nemrod (Fr.)
Name of a style of garnish consisting of fried beef marrow, mushrooms and chestnut purée.

Nepaul Pepper
Pepper ground from yellow capsicums. It possesses a sweet, pungent flavour and forms an important ingredient of Indian curry powders. Grown largely in Hindustan.

Nerole (Néroli, Fr.)
An essential oil distilled from orange blossoms, used for flavouring. Orange flower water is the fragrant liquid collected after the distillation of nerole.

Nesselrode
Name given to a range of iced puddings by Count Nesselrode of France. Iced puddings bearing this name usually denote that chestnuts are embodied in some form.

Nettles
Nettles may be cooked exactly as spinach, and will be found very good and wholesome fare.

Neufchâtel
A soft, fermented and refined, small French cheese, made in and around Neufchâtel in Normandy.

Newburg (Fr.)
Name of a very rich lobster sauce flavoured with madiera wine, enriched with cream and egg yolks. Lobster Newburg is cooked and finished in the same style.

Niçoise (Fr.)
Nice style. Nice—a city of France. Olives, oranges, tomatoes and mulberries are cultivated in the neighbourhood ; hence we find olives and tomatoes in most of the forms of garniture and sauces bearing this name.

As a garniture for meat, it comprises olives, French beans, and tomatoes, served in rich gravy. As a sauce, it contains concentrated tomato purée blended with demi-glace. Consommé Niçois, contains strips of tomato, flageolets and diced potato as its garniture.

Nids (Fr.)
Nests.

Nightcap
A name applied to liquor taken just before going to bed. Spiced ale or mulled wine were popular nightcaps in earlier times. It is now applied to almost any intoxicating spirit or beverage which might induce sleep.

Nip
A small draught of spirits. A quarter bottle or one-twenty-fourth of an imperial gallon.

Nitrogen
An element of the atmosphere, forming four-fifths of its volume. An important element in all proteins and essential to all forms of plant and animal life.

Nivernais
A former province of France. The name, when applied to garnishings for poultry and game, indicates a mixture of small young vegetables and braised lettuce with demi-glace. As a sauce, it comprises Allemande or Velouté with finely shredded young carrots.

Niverolle (Fr.)
Snowbird. As bird shapes of cooked white of egg. (See Neige.)

Noekkelost
A hard, Norwegian, chocolate-coloured cheese, made of goat's milk.

Noggin
A measure of liquor, equal to ¼ pint.

Noisette (Fr.)
Hazel-nut. As a culinary term, it means the best part, the nut or kernel, such as noisette of lamb or mutton, being the middle or best rolled cuts of loin or neck.

Noix (Fr.)
See Walnut.

Noix de Brésil (Fr.)
See Brazil Nut.

Noix de Muscade (Fr.)
See Nutmeg.

Noix de Veau (Fr.)
The kernel, or best part of a leg of veal.

Nonpareilles (Fr.)
Tiny, multi-coloured, seed-like sugar confections, used for decorating luncheon and dinner sweets, and cakes.

Noodles (Nouilles, Fr.)
A product which originated in Germany. They resemble the flat form of Italian paste (macaroni, spaghetti, etc.). Noodles are made of wheat flour, while Italian pastes are made of semolina. (See also Macaroni and Vermicelli.)

Normande, à la (Fr.)
Normandy style. Normandy, a province of France. The name is usually found connected with fish garnishings and sauces. Other than fish dishes, it denotes apple in some form. As a fish garnish, it consists of oysters, mussels, shrimps, mushrooms, in Normande sauce. As a sauce, it comprises rich fish sauce, flavoured with white wine and enriched with cream and egg yolks.

Norvégienne (Fr.)
Norwegian. The name usually implies that fish, eggs or vegetables are embodied in the dish, seldom, if ever, meat. Sauce Norvégienne is a cold sauce composed of eggs, mustard, vinegar and herbs. Potage Norvégienne is a purée of turnips, enriched with milk and cream and garnished with thin strips of beetroot.

Nougat (Fr.)
A sort of almond toffee, made of sugar, lemon juice, almonds or other nuts. Used extensively for show or centre pieces for the dessert course, as it can be so easily shaped into fancy baskets, boats, or almost any shape, in the hands of an expert.

Nouilles (Fr.)
See Noodles.

Nourishment
Foods of nutritive value, which promote growth and development of all, or any, part of the human structure. (See also Diet.)

Noyau (Fr.)
A white, sweet liqueur, flavoured with the kernel of the almond.

Nut
The seed or kernel of fruit enclosed in woody or bony covering not opening when ripe. A highly concentrated food with little waste.

Nut Butter
A spreadable paste made from pounded nuts and moistened with oil, such as pea-nut butter, almond or pecan nut butter.

Nutmeg (Noix de Muscade, Fr.)
The kernel of the fruit of a tropical tree native to the East Indies. The skin enclosing the hard shell surrounding the nut is the popular spice known as mace (which see).

Nut Oil
Almost all nuts yield oils of value for use as a food. Most popular are almond, groundnut and coco-nut.

O

Oatmeal (Gruau d'Avoine, Fr.)
Oatmeal is made from kiln dried oats, from which the husks have been removed, and forms the food that provides porridge. There are three grades, coarse, medium and fine. The oats from Scotland are considered best. The meal of oats produced by grinding.

Oats (Avoine, Fr.)
A cereal which provides us with oatmeal. Considered one of the best of food cereal grains.

Octopus
See Squid.

Œuf
See Egg.

Œufs à la Coque (Fr.)
Boiled eggs.

Œufs Brouillés (Fr.)
Scrambled eggs.

Œufs de Poisson (Fr.)
See Roe, Hard.

Œufs Farcis (Fr.)
Stuffed eggs.

Œufs Frits (Fr.)
Fried eggs.

Œufs Mollets (Fr.)
Soft-boiled eggs.

Œufs Pochés (Fr.)
Poached eggs.

Offal
The edible parts of an animal taken from its inside. Broadly speaking, the term also includes the head, tail and feet, besides heart, liver, kidneys, sweetbreads and stomach.

Oie (Fr.)
See Goose.

Oignon (Fr.)
See Onion.

Oil
See Nut Oil, Olive Oil and Walnut Oil.

Oiseau (Fr.)
Bird.

Oison (Fr.)
Gosling. (See Goose.)

Oka
Small, potato-like vegetables which, when dried in their own country, Peru and Bolivia, are said to taste like dried figs.

Okra, or Gumbo

A herbaceous plant well-known for its ridged, mucilaginous pods, which resemble small immature cucumbers in appearance. It is used to impart a rich, gelatinous nature to soups, casserole dishes and stews. Grown in South America and the West Indies. Americans have taken very favourably to it and their gumbo soups are much esteemed.

Okroschka

A Russian soup.

Old Bird

Applied to birds bred in one year and killed in the next.

Old Fashioned

A favourite American cocktail, consisting of rye whisky, sugar, aromatic bitters, chilled with cubed ice, topped with a maraschino cherry and a thin twist of lemon rind.

Olein

Natural fat found in fatty oils of animals and vegetables.

Oleomargarine

The original name for margarine, which was first made of beef oleo oil, milk and water, with annatto to give colour.

Olio

A rich Spanish stew or pot-au-feu, prepared for special, festive occasions.

Olive (Fr.)

Olive. The fruit which yields the best of all culinary oils ; also used as a garnish for many dishes, and one of the finest aids for cleansing the palate. France, Italy and Spain each provide huge quantities for the ever - growing demand. The Spanish Queen is the largest and most esteemed. In buying, the size is usually denoted by the count per lb,. in the same way as prunes are marketed. The fruit is green until it is full size, then gradually becomes yellow, and finally changes to a dark purplish-brown.

Olive trees often reach a great age—there are trees near Genoa believed to be more than 2,000 years old.

Olive Oil (Huile d'Olive, Fr.)

The best oil is that expressed from fully ripe olives before they turn black. If expressed from under-ripe olives, it is bitter, and if from over-ripe olives, soon becomes rancid. Virgin olive oil is obtained from the first pressing, when only 50% oil is obtained from the olives. Later, the pressing is continued, when up to 70% oil is obtained. The finest quality is of a golden straw colour ; those with a greenish tint indicate a poorer quality or late full pressing. It should be bought in cans, in preference to bottles, to exclude the light, for its keeping qualities.

Olives (Meat)

Very thin slices of meat formed into rolls enclosing forcemeat. In America they are named meat birds, usually braised.

Olivette Potatoes

Small, round, browned potatoes, usually no larger than an olive, used extensively for garnishing all types of dishes, a recipe for which is given below. Cut potatoes with a Parisian potato spoon to the shape of an olive. Put in a vessel with cold water, bring to boiling point, and drain. Melt some butter or other fat in a sauté pan, add the potatoes and bake in oven until a nice golden brown. Drain off fat and season with salt.

Oloroso

A popular, full-bodied, sherry wine. Rather sweet and of golden colour.

Omble

A fresh-water fish, of the salmon tribe, found in the Swiss and Savoy lakes.

Ombre (Fr.)

See Grayling.

Omelet (Omelette, Fr.)

A light pancake preparation of eggs, to which other foods are added to give it substance and flavour. It can be so treated to suit almost any meal, simple to make, yet most cooks fail in its preparation by not getting the pan and butter hot enough to ensure a light, fluffy finish.

Onion (Oignon, Fr.)

A vegetable and a condiment, for next to salt the onion is the most valuable condiment in the science of cookery. When boiled, it loses much of its pungent volatile oil and becomes agreeable and nutritious. Fried or baked, it takes on a slightly different flavour, and in this form will completely change the flavour of a dish, as compared with one containing plain boiled onions. Contrary to many beliefs, it aids digestion and possesses stimulating properties.

Oporto

Second city of Portugal, famous for the export of the wine which bears its name. An act of 29 January, 1906, defined " port " as a wine grown in the Douro district, exported from Oporto, and containing more than 16.5% of alcoholic strength.

Opossum

A small animal about the size of a cat, found in the southern states of America. Recently popularised as a new dish. It is scalded and scraped before roasting and baking, and is said to have the flavour of a young pig.

Orange

The most favoured of all citrus fruits. As a dessert, the best are the seedless Jaffa. For marmalade, the Seville orange is usually chosen. The Navel is the most abundantly grown seedless orange. In packing, oranges are graded and crated in all sizes from 80 to 320 to the crate, the best grades being those between 120 to 160 per crate. The very large have more rind in proportion to pulp, and are used for candied peel.

Orange juice is one of the best known sources of vitamin C, surpassed only by the blackcurrant.

Orangeade

A beverage made of orange juice, similar to lemonade.

Orangeat (Fr.)

Orange peel candied.

Orange Bitters

An extract of sour oranges and their pips.

Orange Flower Water

See Nerole.

Orange Gin

Gin flavoured with orange and of orange colour.

Orange Whisky

A liqueur whisky flavoured with orange.

Oreille (Fr.)

Ear.

Orge (Fr.)

See Barley.

Orientale, à l' (Fr.)

Oriental style, denoting rice, curry or rich spices in the composition of the dish, or intermingling colours when tomato is introduced.

Oriental cookery is characterised by the use of many condiments and the cutting of the food into small pieces before cooking. Confucius refused to accept foods that were not " chopped up properly " and ruled that there must never be more flesh food than vegetables in the composition of his dishes.

Orloff, Orlov

Name of a noted Russian family, prominent from the 16th to the 18th centuries. Many dishes are styled à l'Orloff, but no particular mode can be given, as this varies in almost every dish. It would appear that the name was applied recklessly, no doubt to gain favour in that period ; so recklessly, that cooks did not stop to find out how to spell the name correctly. As with " Demidoff ", the two " f's " should be a " v ", and the name should be " Orlov ".

Orly, à l' (Fr.)

Bernard Van Orley, noted Flemish painter, born 1490, died 1540. Name given to dishes consisting of fish or meat coated with batter and fried in deep fat. Tomato sauce is usually served with such dishes. The " e " has been discarded over the years of time.

Ortolan

These birds, though small and very rare, are much esteemed by epicures for the delicacy of their flesh. They are in season November to February.

When the great Alexis Soyer was once asked to prepare ortolan stuffed with truffles, he replied : " An ortolan cannot be stuffed with truffles, but I will gladly stuff you a truffle with an ortolan ".

The ortolan is almost extinct in these Isles. It is distinguished by its black wings and greenish - grey head. When caught and fattened, it is considered a great delicacy. In size, it is not much bigger than a thrush. The birds are netted in great numbers in some European countries. They are then kept alive in darkened rooms and fattened on oats and millet. In a very short time they become quite fat, and are then marketed. Ortolan is the French name, and is that used in most English-speaking countries.

Os à Moelle (Fr.)
Marrowbone.

Oseille (Fr.)
See Sorrel.

Oswego Tea
See Bergamot.

Otter
Otters were at one time eaten in considerable quantities during Lent, they being inexcusably considered a type of fish. A carnivorous animal, resembling a large weasel, inhabiting rivers and streams. Should be cooked like a badger.

Outarde (Fr.)
Bustard.

Ovale (Fr.)
Oval or egg-shaped.

Ovar
A Hungarian cheese made of cow's milk, of a reddish-yellow colour.

Oven (Four, Fr.)
An insulated chamber, when heated, used for the baking of foods.

Ox Cheek (Mufle de Bœuf, Fr.)
Meat from the cheek of the animal.

Ox Palate (Palais de Bœuf, Fr.)
See Palate.

Ox Tail (Queue de Bœuf, Fr.)
An excellent, nutritious part of the animal for making rich soups and entrées.

Oyster (Huître, Fr.)
Oyster addicts will not have them any way but raw on the half-shell, however many delectable dishes may be made from cooked oysters. Short cooking time is the secret for keeping oysters tender and flavourful. Over - cooking toughens an oyster. Do not wait for the edges to curl. Fried oysters need just one minute of cooking on each side. Oyster stews are always best cooked over water in a double boiler. Always add oysters to any cooked dish as the last ingredients.

To write of oysters and all about them would be a lengthy task. One writer started to do so in 1890, and ran into two volumes containing 1,370 pages.

The reason we may not eat oysters in the months from May to August is simply that this is the close season; they are busily occupied in reproducing their kind. However, Continental oysters are now imported during the English close season, and are to be found in West End restaurants, much to the surprise of the uninitiated. The test of freshness is to see whether the muscle is sunken; if swollen and standing above the rest of the fish, it is unfit.

As to what to drink with oysters —well, if it's a meal of oysters, then stout. Sweet wines should never come near oysters.

Chablis is classic, when procurable. Dry hock or a moselle are good. For myself, I like Black Velvet—being fifty-fifty dry champagne and stout.

The natives from Colchester or Whitstable are most highly esteemed and are usually eaten raw by the epicure. Blue Points, Portuguese, or the large American oyster, are the types generally used for cooking. The relaid oyster has been transferred from its original breeding ground to another, so that it may develop and acquire to some extent the qualities of the aristocrat.

Oyster Plant
Another name for salsify (which see).

Ozone
A form of oxygen. Used commercially for sterilisation of water.

P

Pailles (Fr.)
Straws.

Pailles au Parmesan (Fr.)
Cheese straws.

Pain (Fr.)
Bread. (See also Miche.)

Pain Bis (Fr.)
Brown bread.

Pain Rôti or Pain Grillé (Fr.)
Toast.

Palais de Bœuf (Fr.)
Ox-palate. (See Palate.)

Palate
The roof of the mouth. The ox-palate is generally used as a fricassée.

Palma
Name given to certain sherries, denoting dry, pale, fine sherry.

Palpuszta
A Hungarian cheese with an odour similar to that of the Limberg type.

Pamplemousse (Fr.)
One of the original names for the grapefruit (which see). The other name being shaddock.

Panada (Panade, Fr.)
A preparation of bread soaked in milk or stock, which is then drained and pounded to form the foundation for stuffings and forcemeats. Considered much superior to grated crumbs as used in most English kitchens.

Panais (Fr.)
See Parsnip.

Pan-broiled
To cook uncovered in a hot frying pan, the pan being smeared with the smallest amount of fat to prevent sticking.

Pancake (Crêpe, Fr.)
The French equivalent to our pancake is taken from the English word " crisp ". Thin light flat cakes made of well matured batter fried in butter. If made from unmatured batter the pancake will be tough and leathery. The batter should be smooth, the consistency of cream, and allowed to stand at least 2 hours, to ensure successful Crêpes Suzettes. Originally, pancakes were mixed with beer, to give lightness to the batter.

Pancreas
The sweetbread (which see).

Pandoras
A Spanish delicacy, consisting of fingers of toasted or fried bread spread with a savoury meat mixture dipped in batter and fried.

Pané (Fr.)
Coated with breadcrumbs.

Pannerone (It.)
See Gorgonzola.

Panocha
Name of a type of Persian nut fudge which nowadays contains almost any addition, as coffee panocha, cherry panocha, chocolate panocha. It is like making additions to Turkish delight to give it variety.

Panure (Fr.)
Breadcrumbs, moist or raspings.

Paon (Fr.)
See Peacock.

Paons de Mer (Fr.)
See Ruffs and Reeves.

Papaw (Papaye, Fr.)
A fruit which grows in large clusters on a tree similar to a palm tree. The fruit will vary in weight from 4 to 20 lbs. and has a flesh which resembles that of a musk melon. Both the fruit and the plant itself contain a juice known as papain, which has the peculiar property of rendering the toughest meats tender. This was first realised by the natives, who used to wrap fowls or meats in the leaves overnight, before roasting the food, or to rub green papaw juice over their roasts.

Papier Dentillé (Fr.)
Lace paper. (See Doily.)

Papillotes, en
See En Papillote.

Paprika (Pabrica, Fr.)

There are two kinds of paprika, the pungent produced by drying and grinding the Hungarian capsicum, and the mild made from the Spanish capsicum, a mild cayenne pepper with which it should never be confused.

Paradise Grains

See Grains of Paradise.

Paradise Nut

A sweet oily nut, similar in shape to the Brazil nut, but with a smoother, thinner shell. The nuts—2 lbs. or more of them—are formed inside an urn-shaped pod 8 to 12 inches in diameter, which weighs 6 to 12 lb. This urn-shaped pod has a sort of lid, which when it falls to the ground emits a loud report, which brings all the monkeys within hearing quickly to the spot. Hence the urn is called a monkey pot, and the reason why so few of these nuts reach the market.

Paradise Pepper

See Shot Pepper.

Parboil

To boil partially, or for just a short time.

Parfait (Fr.)

Perfect. A soft, light, rich dish of ice cream, of a soufflé character. The term is also applied to soufflés of meat, fish, game or poultry, but in the U.S.A. and England the term is only applied to fancy dishes of ice cream.

Parisienne, à la (Fr.)

Parisian style. A term applied at random to dishes of an elaborate character. No particular mode of garnish is claimed for dishes bearing this title. As a sauce, it consists of rich brown Madeira, with chopped shallots and parsley added, and enriched with butter.

Parkin

A type of ginger cake made with oatmeal. The quality, shape and flavour vary considerably in the northern counties. Some are made as round flat cakes, others square, while another type is made in a large cake and cut into small squares when cold.

Parmentier (Fr.)

Name of one who introduced the potato to France in 1786. All dishes bearing his name denote that potatoes have been embodied in the dish, Potage Parmentier being a potato cream soup.

Parmesan

Name of a delicate flavoured Italian cheese, used extensively for culinary purposes. Pertaining to Parma in Italy.

Parsley (Persil, F.)

There are two varieties of parsley, the straight-leaved and the curly-leaved. The straight-leaved is better known as chervil. Parsley is popular as a kitchen herb for garnishing and flavouring. It has a high percentage of vitamin A and C, and ranks higher than spinach in its iron content. Parsley oil is mildly stimulating and an excellent preservative.

Parsnip (Panais, Fr.)
A root vegetable of the carrot family, possessing a peculiar pleasing flavour, especially when roasted. Its flesh is dingy white to yellow in colour. It is best left in the ground till wanted, to ensure a good firm root; being one of the few vegetables which will withstand a hard winter. It is high in calcium, phosphorus and iron content, and easy to digest.

Parson's or Pope's Nose
The name given to the rump of poultry or game birds. The tail end of a bird.

Partridge (Perdreau, Perdrix, Fr.)
The common or grey partridge is considered the finest from the gastronome's point of view, and is the kind usually marketed in the British Isles.
The partridge is one of the few game birds which should not be hung more than 3 to 4 days. If stored longer and left to get high, it will lose its delicate flavour, possessed only by the young birds. To bring out the finest flavour, take a small bunch of vine leaves, douse lightly with brandy, stuff inside the vent and roast like a pheasant. Remove vine leaves and throw away, and serve with sauerkraut cooked in champagne.

Young birds—being those shot from 1 September to end of December in the same year as bred—are easily distinguished from the adult. In adult birds the first flight feather is rounded, while in the young it is pointed at the tip; also, until the colder weather sets in, the feet of the young are yellowish-brown, turning to pale bluish-grey with age and colder climate.
Strange to relate, the partridge has largely increased in numbers during the last century, while the game birds most prized in the 14th, 15th and 16th centuries have almost disappeared. Whilst the price of the partridge has considerably increased, that of most other game birds has decreased—some are now even scorned.

Passion Fruit
A fruit grown in Australia, New Zealand, and extensively in Central America. It is the size of a large Victoria plum, with a tough, purplish skin, enclosing a seedy, orange-coloured pulp of exquisite flavour.

Passion Gin
Gin flavoured with passion fruit, yellow in colour.

Passoire (Fr.)
A strainer or colander.

Passover Bread
See Matzoth.

Pastèque (Fr.)
Water melon.

Pasteurize
To sterilize partially a liquid at a temperature of 140°-180°F. which destroys certain pathogenic organisms and arrests fermentation.

Pastillage (Fr.)
Gum paste used for shaping into decorative show pieces for wedding or other celebration cakes. It consists of very stiff royale icing mixed with softened gum tragacanth worked to a very smooth paste.

Pastilles
A title for small, flat, rounded gum lozenges, usually claiming to be flavoured with concentrated fresh fruit juices.

Pastry (Pâtisserie, Fr.)
Pastry is usually made up under one of the six headings : plain short crust, rich short crust, flaky pastry, puff pastry, suet pastry, savoury pastry. The first two are usually employed in tarts or tartlets of a sweet nature ; the second two for patties, light fancy pastries, and the covering of meat pies ; suet pastry for steamed meat or fruit puddings and dumplings ; savoury pastry for croûtes of a savoury nature and, when cheese is added, for cheese straws.
The eating qualities will vary considerably according to the amount of fat or shortening employed, the strength of the flour used, and, of course, the experience of the manipulator. (See also Puff Pastry.)

Pâte (Fr.)
Paste.

Pâté (Fr.)
Pie, covered or raised. (See Patty.)

Pâte d'Amandes (Fr.)
See Almond Paste.

Pâte d'Anchois (Fr.).
Anchovy paste.

Pâté de Bifteck (Fr.)
Beefsteak pie.

Pâté de Foie-gras (Fr.)
Pie or paste of fattened goose livers. Highly esteemed by epicures, the best being made at Strasburg. Obtained by the scientific fattening of geese for the enlargement of their livers. It is packed and exported in four forms, Foie-gras au Naturel, Pâté de Foie-gras, Purée de Foie-gras and Saucisson de Foie-gras. The first three readily denote their contents. The fourth consists of liver cut up in very small pieces and mixed with pork trimmings and packed in sausage shape in cans.

Pâte Feuilletée
Puff paste (which see).

Pâte Frisée
Short paste.

Pâtisserie (Fr.)
Pastry, pastry-cook's shop.

Pâtissier (Fr.)
Pastry cook.

Patty (Pâté, Fr.)
Small shells of puff pastry usually filled with savoury mixtures of fish, fowl or game, favourites being oyster, lobster or chicken patties.

Paupiettes (Fr.)
Thin slices of meat (usually veal) rolled with a forcemeat filling in sausage shape—as Paupiettes de Veau, which in America are known as Veal Birds, as when cooked they resemble small headless birds.

Pavot (Fr.)
See Poppy Seed.

Paysanne, à la (Fr.)
Peasant style. Foods prepared in simple manner.
Consomme Paysanne is a clear gravy soup, garnished with shredded lettuce and diced root vegetables.

Pea, Green
Sea Peas.

Peach (Pêche, Fr.)
There are the white fleshed and yellow fleshed, the freestone and clingstone peaches ; the freestone with flesh pulling freely from the stone and the clingstone being those with flesh which adheres to the stone. Most of the yellow clingstone peaches are canned. The Chinese wrote about peaches ten centuries before Christ and they were at one time known as the Persian apple. Peaches quickly deteriorate, bruising easily if not carefully handled.

Peach Bitters
An extract of peach kernels.

Peacock (Paon, Fr.)
The peacock was formerly much esteemed for the table, it being imported from India and Ceylon to aviaries and parks in all parts of the world. During the Middle Ages, it frequently graced the banquet table, cooked whole and served with its own gorgeous plumage as decoration.
The flesh is abundant in proportion to the bone, but the quality is a matter of individual opinion. The preference seems to be for a young peahen, the flesh being more delicate and not so dry as that of the cock bird.

Pea-flour
Dried ripe peas milled for use in soups and as a thickener for sauces.

Peahen (Paonne, Fr.)
The peahen is at its best February to May, and when young and well kept tastes not unlike pheasant. It is much more frequently served than the cock, it being usual to dress it with the tail feathers from the cock bird as decoration.

Pea-nut (Arachide, Fr.)
These nuts yield from 40% to 50% of oil by cold expression, and a greater quantity is obtained if heat is applied, but this is of inferior quality. The

oil so obtained is used in pea-nut butter, margarine and as a frying oil. The nuts may be eaten plain, roasted or salted, and are very nutritious. The plant flowers droop to the ground as they wither and the seed or nut is formed under the soil—hence the alternative names of ground-nut and earth-nut.

Pea-nut Butter
In its production, the pea-nuts are roasted, skinned, de-germed and ground to a paste and mixed with pea-nut oil. It has a very pleasant flavour and is very nutritious. (See also Nut Butter.)

Pear (Poire, Fr.)
A most delicate and perishable fruit. The William, Comice and Bartlett are considered some of the best for dessert. The pink tint in cooked pears is a sign of over-cooking. To retain the whiteness in cooking pears, after peeling let them stand 1 hour in slightly salted water.

Pearl Barley
Barley that has been specially treated to separate it from its husk. Husked barley.

Peas (Pois, Fr.)
Generally considered our most valuable and nutritious vegetable. Peas with green wrinkled pods are usually sweeter than the more attractive smooth pods. To be enjoyed at their best green peas need to be eaten within a few hours of gathering. If gathered and kept too long in bags, peas generate heat, causing considerable loss of flavour and waste. Dried peas, when soaked and cooked properly, are high in food value.

Peas, Processed
Peas which have been thrashed and dried by a process of dehydration and then soaked to restore the lost moisture, and canned out of season. Canners must disclose this fact on all labels of cans containing peas packed by this process and not being fresh garden peas (packed as picked).

Peas, Split (Pois Cassés, Fr.)
Green peas dried and with the outer skin removed, which renders them more easy to cook. Husked peas.

Pecan Nut
A species of hickory nut. Olive shaped, rich brown in colour, with an agreeable flavour. Somewhat resembles a poor quality walnut when shelled. It ranks higher in fat content than most nuts, having a 70% fat content.
PECAN CAKES (see Allegretti Pecan Cakes.)

Pêche (Fr.)
See Peach.

Pectin
A substance found in the leaves, bark, roots, stalks and fruits of plants, which increases as the fruit ripens. It is extracted and used for jam and jelly manufacture, to assist in rapid thickening or jelling.

Peewit (Vanneau, Fr.)
See Lapwing.

Pekoe Tea
Under the title of Pekoe fall almost all the fancy China teas, as Flowery Pekoe—small, evenly folded, olive-coloured; Orange Pekoe—small black leaves with yellowish ends; and Pekoe—small with whitish tips. These fancy teas are usually perfumed, generally after manufacture by contact with chulan blossoms, which have an odour similar to that of jasmine.

Pelardon
A fermented French cheese made in Languedoc.

Pemmican
Dried meat of the buffalo or deer, ground to a powder, mixed with fat or oil, acid berries or currants, and used as a food by Canadian and American Indians.

Penguin (Pingouin, Fr.)
The eggs of the penguin are more highly esteemed than its flesh, as a food. In texture and flavour they resemble plovers' eggs and are very rich.

Pennyroyal
A member of the mint family, less pungent than peppermint or spearmint.

Pepper (Poivre, Fr.)
A name given to several pungent spices, such as black, white, cayenne or red, Ashanti and Jamaica pepper, but derived from three different orders of plants. White and black pepper are the seed of the same shrub, the only difference being that the white has the outer dark husks removed. The cayenne or red peppers are prepared from the small-fruited capsicums. (See also Paprika and Capsicum.)

Pepper, Mignonette or Paradise
Other names for Shot Pepper (which see).

Pepper Corn
The seed of the pepper plant. Whole pepper. Generally used with its black husk on for culinary purposes.

Peppermint
See Mint.

Pepper-pot
A West Indian highly spiced stew of meat, poultry, fish or game, rendered hot with cayenne, cassareep and other hot spices and condiments. Philadelphia pepper-pot consists of stewed tripe and dumplings, highly seasoned.

Pepper Sauce (Sauce Poivrade, Fr.)
See Poivrade.

Perch (Perche, Fr.)

The perch is one of the most common of our fresh-water fish ; at the same time, it is one of the best. It is to be found in almost all the lakes and rivers of the British Isles. Specimens weighing 8 or 9 lbs. have been caught, but one weighing 1 lb. is a good fish.

The flesh is white, firm, of a good flavour and easily digested. The peculiarity about the flesh of the perch is that it is difficult to scale, so much so that some cooks boil the fish first and scale it afterwards The best way is to plunge the fish into boiling water for a minute and then scale it. When fresh, the body has a bright shining appearance and the gills are rosy red.

Perch is in season from the end of May until the beginning of February.

Be careful when handling, as the little spikes of the dorsal fin are dangerous and may cause pain.

Perdreau (Fr.)

Young partridge. (See Partridge.)

Perdrix (Fr.)

Partridge in its second season. (See Partridge.)

Périgord (Fr.)

See Périgueux.

Périgueux (Fr.)

Périgueux is a town of south-western France and was formerly the capital of the old province of Périgord. À la Périgueux implies that truffle has been employed in the composition of the dish or sauce. Truffles and pâtés de Périgord are chief products of the town.

Periwinkle (Bigorneau, Fr.)

The periwinkle is in season all the year round, being very abundant around the coast of England and Scotland. It has a small round black shell, inside which is a small sea snail.

They should be boiled for about 20 minutes in salted water and allowed to cool quickly. First, one must be armed with good long pins, remove the operculum, insert the pin diagonally, and then, with a cunning circular movement of the wrist the succulent little animal is extracted, complete to its tapering tail if you are clever. Eaten with bread and butter, they are the children's delight, and also the grown-ups' secret longing, if only they can manipulate them on a quiet Sunday afternoon.

Perles de Japon (Fr.)

See Perles de Nizam.

Perles de Nizam (Fr.)

Extra polished, extra quality pearl barley. Large pearl barley husked and polished.

Perrier Water
One of the best of table waters. A natural mineral water from the south of France, colourless and tasteless.

Perry
An alcoholic beverage made from pears. A product bearing the same relation to the pear as cider does to the apple, but not quite so alcoholic.

Persil (Fr.)
See Parsley.

Persillade (Fr.)
Thick white sauce to which has been added a large quantity of freshly chopped young green parsley.

Persimmon
An egg-shaped fruit with a flattened end nearest the stem, yellow in colour and 1 to 2 inches in diameter. Its astringency decreases as it ripens, until it virtually becomes a sugar plum, which has earned for it the nickname of date plum.

Pestle
An instrument for pounding anything in a mortar (see Mortar.)

Petite Marmite (Fr.)
A French broth cooked and served in individual earthenware pots. Usually served with toasted bread crusts added at the last minute, with a flick of grated cheese.

Petit Gruyère (Fr.)
A small processed cheese wrapped in tinfoil.

Petit Lait (Fr.)
Whey (which see).

Petit Pain (Fr.)
An indvidual bread roll.

Petit Poussin (Fr)
The French term of baby chicken. Not to be confused by students with " poisson " the French for fish. (see also Chicken.)

Petit Salé (Fr.)
Belly or streaky bacon.

Petits-fours (Fr.)
A general term for all sorts of tiny decorated cakes, sugared fruits and bonbons.

Petits Pois (Fr.)
Small peas.

Petits Pois au Beurre (Fr.)
Green peas tossed in butter.

Petits Pois Verts (Fr.)
Small green peas.

Pétoncle (Fr.)
See Scallop.

Pettitoes
Pig's trotters.

Pheasant (Faisan, Fr.)
Pheasants have many claims to interest. They are " good sport ", their flesh is excellent, and some varieties, especially the cock birds, are extremely beautiful. The English ring-neck is primarily a naturalised cross of the Chinese and common pheasant, and its introduction to England is attributed to the Romans. The male is a handsome bird, with brilliant plumage, the female protectively coloured in mottled

brown. A brace of pheasants always constitutes one male and one female bird, and in no other game is the distinction between the sexes so marked, with the exception of the peacock and peahen.

At table, the pheasant owes all its virtue to the length of time it is hung after being shot. How long should a pheasant be hung ?—1, 2 or 3 weeks, depending on the weather and how shot. It should be allowed to mature fully, but not decay. Game of any kind can be hung too long, and should decay set in, then the true flavour is completely lost and it tastes bitter. The young cock bird is recognised by its short spurs. Long, sharp spurs denote age and toughness. The hen bird, while not so beautiful in appearance, is more tender and usually fatter than the cock. The young hen can be recognised by its soft, pliable feet and light plumage. An old hen has hard, rough feet, which are less pliable, the plumage darkens with age. The season for pheasants is from the beginning of October to February. They are at their best from mid-October to mid-January.

Phoque (Fr.)
See Seal.

Piccalilli
A mixture of chopped vegetables preserved in a mustard and vinegar sauce.

Pickle, to
To preserve flesh, fish or vegetables in a solution of salt and water or vinegar. To brine used for preserving meats, saltpetre is added to give the meats that pinkish appearance, which would otherwise be an uninteresting grey.

Picnic
Entertainment taken in the open air with al fresco meals.

Pie (Pâté, Fr.)
The basic idea of the covered pie is of very old standing, and was the very early method of preservation of foods by covering with a paste or dough to exclude air, in the same manner as a layer of fat on liquids will lengthen its keeping qualities. Thus, sheets of plain dough were laid over meats and other foods to exclude air, in very early times. In some instances, the paste or dough must have absorbed the fats rising to the top of the vessels of food, so that when the foods were baked with the unleavened dough upon them, the crust was found to be agreeable and palatable, according to the amount of fat the dough had absorbed.

Left-over meats, poultry and game, will therefore keep much longer if baked under a crust as a pie, and of course, the richer the crust, the more palatable and agreeable the whole will become.

Fruits of all kinds are also used as fillings for pies.

Pièce de Résistance (Fr.)
The most important course of the meal. The dish by which the chef reveals his culinary skill to the full.

Pied (Fr.)
Foot.

Pieds de Veau (Fr.)
Calf's feet.

Piémontaise (Fr.)
Name given to a style of garnish for entrées consisting of, rizotto with truffles cut julienne style. Originating from Piémont (Piedmont) in France.

Pig
Name applied to swine, both hogs and sows, before they reach mature age. A wonderful provider of food, for it has been truly said that almost every part of the pig can be utilised except its squeal. It provides more side dishes than any other animal.

Pigeon (Pigeon, Fr.)
In the Middle Ages the pigeon loft supplied meat daily to wealthy houses, at least for a good part of the year. Pigeon houses standing alone in a field can still be found on the estates of many old houses or halls in Essex.
A pigeon needs to be young to be appreciated at table. Old birds which can only be stewed or cooked in casserole are dry and insipid. In the south of France, many establishments have a dovecote to ensure a regular supply of young birds which, cruel to relate, are smothered to death. This is supposed to save any loss of blood in killing, resulting in a better flavoured bird. We in England choose to buy them from the poulterer or market, but all too often they are found to be old and tough. Young pigeon roasted or baked whole in a pie can be really delicious fare, but alas, how often are we offered young birds. Hence a prejudice against the pigeon. (See also Wood Pigeon.)

Pigeonneau (Fr.)
See Squab.

Pig's Fry
The interior parts of the pig, usually cut in long thin slices and mixed together to form a rich succulent stew.

Pike (Brochet, Fr.)
The pike is often referred to as the fresh-water shark, because it not only devours fish of other kinds, but also of its own kind. The size of the English pike is considerable. Instances have been known of its attaining a length of 3 ft., and a weight of 40 lbs. Its usual colour is a pale olive-grey, deepest on the back, and marked on the sides by several yellowish spots or patches ; the abdomen is white, slightly spotted with black.
The names " pike " and " jack " refer only to the age of the fish. A jack is a pike which has not attained more than 3 lbs. in weight or does not exceed 2 ft. in length.

It ought to be better known
that it is dangerous to swallow
the bones of the pike, as they
are sharp and of so peculiarly
hard a texture that they will
not dissolve in the stomach.
The flesh of the large pike is
dry, rather coarse, and very
bony. Fish weighing 4 to 8
lbs. are best for table. Before a
pike is cooked, it should be well
salted 12 hours before-hand.
This can be done by hanging the
fish by the jaw and forcing as
much salt as possible down its
throat, or cutting it into steaks
and salting the steaks either side.

Pikelet
The northern name for crumpet
(which see).

Pilau, Pilaw, Pilaf (Fr.)
Rice stewed with meat, poultry
or fish, spices, etc.

Pilchard (Royan, Fr.)
The pilchard resembles the
herring in many respects and is
caught chiefly off Devon and
Cornwall. It is a smaller fish
than the common herring. The
dorsal fin of the pilchard is
nearer the centre, while that of
the herring is farther back.
Thus, if a herring is picked up
by the first dorsal fin, the head
dips forward, whereas the pilchard preserves its equilibrium,
as the dorsal fin occupies
exactly the centre of gravity.
The pilchard is at its best
between July and the end of
December. Its taste is very
like that of the herring.

Pilet (Fr.)
See Pintail.

Pilot Bread
Another name for ship's biscui
or hard tack.

Pimento
The colourful aromatic berry
of the pimento tree, used fo:
the Hungarian paprika.

Pimiento
The large-fruited Spanish cap
sicum, used for the mild pa
prika (which see).

Pimms Cups
Name of four well-known cups
No. 1 has gin as its base ; No. 2,
whisky ; No. 3, brandy ; No
4, rum.

Pimpernelle (Fr.)
See Burnet.

Pineapple (Ananas, Fr.)
A fruit which takes its name
from its resemblance to the pine
cone, but as the pine cone grows
high up the pineapple grows on
a low plant with long spreading leaves. A rich, juicy fruit
with a brownish-yellow skin
and a strong, pleasant aroma.
Canned pineapple is used in
far greater quantities than the
fresh and is one of the few
foods which change very little
in colour, flavour or aroma in
their canned form. It is
packed in slices, cubes, spears or
arrows, and its juice is also
agreeable when canned.
The best pineapples are the
Hawaiian, the African being
smaller and not so juicy.

Pingouin (Fr.)
See Penguin.

Pint
One-eighth of a gallon. Contents 34.659 cubic inches.

Pintade (Fr.)
See Guinea Fowl.

Pintail (Pilet, Fr.)
The pintail is a wild waterfowl, popularly so named because of its long tail feathers of greenish-black. The head and throat of the male are of greenish-brown, the neck is especially long and slender, the back being marked with waving black lines. The breast and under parts are white. The upper part of the female is mottled grey, yellow and brown, its tail shorter than that of the cock bird. It is highly esteemed by epicures.

Pipe
The standard cask for port in this country, containing 115 gallons.

Piping
A term applied to the decoration of cakes, meats, etc. when the decorating medium is forced through tubes or small pipes to form the intricate shapes and forms built up as a lace or network. Icing forced through tubes in fancy pattern or shape.

Piping Bag
A bag made of linen or grease-proof paper, for holding the piping tubes and ingredients for decorating.

Pippin
Name given to certain types of apple, a few of which are Cox's orange pippin, Ribston pippin, Newton pippin and golden pippin.

Piquante (Fr.)
Piquant. Pleasantly pungent ; appetising. Sauce Piquante is a sharp sauce consisting of Espagnole with chopped gherkins, capers and shallots, seasoned with pepper and anchovy essence.

Pistache (Fr.)
See Pistachio Nut.

Pistachio Nut (Green Almond)
The kernel of the small reddish fruit of the pistachio tree. The quality of the kernel varies considerably ; in the best the nut is a greenish colour inside. Used extensively for flavouring or decorating meats and confections.

Pisto Manchego
A Spanish pork stew.

Pitcaithly Bannock
A type of almond shortbread containing caraway seeds and finely chopped peel.

Pithiviers
A town of France well noted for its speciality of lark pies and dainty pastries.

Plaice (Plie, Fr.)

Fried plaice and chips is the favourite dish in most provincial English restaurants when the joint is off, and this is the most satisfactory way of cooking it.

Plaice is at its best between June and the end of December. That marketed February to May is thin and lacks good taste, as it is the spawning season. Hence the strong flavour in some plaice during this period. A fish of 8 lbs. is considered large. A fish of 2 lbs. will give four 4-oz. fillets, for almost all flat fish will lose half its weight in cleaning and filleting.

Plaice can be recognised by its yellow to reddish-brown spots on the dark side, the other side being white. The age of plaice is determined by the number of rings in the otolith " earstone ".

Planked Steak

This consists of a thick steak placed on a well oiled, well seasoned oak plank, the size of a small boy's cricket bat. It is surrounded with creamed potatoes and other colourful vegetables and cooked under a grill or broiler. When cooked it is tastefully garnished and served to the guest on the plank. A fine idea for serving foods really hot.

Plantain

A fruit strongly resembling the banana, both in appearance and flavour, when baked. It is seldom eaten raw.

Platter

A large flat plate or dish, in earthenware, glass or metal.

Plover (Pluvier, Fr.)

There are three members of the Plover available to gastro-nomes of these Islands, the greatest merit being bestowed upon the golden plover for its delicacy of flavour. Next in order of merit is the grey plover. These two are still fairly plentiful in northern counties.

The green plover, which is better known under the name of lapwing or peewit, is not so abundant and lacks in flavour. Its size is not much bigger than that of a sparrow, while the grey plover will grow to the size of a woodcock.

The golden plover is so called from its golden-speckled upper plumage, and is especially distinguished by the great spread of its wings.

The grey plover can be distinguished by its black and white upper plumage, with no yellow spots. In young birds the plumage markings are less well defined, but this is no drawback to distinguishing the grey plover, which has only three toes—it develops no hind toe—and, of course, is larger than the golden plover.

Plovers' eggs may no longer be sold by law. (See also Lapwing.)

Pluche (Fr.)
A mixture of herbs snipped or cut small, used for garnishing soups.

Pluck
The lights, liver and heart of sheep, ox, or other animal.

Plum (Prune, Fr.)
A stone fruit extensively cultivated in England and many European countries. Of the dessert kinds, the Victoria is placed high on the list. A useful fruit for stewing and pies. Care should be taken to use only sound, ripe fruit.

Plum Pudding
See Christmas Pudding.

Poaching
Poaching is a form of simmering which takes place at 205° to 210°F. or just below boiling point, which is 212°F.
Meat or poultry are never boiled continuously. The liquor in which the food is to be cooked is brought to a rapid boil, the food lowered into it, and the heat reduced at once, so that the liquor is just kept on the move (simmering).
Never use more liquor than is needed, just enough to cover the food, especially so if cooking in wine or cider, or when the liquor is to be used for sauce making.

Pocher (Fr.)
To simmer or parboil slightly, as in the process of poaching fish or eggs.

Poêle (Fr.)
A kitchen pot.

Point, à (Fr.)
Cooked to the exact degree of done-ness--to the turn.

Points d'Asperges (Fr.)
The young green tips of asparagus. The term is much used for garnishings.

Poire (Fr.)
See Pear.

Poireau (Fr.)
See Leek.

Pois (Fr.)
See Peas and Petits Pois.

Pois Cassés (Fr.)
See Peas, Split.

Poisson
The French for fish. Not to be confused by students with " poussin ", being French for young chicken.

Poissonière (Fr.)
Fish kettle or pan.

Poisson Rouge (Fr.)
See Char.

Poitrine (Fr.)
Breast.

Poivrade Sauce
A rich brown peppery sauce flavoured with ham, onions and herbs. Used extensively in French meat and game dishes.

Poivre (Fr.)
See Pepper.

Poivré (Fr.)
Peppered. Sauce Poivrade—pepper sauce.

Polenta

An Italian pudding, at one time made of chestnut meal but now generally made of semolina. When cold it is sliced and served with grated cheese and condiments.

Polignac

Name of an ancient French family which can be traced back to the 9th century. In the 14th century the male line became extinct. A number of dishes bear this name. As a sauce, it consists of a very rich white sauce with finely sliced mushrooms added.

Pollan or Pullan

This fish is caught in great quantities off the Irish coast. The cry " fresh pollan " is as well known to the Irish as that of " fresh herring " to the English. It is at its best from March to September. Cook as a trout.

Pollitos Salteados

A Spanish dish of chicken sauté.

Pollock or Pollack

This is a member of the codfish family. It is considered inferior to the cod. Big specimens will weigh 25 lbs. and upwards, and will be 3 ft. in length or more. The smaller fish are sometimes referred to as pollock whiting.

The pollock can be recognised by the under jaw which projects beyond the upper.

Polonaise, à la (Fr.)

Polish style. Dishes under this title usually have beetroot, sour cream, red cabbage or horseradish embodied.

Polony

Name given to various kinds of partly cooked sausages.

Pomegranate (Grenade, Fr.)

A fruit which is mentioned in earliest religious and mythological writings. Solomon sang of an orchard of pomegranates. The fruit is the size of a large orange, with a thick leathery skin, in colour light yellow to deep purplish-red. Its interior consists of a subacid pink to red pulp, enclosing in mass formation seeds of purplish-white. It is most refreshing in warm weather.

Pomme (Fr.)

See Apple.

Pomme Cannelle (Fr.)

See Custard Apple.

Pomme de Terre (Fr.)

See Potato.

Pomme Sauvage (Fr.)

See Crab Apple.

Pompadour

The Marquise de Pompadour gave her name to many French dishes. Known for her lavishness as a hostess, the garnishings and sauces are considered most extravagant compared with present-day standards. All sauces are enriched with butter, cream and egg yolks.

ompano or Pampano
This fish is only included here because it is often included in English recipe books, when in fact it is a fish of the South Atlantic and not available to us in these Isles. It is one of the most delicious of the fishes of South America, whither one has to travel to appreciate it at its best. It is noted for its fine nutty flavour.

ont-l'Évêque (Fr.)
A half cooked, fermented French cheese, of mild flavour, yellow in colour, packed in small, square, flat boxes.

•op-corn
Grains from Indian Corn heated over fire until they expand and burst, releasing the puffed white starchy interior.

•ope's Eye
A certain Pope was said to have his nose and eye everywhere. The term Pope's or Parson's Nose is well known. The name Pope's Eye is given to the circle of fat found in the centre of a leg of pork or mutton, for it is said he had his nose and eye on everything.

Pope's Nose
See Parson's Nose.

?op-overs
Very light puddings made from rich Yorkshire Pudding batter. They are cooked in very hot

dariole moulds, to make the batter rise and pop-over the top of the mould.

Poppy Seed (Pavot, Fr.)
The seeds of the large poppy are used for stuffings, coating Continental breads and confectionery. The seeds contain little opium, which is found in the casing containing the seed.

Pork (Porc, Fr.)
The flesh of swine which is used for food, fresh, salted and smoked. It makes up nearly half the meat used in these islands, partly because of its high caloric value so essential to our cool climate. The breakfast bacon habit of England is a natural instinct to start the day with fatty food.

Porpoise
The porpoise, antiquarians tell us, was once a favourite at the feasts of King Henry VIII. In some countries it is still eaten, and the flesh of the young has been compared to veal. Porpoises are sometimes brought to Billingsgate Market, but instead of being food for kings, not even the beggar will touch it ; it is bought only for show and probable publicity, if the evening newspapers have space to show a photo of this curiosity from time to time.
It is best sliced thin, egged and breadcrumbed, and fried.
The porpoise is a mammal, and not a fish.

Porridge

A corruption of the Biblical " pottage ". An every-day Scottish breakfast dish of cooked oatmeal served with milk and sugar or salt. Nutritious and palatable.

Porter

The beer between ale and stout. The original 'arf and 'arf for the porter.

Porterhouse Steak

A thick steak cut from the thick end of the sirloin. Its title originating from the old Porter-house.

Portugaise (Fr.)

Portuguese style. Nearly all dishes bearing this title have tomato, onion or garlic as one of the prominent ingredients.

Posset

Milk curdled with dry wine— sweetened with sugar or molasses. Sometimes thickened with grated bread.

Potable

Drinkable. Something that may be drunk.

Potage (Fr.)

See Pottage.

Pot-ale

The residue from a grain distillery turned out as pig food.

Potato (Pomme de Terre, Fr.

Potatoes were cultivated i Spain as long ago as 1584 an in Belgium in 1588, the origina supplies coming from Peru The yellow-fleshed waxy vari eties are best for frying and th white floury type best suite for boiling, the best dual pur pose potatoes being the red skinned varieties. To-day w take the potato very much fo granted, but one can hardl imagine the Sunday dinner o the 16th century in England that never knew a potato. Nov used every day of the year, i is the one vegetable that th white races never tire of, as i can be cooked and prepare in so very many interestin ways.

Potato, Sweet

A root tuber largely cultivate in Southern America and the East Indies. Botanically it i not related to the ordinar potato. It has a light to dee yellow coloured flesh, whicl is of a soft, sugary consist ence.

Pot-au-feu (Fr.)

The national soup of France, claimed from Spain. Spain's great households always had the perpetual pot of boiling meats and vegetables con stantly simmering on the hearth. As the noble lords of Spain brought their cooks on to French soil, the French were quick to take up and improve upon the idea of the pot on the fire, extracting all the goodness from meat and vegetables.

There are many variations of the pot-au-feu, which all have the same idea except that the type of meat used differs.

Potiron (Fr.)
See Pumpkin.

Pot-pourri (Fr.)
A favourite dish in Spain, consisting of stewed meats highly seasoned.

Pot-roasting
A method of cooking tough cuts of meat and birds not of the best quality. The meat is first fried on all sides in an iron saucepan with enough dripping to cover the bottom. A little stock or water is then added, with seasoning ; the lid is put on tightly, and cooking is then continued in the oven very slowly at no more than 300° F. (Regulo 1½) at the rate of 1 hour to the lb.

Pottage (Potage, Fr.)
Meat or vegetables boiled to softness in water or stock, usually with barley or similar cereal. Compare Esau's mess of pottage.

Potted
Fish, meat, poultry or game pounded to a smooth paste and preserved in pots or jars.

Pottle
A wine measure recognised in England as ½ gallon.

Pou de Mer (Fr.)
See Whelk.

Pouding (Fr.)
See Pudding.

Pouding de Noel (Fr.)
See Christmas Pudding.

Poudre de Levure (Fr.)
See Baking Powder.

Poularde (Fr.)
Fat fowl. (See Chicken.)

Poule (Fr.)
Boiling fowl. (See Chicken.)

Poulet (Fr.)
Cock chicken. (See Chicken.)

Poulet de Grain (Fr.)
Spring chicken. (See Chicken.)

Poulet Dinde (Fr.)
Young turkey. (See Turkey.)

Poulette (Fr.)
Hen chicken. (See Chicken.)

Poulette, à la (Fr.)
A white stew made with chicken stock enriched with butter, cream and egg yolks. Sauce Poulette being a Velouté.

Poultry (Volaille, Fr.)
Domesticated fowls. (See Volaille.)

N

Pourpier (Fr.)

See Purslane.

Poussin (Fr.)

See Petit Poussin.

Praline (Fr.)

A rich paste of pulverised nuts and sugar, that made from hazel-nuts or filberts having a most agreeable, aromatic flavour for chocolate centres.

Prawn (Crevette, Fr.)

The prawn is a delicate shell-fish, very much like the shrimp, but larger and more delicate in flavour.

They are in season all the year round, and at their best from February to October. They are largely used for garnishing other fish dishes, and make an excellent sauce. When taken from the water, they are whitish in colour, but they are generally boiled before they reach the market, and in that condition they are pink or red. The tails are the only portion ordinarily eaten, the heads usually being pounded and used for soups.

Pré Salé (Fr.)

Name applied to first quality, Southdown mutton. The word originating from the French term " salt field ".

Preservation of Food

The four most common methods by which food is preserved are :

the use of chemical agents or antiseptics, the application of cold or refrigeration, drying or desiccation, and the application of heat. Modern science applies the method best suited to the foods to be preserved and harvests gathered 10 years ago can safely be used out of cans to-day.

Pressure Cooker

A cooking vessel with a tightly fitting lid to prevent the escape of steam, and controlled by a pressure valve. Very little water is used in the vessel and steam is generated under very high pressure which reaches a temperature considerably more than that of boiling water. Because of this high moist temperature being generated under pressure, the foods are cooked in a much shorter time, just as foods cooked at high altitudes cook in less time than at sea level. For explanation of this, see Boil and Boiling.

Présure (Fr.)

See Rennet.

Pretzels

Hard, brittle German biscuits originally called Bretzels, and to this day the hard, brittle twists of dough are shaped into a knot-like letter B. The curls of dough are dipped in hot lye, salted and baked.

Prickly Pear

Indian fig or barberry fig. Pear-shaped fruits marked by small spicules or spines. The fruit varies in colour and is found in yellow, red, purple and other colours. The flavour is distinctly refreshing and in size they vary from 1 oz. up to 1 lb. in weight. The best are those with the thinnest skin.

Primeur (Fr.)

First early forced fruits and vegetables which arrive before their natural season, are given this title.

Princesse (Fr.)

Name of a style of garnish consisting of artichoke bottoms filled with asparagus tips with noisette potatoes.

Printanier (Fr.)

Spring style. This always implies that fresh spring vegetables are embodied in the dish in some form. It is usual to obtain very small, early spring vegetables, and to cook them whole to avoid cutting them, or to pare the vegetables small enough to avoid dicing. Only in Sauce or Potage Printanière are the vegetables pulped or diced.

Printemps (Fr.)

Spring.

Profiterole (Fr.)

Tiny éclairs or pea-sized cakes made from cream bun or choux paste, filled with creamed foods, and used as a garnish for clear soups.

Promessi

An Italian soft cream cheese.

Protein

A Greek word meaning " first ", being the first element in any compound. The group of bodies which form the most essential articles of food which go to make up the soft tissues of animals and vegetables, for they are essential to all life, both plant and animal.

Protein of high food value is contained in meat, fish, milk, cheese and eggs. Ripe peas and beans show a high protein content, but it is of deficient quality. Soy beans and peanuts take a high place for protein content.

Provençale, à la (Fr.)

Province, a former province of southern France. The term is applied to dishes of southern France, containing garlic or onion and olive oil.

Prune (Pruneau, Fr.)

The principal source of supply of this agreeable food comes from California. The plums are fully ripened on the tree to obtain the maximum sugar content, and allowed to dry and fall off the tree of their own accord without fermenting. Prunes are excellent energy producers, because of their high sugar content. They are usually graded in boxes weighing 20 to 30 to the pound up to 80 to 90 to the pound. This grading mark can be seen on all cases of prunes and is an indication to the buyers of the size of prune the case contains. The 20 to 30 size is a beautiful rich plump prune.

(Prune is also the French for plum.)

Pruneau (Fr.)
The dried plum.   (See Prune.)

Prunelle (Fr.)
See Sloe. Also a name given to a pale green liqueur with the flavour of sloes—Crème de Prunelles.

Ptarmigan or Mountain Grouse
(Perdrix Blanche, Fr.)

By some the ptarmigan is considered inferior gastronomically to the grouse, but having tasted it at perfection I just cannot agree. Its flesh has a peculiar bitter taste, much relished by epicures. It should be stuffed with a bunch of parsley or chervil, or both, before roasting. If not badly shot, and hung 10 to 14 days, it reaches perfection, and I would much prefer a properly prepared ptarmigan to an over-roasted young grouse. There are only two ways of cooking a ptarmigan, and these are to roast the young birds and braise the older ones.

It is to be found in Scotland at heights over 2,500 ft., and is the only English bird which turns white during winter. It is about the same size as the red grouse. In Gaelic it is " tarmachan ".

Ptomaine
A term invented by an Italian chemist, Selmi, for the basic substances produced in putrefaction which cause food poisoning. The inanimate poisonous substances resembling alkaloids resulting from decomposition of proteins. Many food poisonings are due to bacteria or their products.

Pudding (Pouding, Fr.)
As a culinary term pudding usually denotes a sweet dish. It is also used in connection with meat, but in such instances is restricted to meat cooked inside a suet crust or an intestine stuffed with meat. Milk, suet, sponge and fruit puddings all have their place in English cookery, but none has such an important place as the traditional Christmas Pudding, a formula for which is given under that heading, this particular formula having gained several gold medals at important exhibitions.

Puff Pastry

A very light, rich paste, which so few cooks can make properly. Two methods of manufacture are set out below :

No. 1.

Never attempt to make puff pastry in a warm kitchen, and always see that the butter to be used is placed in the refrigerator the night before. Imported tub butter is better than soft fresh farm butter, for the tougher the fat is, the better the puff pastry.

Sift 1 lb. of flour on to a board and rub in 2 ozs. of lard, mix to a smooth dough with 16 ozs. of water. Let the paste rest 20 minutes. Roll the paste out oblong shape 12 inches by 8 inches, and spread with 14 ozs. firm butter. Fold in three, roll out oblong shape 12 inches by 8 inches and fold in three once more. Let rest 20 minutes. Repeat this process 3 times, allowing 20 minutes' rest between each double fold. Keep the pastry cool and covered with a damp cloth at every stage. It is now ready to make into patty, vol-au-vent cases, or tartlets.

No. 2.

Proceed as above, using 10 ozs. of butter. This pastry will not rise as high as No. 1, but is quite suitable for many purposes, such as cannelons, rissoles, turnovers, etc., where a rich puff pastry is not required.

Puits d'Amour (Fr.)

Small, French pastries made of light puff paste.

Pullan

See Pollan.

Pulled Bread (Pain Tiré, Fr.)

See Bread, Pulled.

Pulled Sugar (Sucre Tiré, Fr.)

See Sugar, Pulled.

Pullet

A hen chicken. (See Chicken for full terms.)

Pulque

The national drink of Mexico. Made from the fermented juice of the Maguey plant. It is a yellowish, sweetish, rather pleasing beverage and is also known as " honey water ".

Pulses

Seeds of leguminous plants— as peas, beans, etc.

Pulverise, To

To powder finely, as icing sugar.

Pumpernickel (Ger.)

A Westphalian black bread made of coarse rye flour. Really only the crust takes on a black appearance, the crumb is very dark brown.

Pumpkin (Potiron, Fr.)

It is in the form of pumpkin pie that this fruit has achieved the highest fame, rather than as a vegetable. Resembling a very large, yellow melon, specimens for exhibition purposes have reached 200 lbs. in weight. They are about 90% water and 5% to 7 % carbohydrate.

Punch

From the original "panch" made by the Hindoos, consisting of arrack, spice, sugar, lemon juice and water. The English punch bowl has come a long way. In its simplest form hot punch has as its ingredients rum, lemon juice, sugar and water. There are many other versions which contain brandy, ale, milk, etc.

Pungent

A term implying agreeably acrid or sharp, when applied to odour or taste.

Purée (Fr.)

Cooked food forced through a sieve or reduced to a pulp. A soup thickened by such treatment.

Purée de Légumes (Fr.)

Purée of vegetables.

Purée de Pommes de Terre (Fr.)

Mashed or puréed potatoes.

Purl

An old-fashioned winter drink made of ale and beer heated and added to gin and bitters.

Purslane or Purslain (Pourpier, Fr.)

A pot herb used in salads and pickles. The young shoots and succulent leaves are most refreshing in warm weather, eaten raw.

Pyrometer

An instrument for measuring degrees of heat above those indicated on a mercurial thermometer.

Q

Quadrillé (Fr.)

Thin stripes of paste laid in checkered or net fashion across jam or fruit tarts and flans.

Quail (Caille, Fr.)

Most quails offered for sale in this country are imported from Egypt. They are chiefly brought over alive, fattened and sent to market. Few, if any, are caught here nowadays in their wild state.

They are tiny birds, and best roasted wrapped in vine leaves. As a meal they are useless, but served as a course at a banquet they are just tantalising enough to make one wish for another. Stuffed, cooked and dressed in aspic, they are much sought after at hunt and county balls, but how many present-day débutantes have ever set eyes on one ?

Such quails as come your way will keep for several days before they are dressed.

The Romans rather feared quails, thinking they caused epileptic fits. Not so the Greeks, who devoured them in large quantities.

Quart

The imperial quart is equal to a quarter of a gallon, or 69.318 cubic inches. The reputed quart is only one-sixth of the imperial gallon.

Quartier d'Agneau (Fr.)

Quarter of lamb.

Quartier de Derrière (Fr.)
Hindquarter.

Quartier de Devant (Fr.)
Forequarter.

Quass
See Kvass.

Quassia
A tree of the South Americas, the bitter bark and wood of which are used as a tonic. So named after a negro who discovered its value against fever.

Quassia Cup
A sweet alcoholic cup made with an infusion of quassia chips and flavoured with orange peel, borage and spices.

Quenelles (Fr.)
Forcemeat of different kinds, composed of fish, poultry, meats or game, shaped into tiny, olive-shaped balls. They are used for garnishing dishes.

Quetch
A French liqueur the colour of gin with a flavour of plums.

Queue (Fr.)
See Tail.

Queue de Bœuf (Fr.)
Ox tail.

Queue de Veau (Fr.)
Calf's tail.

Quick Frozen Foods
Foods labelled as quick frozen are frozen in a few minutes or in a number of hours, depending on their size and internal temperature. Under present-day quick freezing methods, small fruits can be frozen to minus 10° in as little as 60 to 90 minutes. Pre-cooked frozen foods are frozen in 1½ to 2½ hours. The quicker the freezing the more successful will the food be in use when defrosted. Slow freezing breaks down the tissues of the food, causing it to collapse when defrosted.

Quince (Coing, Fr.)
A pear-shaped, sour, astringent fruit, with a yellowish-green skin, and flesh similar to that of the apple. Its flavour is too harsh to be enjoyed raw, but a little grated in an apple pie gives a most pleasant and agreeable flavour. Used chiefly in jams and jellies.

Quinoa
A large plant with woolly leaves, cultivated in Chile and Peru for its glutinous seeds, which are made into a form of bread which has quite a high food value.

Quoorma
Name of a delicate Indian curry.

Quo Vadis (L.)
Name given to a certain style of finishing fish dishes with white wine sauce and a garnish of crayfish tails and sliced truffle.

Qutaif
A romantic Arabian dish consisting of tissue-thin pancakes, fried in virgin almond oil, sprinkled with rose water and served with a rich honey-like syrup.

R

Rabbit (Lapin, Fr.)

The rabbit is distinguished from the hare by its shorter ears and feet and absence of black on the ears, and by its shorter body. The wild rabbit weighs from 2 to 3 lbs. while the tame variety reaches 6 lbs or more in as many months. Some specimens range in mature weight from 8 to 20 lbs.

The flesh of the young plump rabbit makes quite good eating, both wild and tame. Those who enjoy a delicate gamey flavour will prefer the darker meat of the wild animals, while others will find enjoyment in the mild, white flesh of the domesticated. Young rabbit is delicious sautéed, when far too often it is merely stewed. It ranks high in food value, and should never be despised because of its cheapness.

Racahout

An Arabian beverage made from roasted crushed acorns, sweetened with sugar and delicately spiced. Also the name of an invalid beverage made from tapioca and arrowroot prepared for those with delicate digestion.

Raccoon

A North American wild game about the size of a large cat.

Radicchio (Rampion)

A favourite vegetable with Italians. Its white tender root may be boiled or steamed, or it may be sliced and served as a salad with its young green leaves. The root is a foot or so in length and resembles a long radish.

Radish (Radis, Fr.)

A pungent, succulent salad plant grown in many varieties. It has a small tapering or globular root, white, pink or scarlet in colour, with a pleasing peppery taste, the globular or turnip radish being the most common in use.

Raffinade

A term applied to the best quality refined sugar.

Ragoût

A rich stew of meat, made with vegetables (a goulash). The French equivalent of Irish Stew, but usually browned and thickened.

Rahat Lakoum

See Turkish Delight.

Raie (Fr.)

See Skate.

Raifort (Fr.)

See Horseradish.

Rail (Râle, Fr.)

The rail abounds in this country and is excellent fare roasted or cooked in a pie.

The body is broad and blunt behind and very narrow in front, this shape enabling the bird more readily to make its way in, through, and around the tall reeds of its marshy home. The plumage is of various shades of brown above and yellowish-white below, rendering it very inconspicuous. Its beak is long and partly red. Plucked and ready for market, rails average 2½ to 3 lbs. per dozen.

Raisin (Fr.)
The dried fruit of the grape vine, best of which come to us from California. Sun raisins are those obtained by leaving the fruit of the vine till the clusters dry on the stalks. The finest are White Muscat and Thompson Seedless.

Raisinée (Fr.)
A thin syrupy jam made by very slowly cooking pears with a small proportion of quince in sweet wine or cider. There is a second type made with grapes and quince.

Ràkia
A sweet Hungarian liqueur made from fully ripened grapes.

Rakpaprikas
A Hungarian dish consisting of crayfish, tomato purée and spices flavoured prominently with paprika.

Râle (Fr.)
See Rail.

Ram
The male sheep.

Ramakin (Ramequin, Fr.)
The porcelain or earthenware mould in which a mixture is baked and brought to the table. Paper soufflé cases are nowadays called ramakin cases.

Ramier (Fr.)
See Wood Pigeon.

Rampion
See Radicchio.

Rancid
Decomposition, which produces a rank taste in foods high in fat content, such as butter, cheese and oils, caused by chemical changes of the food.

Rangpar
A citrus fruit about the size of a lemon but with compressed ends. It has a reddish skin and an orange-coloured flesh.

Rape
A plant cultivated in most European countries for its oil-producing seeds. Its leaves are also consumed as a substitute for spinach. Rape oil is obtained from the crushed rape seed.

Raspberry (Framboise, Fr.)
Small red berries with a delicate pulp and pleasing, slightly acid flavour. They are easily bruised and spoil very quickly. They are an excellent source of vitamin C and a good source of iron. Eaten fresh or cooked with care, they form an excellent dessert sweet.

Raspberry Vinegar

An infusion of raspberries, vinegar and sugar. Excellent when served with Yorkshire Pudding.

Rassolnick

A Russian soup made of cucumbers, very salty.

Ratafia

Name of a flavouring essence made from bitter almonds, also a small light macaroon biscuit used in trifles. There is also a liqueur flavoured with plum, peach and apricot kernels and bitter almonds, of this name.

Ration

A term originally applied to a soldier's or sailor's daily allowance of provisions, but as modern warfare is carried to the homes of the people the term is now applied to an allowance of provisions to last over a stated period, which can be for a day or a year. It is interesting to note that at one time a soldier's ration at home was ¾ lb. of meat and 1 lb. of bread per day. In 1949, the English housewife was lucky if she got that amount of meat per week.

Ravigote (Fr.)

A rich French salad dressing, made of olive oil, vinegar, chopped fresh green herbs, garlic, and delicately seasoned. Also the name of a hot sauce.

Ravioli

A savoury meat mixture enclosed in noodle dough and cooked in boiling water. It is usual to serve finely grated cheese with this dish.

Ray

A fish of the same genus as the skate or thornback. It should be hung for at least a day before it is dressed. The wings are cut into strips and kept in salt and water for 5 or 6 hours before they are used. Ray may be boiled or fried, in the same manner as skate.
It is best from September to February.

Rayon de Miel (Fr.)

See Honeycomb.

Receipt

A written formula for the preparation of food—but see Recipe.

Réchaud (Fr.)

A chafing dish.

Réchauffé (Fr.)

Food re-heated—a warmed up dish of food.

Recherché (Fr.)

Refined. Particularly choice or rare.

Recipe

A term originally applied to a formula for a medical prescription, now the principal term given to any formula which sets out details for the preparation in cookery.

Recrépi (Fr.)
Crimped. As applied to crimped fish.

Red Cabbage (Chou Rouge, Fr.)
See Cabbage, Red.

Red Herring
See Herring.

Red Mullet (Rouget, Fr.).
See Mullet, Red.

Réduire (Fr.)
To reduce or concentrate liquids by boiling.

Reeves (Paonnes de Mer, Fr.)
See Ruffs and Reeves.

Réforme, à la (Fr.)
Name given by a French chef to certain dishes which he prepared while at the Reform Club, London, most famous of which is the now well-established Cutlets Réforme. The garnish consists of carrot, truffle, ham and hard-boiled white of egg, all cut julienne style and served in rich Espagnole sauce.

Refrigerator
An insulated cabinet or chamber mechanically controlled to lower the temperature of the enclosed air, for the preservation of food. Usually such plants are run at a temperature of from 40° to 45° Fahrenheit, and do not, as a rule, freeze the foods.

Refroidi (Fr.)
See Chilled.

Régal (Fr.)
A feast or banquet.

Régence
Name of a popular fish sauce consisting of Sauce Normande reduced with wine, garnished with sliced mushrooms and truffles. If the name is applied to poultry, the basis is Sauce Suprême.

Reggiano
An Italian cheese similar to Parmesan, but more aromatic and highly flavoured. It improves with age and is not usually marketed until a year or 18 months after maturing.

Reginette
Wavy noodles, very thin, used like ordinary noodles.

Réglisse (Fr.)
See Licorice.

Regulo
A regulating dial affixed to modern gas stoves for controlling the flow of gas to the roasting chamber. The numbers equal the following temperatures in degrees Fahrenheit:

$\frac{1}{2}$	1	2	3	4	5	6
250	275	315	325	350	375	400

7	8	9	10	11	12
425	450	475	500	525	550

The temperatures will vary somewhat depending upon the pressure of gas in the particular district.

Rehoboam
A bottle equal in size to 6 ordinary wine bottles, containing 1 gallon. (See Bottle.)

Reindeer (Renne, Fr.)
It may come as a surprise to many to learn that reindeer tongues, imported from Russia and Lapland, were sold extensively under the guise of ox tongues in England before the war. They are delicious eating, and to those who appreciate good fare they are always preferred to the Argentine packed ox tongues, which are usually over-salted in cooking.
Both sexes of reindeer are antlered. The meat of cows and steers is like mild venison. That of a three-year-old steer is generally considered best. The meat of the buck is too strong in taste to please.

Reine Claude (Fr.)
See Greengage.

Reinette (Fr.)
See Russet Apple.

Relevé (Fr.)
A French term for a course of a substantial nature, consisting of large joints of meat, game, and occasionally fish.

Relish (Goût Piquant, Fr.)
A highly flavoured or seasoned food used with other foods to make them more palatable or to stimulate the appetite.

Remouillage (Fr.)
The thinner, second stock.

Rémoulade (Fr.)
Name given to a rich cold savoury sauce, similar in character to mayonnaise sauce. Used as a salad dressing.

Render
To free fat from connective tissue by the application of heat.

Renne (Fr.)
See Reindeer.

Rennet (Présure, Fr.)
An infusion of the inner skin of a calf's stomach. The best quality being obtained from animals that have received no other food than milk. Rennet's chief importance from a food standpoint is its unique property of coagulating milk for cheese manufacture and the jellying of milk for junket.

Repassé (Fr.)
Repeatedly strained. As carried out for aspics and fine sauces.

Restaurant (Fr.)
Name of a tavern opened in the Rue des Poulies, Paris, in 1765, by one Boulanger, for the serving of restorative broths to ladies unaccompanied by gentlemen. Re-staurants for ladies needing light refreshment. Later more substantial foods were served under licence, and gradually the catering establishments as we know them to-day were evolved, where meals of a substantial nature are served.

Rhubarb (Rhubarbe, Fr.)
Name applied to both a drug and a vegetable. Rhubarb as a vegetable consists of a leaf stalk which possesses a rather pleasing acid flavour and is used stewed, in pies and puddings. It being the stalk of the plant, it is a mistaken notion to call it a fruit. All the same, it is eagerly awaited each spring to herald in the first of the fresh pie or pudding fillings, and by many is looked upon as the first fruit of the season. The drug is an extract of the root of the plant, there being two kinds, the kiln-dried and the sun-dried. It has natural purgative qualities.

Rhum (Fr.)
See Rum.

Ribs of Beef (Côtes de Bœuf, Fr.)
In England we have five joints that come under the heading of ribs of beef—(1) wing rib ; (2) top ribs ; (3) fore ribs ; (4) back ribs ; and (5) flat ribs. The wing rib is the cut most esteemed and commands a higher price than the other cuts.

Rice (Riz, Fr.)
As a wheat-growing country it is difficult perhaps to realise that rice is more extensively used for human food than any other grain. In China, Japan and India it is the staple food, and is the principal food of more than one-third of the entire population of the world.

There are many varieties of rice, in fact, more than of wheat and corn put together. The grains vary from fine long slender ones to short fat ones. The grain is chiefly marketed with the outer layers removed, and contains an average of nearly 88% of nutrients, a little more than wheat. The rice when threshed is brown, and the husk is removed by milling, which produces the white rice. The best grade of rice consists of polished, unbroken grains of a white, creamy colour. In other grades there are broken kernels and other defects which affect the price. The finest marketed in England is Carolina.

Rice, Burst
Rice put into cold water. On reaching boiling point the grains burst.

Rice, Wild
A rather long, thin grain, chiefly greenish, with a peculiar, slightly smoky flavour, which is very pleasing to the palate. Careful cooking is required to bring out the best qualities of wild rice. Grown extensively in the southern States of America, it has always been relished as a food by Indians, and in recent years it has become quite popular in American restaurants. Also known as zizanie.

Rice Flour
Ground rice made from defective rice broken in the husking stage.

Rice Paper
A white, smooth, glossy paper made in China from the pith of a tree peculiar to Formosa. It is edible, and macaroons and other like biscuits are baked on it.

Richelieu
Name of a noted French Cardinal, also of two famous French statesmen, all three celebrated gourmets. Cardinal Richelieu is credited with having created the popular mayonnaise sauce, besides giving his name to many French dishes.

As a sauce, this style consists of a rich brown game gravy reduced with madeira wine and enriched with meat extract. As a garnish for poultry and game, it comprises mushrooms, artichoke bottoms, chicken quenelles enriched with demi-glace. Consommé Richelieu is a fish-flavoured consommé garnished with lobster quenelles.

Ries Würstchen (Ger.)
A type of Austrian rice sausage.

Rigatoni (It.)
Fluted elbow-shaped pieces of macaroni. The largest fluted elbow-shaped macaroni made.

Rillottes (Fr.)
Pork pounded to a paste, highly seasoned. Used in France for hors d'œuvre.

Rillottes and Rillons de Tours enjoy the greatest popularity.

Ris d'Agneau (Fr.)
Lamb's sweetbreads.

Ris de Veau (Fr.)
Calf's sweetbreads.

Ris de Veau Piqué (Fr.)
Larded sweetbreads.

Risengrod
A Danish dish of rice porridge.

Risotto
An Italian stew of butter, rice, cheese and tomatoes, usually flavoured with garlic.

Ris Pisi
A favourite Italian soup containing rice and green peas.

Rissoles (Fr.)
A savoury meat or fish mixture enclosed in rich pastry, formed into half-moon shapes, usually egg and crumbed or rolled in finely crushed vermicelli and fried. (See also Croquettes.)

Riz (Fr.)
See Rice.

Roach (Gardon, Fr.)
The roach is a fish which inhabits shallow and gently flowing streams. It seldom weighs more than $1\frac{1}{2}$ lbs. The colour of its upper part is dusty green, with blue reflections, becoming lighter on the sides, and passing into silvery white on the belly. Its flesh is white, but turns red when boiled.

It is in season from September to March, and at its best from October, but is not much sought for the table as it is very bony. All the same, it makes good fish soups.

Roast, To (Rôtir, Fr.)
To cook before an open fire or radiated heat. The only method of cooking available to the ancients before the invention of pots, pans and ovens. The most natural way of cooking foods and undoubtedly still the best. One can well imagine prehistoric man dragging his kill up the mountainside to his cave, dropping the animal too near the fire and falling down utterly exhausted to sleep. He would no doubt awake to find his food roasted —emitting a mouth-watering odour—and for the first time taste roast meat.

Roasting Jack
A mechanical device for turning the spit upon which the meat is hung by means of hooks for roasting. (See also Spit.)

Robert (Fr.)
Name of a rich brown spicy sauce with chopped brown onions, chili vinegar and mustard, served with pork and other rich meats. Invented by a French restaurant keeper.

Rocambole (Fr.)
A member of the onion family which bears its fruit at the top of its stem, not quite so pungent as garlic.

Rockling (Baudroie, Fr.)
This fish is sometimes referred to as the sea loach. It is a much larger fish, however, averaging a length of between 1 foot and 18 inches. In the young, the colour is a uniform brown, but as it approaches maturity it becomes of a rich yellowish-brown, spotted on the upper part of the body with deep chestnut brown.
As its flesh is of little value, developing an unpleasant smell shortly after death, it is seldom to be seen at the market. It should be cooked like hake.

Rock Salmon
A name given to the ordinary coalfish, which should be stopped. Many housewives and caterers have been enticed to buy fish under this name, with bitter disappointment. It is misleading, and should be shunned. It is also known as saithe, flake and dogfish. (See Coalfish.)

Roe, Hard (Œufs de Poisson, Fr.)
All types of caviare are made from the hard roes of fish.

Roe, Soft (Laitance, Fr.)
The soft roe is that of the male fish. The hard roe is that of the female, being the eggs.

Rognon (Fr.)
Kidney.

Rognon de Coq (Fr.)
Cock's kernel. A euphemistic name for fowls' testicles sold in bottles, separate and mixed with cocks' combs.

Rognon de Mouton (Fr.)
Sheep's kidney.

Rognon de Veau (Fr.)
Calf's kidney.

Rokelax
Norwegian smoked salmon.

Roll Mops
See Herring, Roll Mops.

Roly-Poly
A suet pudding, rolled out in sheet form, spread with jam, dried fruit, etc., and rolled up Swiss roll fashion. Usually boiled or steamed.

Romaine (Fr.)
The long-leaved cos lettuce.

Romaine, à la (Fr.)
Roman style. As a sauce, it consists of Espagnole sauce mixed with currants, sultanas, Italian pine seeds and diluted with wine vinegar. Potage Romain is a thick white cream soup garnished with rice quenelles.

Romanoff
Name of a Russian Imperial family, whose name has been given to a number of French dishes. As a garnish for meats, it comprises stuffed and braised cubes of cucumber, tiny potatoes, celeriac and mushrooms in demi-glace.

Romarin (Fr.)
See Rosemary.

Rook (Corbeau, Fr.)
Rural England still takes kindly to rook pies and puddings.
The rook may be distinguished from the crow by the lack of feathers on its face, which are lost at an early age, leaving a bare, scabrous and greyish-white skin, which can be detected at a great distance. Its black plumage has a rich purple gloss on head and neck.
Rooks are used extensively as fillers for game pies, giving bulk but not flavour. During the late war they reached the fantastic price of 2/10 each, and as the demand for them fell, butchers resorted to stuffing them to sell at 2/9 each. Although the meat ration was reduced in the post-war period, the price had dropped to 9d. per bird by 1949, with few buyers, the public having had their fill of this uninteresting fare.

Root Beer
A beverage made by an infusion of roots, barks and herbs, which is fermented with yeast. Mixtures of various roots are retailed in packages for the making of this homely beverage.

Rope, in Bread
A souring of the bread dough caused by using green or sprouting wheat, which causes stringiness in bread when baked. The bread, when cooked, develops an objectionable pungent sour smell and is unfit for consumption.

Roquefort (Fr.)
A noted French cheese made from sheep's milk. Rather pungent in flavour and a little too salty for the average English taste.

Rosemary (Romarin, Fr.)
An evergreen shrub with leaves deep green above, white underneath, and curled at the edges. It is very fragrant and in medicine is used as a stimulant. Occasionally employed for seasoning and in the manufacture of preserves.

Rosetbakkels or Rosettes
A type of German waffle, fried on small, rosette-shaped irons in deep fat or, alternatively, baked in special-shaped waffle plates. Usually served with honey or syrup.

Rossini
Name of a famous musician and gastronome who invented culinary dishes in between composing his music. His most famous dish which he invented being Filet de Bœuf Rossini, consisting of grilled fillets with slices of foie-gras and truffle placed on top, served with Sauce Périgueux.

Rôti (Fr.)
The roast, roasted.

Rôtie (Fr.)
Slice of toast.

Rouennaise, à la (Fr.)
Rouen style. As a sauce, it comprises rich Madeira sauce blended with pounded duck liver. Potage Rouennais consists of a purée of duck and lentils. Rouen being famous for its ducks, sauces, soups and other dishes usually embody duck in some form.

Rouget (Fr.)
See Red Mullet.

Roughage
The fibre of cereals, fruits and vegetables which act as an aid to intestinal elimination if eaten in reasonable quantities. Certain cereals are sold in package form claiming these qualities, but one should be warned that plenty of liquid in the form of milk or water should be added to such cereals.

Roulade (Fr.)
Meat roll, or galantine.

Roulé (Fr.)
Rolled.

Roussette or Chien de Mer (Fr.)
See Dogfish.

Roux (Fr.)
Roux is one of the basic thickening mediums for sauces. It is a mixture of flour and butter, but economy compels cooks to substitute margarine for butter. In fish cookery, the butter and flour are nearly always creamed together cold, and added to the hot liquid as a thickener to make the sauce. For brown sauces the liquid is usually added to the cooked browned roux. (See also Cream, to.)

O

Royal (Royale, Fr.)

Name given to a savoury egg custard which can be prepared in a variety of flavours and colours, used for garnishing a variety of clear soups. Consommé à la Royale is always served with plain egg custard cut into dice or other fancy shapes.

Royale Icing

The harding type of icing used for coating wedding, birthday and celebration cakes ; it being almost an airtight casing, cakes coated with this type of icing will usually keep for a very long time. It consists of icing sugar and whites of eggs beaten together until they become almost as light and pliable as stiffly whipped cream. A little blue is sometimes added to give that expert whiteness, and acetic acid to hasten its drying or hardening powers.

Ruban (Fr.)

Ribbon.

Rubané (Fr.)

Ribbon-like, as Crème Rubanée, being ribbon-like layers of different coloured cream built one on top of the other.

Rudd

Of the same family as the roach, being a fresh-water fish, it is not of good flavour, and is very bony. It is best used for fish soups. If you must cook it, then fry it as for roach.

Ruffs and Reeves (Paons de Mer, Fr.)

These little birds, of which the ruff is the male and the reeve the female, take their name from the long feathers which show around the neck of the male bird, in appearance resembling the old-fashioned ruff once worn by ladies.

Ruffs are seldom offered for sale in England to-day, although in earlier times they were highly esteemed and fetched very high prices. They were caught extensively in the Midland counties, where they were quickly fattened and marketed. They are now gradually becoming scarcer in England, due to the destruction of their favourite haunts, the fens, by drainage.

All recipes usually given for cooking woodcock may be used for cooking the ruff, with the exception that, unlike the woodcock, the ruff must be drawn.

Rum

A potable alcoholic liquor distilled from the by-products obtained from the manufacture of cane sugar. There are two main types — Jamaica and Demerara. The Demerara is smoother and of lighter flavour than the Jamaica rum.

Rumkin

A type of drinking vessel.

Rundergehakt
A Danish dish of minced beef.

Runderlappen
A Danish dish of stewed steak.

Runner Bean
A climbing bean bearing green pods larger than those of the French bean. If picked when small they are nearly equal in flavour to the French bean. When allowed to grow too long they become coarse and stringy, with large, scarlet-coloured beans.

Rusks
A term applied to a variety of small light cakes and slightly sweetened, twice-baked bread, to render it crisp and longer-keeping. Long-shaped rolls are baked, cooled, sliced and re-baked very steadily until the pieces have a very dry toast-like appearance.

Russe, à la (Fr.)
Russian style. Dishes bearing this name usually indicate that horseradish, sour cream, beetroot juice or shredded beet-root, has been embodied in the composition.

Russet Apple (Reinette, Fr.)
A delicious flavoured, dull, rough-skinned apple, highly prized as an English dessert apple.

Russian Dressing
Mayonnaise cream dressing to which have been added Worcestershire Sauce, chili sauce, chopped pickles and a variety of seasonings.

Russian Sauce (Sauce Russe, Fr.)
Allemande sauce with grated horseradish, finely chopped ham, reduced with vinegar and white wine, seasoned with some cream, sugar, pepper and salt.

Rutabaga
A Swedish turnip with a strong flavour somewhat similar to kohl rabi. The flesh is yellow in some types and white in others.

Rye (Seigle, Fr.)
In England rye is chiefly cultivated as a forage plant for cattle and horses. In Russia and parts of Germany rye is the principal bread corn. It is of relatively high gluten content and nutritive value. In Canada and America whisky is distilled from it. Canadian rye whisky has a very pleasant flavour. The Russians make a drink from rye and other ingredients, which they call kvass. The grain is similar in appearance to barley. (See Kvass.)

Rye Bread (Pain de Seigle, Fr.)
In Northern Europe rye is the principal bread corn and in nutrititive value it stands next to wheat bread, which explains why it is used so extensively in countries of northern latitude ill-suited to the cultivation of wheat, rye being one of the hardiest of cereals. Rye bread is very dark in colour but has a pleasing, nutty flavour.

S

Sable (Fr.)
A light, short-eating cake usually baked in ring shape as a sand cake.

Saccharine, Saccharin
First discovered in 1879 by accident by Ira Remsen and C. Fahlberg at the John Hopkins University, U.S.A. It has 400 to 500 times more sweetening power than sugar. As a food it is valueless as it passes through the system unchanged. As such, it is ideal for sweetening cooling beverages, thus avoiding the consumption of heat-making sugar. It is a coal tar derivative.

Saccharometer
An instrument for measuring the volume of sugar in liquids. (See Baume Saccharometer.)

Saddle of Mutton (Selle de Mouton, Fr.)
The two loins complete with kidneys not cut asunder. In lamb or young mutton, it is considered the finest part of the animal.

Saffron (Safran, Fr.)
The dried stigma from the flower of the crocus plant. It is of a deep orange colour, with a sweetish aromatic odour. It gives a pale yellow colour to sauces and cakes.

Safran (Fr.)
See Saffron.

Sage (Sauge, Fr.)
There are three forms of this evergreen sub-shrub ; the red-leaved, common silver, and the narrow - leaved silver. The last is the herb most used for culinary purposes.

Sago (Sagou, Fr.)
A food starch obtained from the split trunk of the sago palm. The starchy pith is extracted and ground to powder, which in turn is kneaded with water. The starchy mass is then run through sieves varying in mesh to produce seed, pearl and bullet sago. The principal supplies come to us from Borneo, and it has no relation whatsoever to tapioca, which see.

Sagou (Fr.)
See Sago.

Saignant (Fr.)
Denoting underdone.

St. Cloud
A noted village of France which gives its name to a number of French dishes—as Potage St. Cloud, a bean soup garnished with finely chopped lettuce.

St. Germain (Fr.)
The name given to a favourite pea soup enriched with cream. As a garnish it consists of a purée of green peas.

St. Hubert (Fr.)
Dishes bearing this name are made with game. St. Hubert —the patron saint of hunters. Potage St. Hubert is a purée of game garnished with dice-cut fillets of game.

St. Pierre (Fr.)
See John Dory and Samphire.

Saithe
Just another name for the coal-fish. This time it is the Scottish way of naming it.

Saki
A Japanese spirit distilled from rice.

Salad (Salade, Fr.)
A preparation of fresh or cooked herbs, vegetables or other ingredients served with oil, vinegar and seasonings, or a combination of fruits usually iced and served with liqueur. Fish, meats, poultry and eggs may be included with vegetable salads or a combination of fruits and vegetables, e.g. lobster salad (Salade de Homard), green salad (Salade Verte), chicken salad (Salade de Volaille), etc. (Names of other particular salads will be found in their alphabetical order.)

Salad Dressing
Salad dressing should be varied to suit the dish which the salad is to accompany. A light oil and vinegar dressing is ideal for dinner salads when served with hot chicken and the like. Salads served with cold foods are usually dressed with the creamy type of dressing.

Salamandre (Fr.)
A utensil which was at one time filled with red-hot coals and used for browning the surface of dishes. The gas and electric grills have driven it into the antique shop.

Salami
An Italian sausage highly spiced which keeps for a very long time if properly dried. The best grades contain red wine and are much esteemed for use as hors d'œuvre.

Salé (Fr.)
Salted, as hareng salé, salted herring. Corned, as corned beef (which see).

Salenyia Gribi
A Russian dish of salted mushrooms eaten as an hors d'œuvre.

Salisbury Steak
Minced lean beef mixed with bread, eggs and milk, seasoned, formed into hamburger style cakes and fried.

Sally Lunn
A sweet spongy yeast cake, first made about 1788 by a girl named Sally Lunn who became famous for her baking of fine tea cakes, which she hawked around the streets of Bath.

Salmagundi
A very old English dish, consisting of diced fresh and salt meats mixed with hard-boiled eggs, pickled vegetables and spices, dressed on a bed of salad.

Salmanazar
A large bottle equal in size to 12 ordinary wine bottles, capacity 2 gallons. (See Bottles.)

Salmi (Fr.)

A highly finished hash, made with game or wildfowl, cut up and prepared in either rich gravy or sauce.

Salmon (Saumon, Fr.)

The salmon is the most popular fish among all who love sport and good food, whether it be cooking or eating it. How eagerly the opening of the salmon season is awaited by sportsman, chef and diner. Izaak Walton describes it as the king of fresh-water fish.

So much has already been written about the salmon and its habits, that I propose to dwell only on those points which interest the chef or cook. The flesh of the salmon is rich and delicious in flavour. To be eaten in perfection, it should be dressed before it has lost tide. If this is done, there will be found between the flakes a white creamy substance, which is highly esteemed and known as the curd. Nevertheless, it is rather indigestible at this stage, and is best when kept a day or two. When the curd takes a change and melts down, and though less delicious in flavour, the fish becomes richer and much more wholesome. The flesh of the male has the best flavour, and has more curd than the female.

To recognise it at its best, it must be very stiff, shiny and red in the gills, with scales bright and silvery. The medium-sized fish are best— 14 to 16 lbs.—the larger fish are likely to be coarse. The Norwegian salmon are considered better than those caught in Scottish waters. Next in order of merit comes the Canadian. Salmon may be cooked in almost any manner, baked, boiled, broiled, fried, grilled, stewed or poached, for it has an eye appeal all its own. Truly the king of fish for the table.

It is in season from the beginning of February to the end of August and is generally cheapest in July and August.

Salmon Trout (Truite Saumonée, Fr.)

Salmon trout, though resembling salmon in flavour in certain respects, and in appearance, are not really of the same species. They seldom exceed 2 to 3 lbs. in weight. They are justly esteemed a delicacy and may be dressed according to recipes given both for salmon and trout. Boiling is the least agreeable form of cooking this fish.

It is a sea-fish, and when large it is white and is little valued ; but when small, it is generally red, but it is never so red as salmon. Look at the inside of the throat through the gills, where the colour of the throat may be seen. If very red, the flesh will prove red, and this is the kind which is most prized. In season March to August.

Salpicon (Fr.)

Meat, poultry or game minced, seasoned and mixed with mushroom sauce to bind it, used for rissoles, croquettes or Côtelettes Salpicon.

Salsifis (Fr.)

See Salsify.

Salsify (Salsifis, Fr.)

A vegetable plant with thin, long, tapering white roots, which when boiled form a good winter vegetable. At one time called the oyster plant, why, one can hardly imagine, for it does not resemble the oyster in flavour. When cut small and cooked, it has an osyter-like appearance, so it may have been more from appearance than flavour that it gained its other name.

Salt (Sel, Fr.)

At one time almost all salt was produced by the evaporation of sea water, and sea salt still forms a staple commodity in many countries surrounded by sea and where the climate is dry and the summer of long duration. Most of the salt in commercial use to-day is manufactured from rock salt, chiefly in the Middlesborough district, the process of manufacture being to run water into large bore holes in the rock salt, where it is allowed to remain until it is saturated with salt.

This brine is then pumped up and heated in pans to drive off the moisture, leaving the salt in crystallised form. The various grades of lump, stoved or superfine are obtained by various processes of boiling to obtain coarse, medium or fine crystals. (See also Bay Salt.)

Salted Herring

See Herring, Salted.

Saltpetre (Salpêtre, Fr.)

Potassium nitrate, used in preserving meats. Sodium nitrate has replaced saltpetre to a large extent. The red colour of hams, salt beef, and sausage, is intensified by it.

Salzgurken (Ger.)

A German pickle made of sour cucumbers served with boiled or roast meats.

Salzstangen (Ger.)

Small Vienna style rolls sprinkled with salt and frequently with poppy seed.

Samp

A term applied to hulled Indian corn. Marketed as whole kernel samp or, if broken, half kernel samp. Also applied to a type of porridge made of the hulled corn.

Samphire (St. Pierre, Fr.)

An aromatic salad herb which grows wild mostly on cliffs near the seashore.

Samshu
A Chinese beer brewed from rice.

Samztah
An Arab dish made of sweet dates and cream thickened a little with cornflour.

Sandwich (Tartine, Fr.)
Originally two slices of buttered bread with sliced meat, game, or paste placed between them, said to have been invented by the 4th Earl of Sandwich as a means of eating his meals quickly during his bouts of gambling. To-day, there are many forms of sandwiches made of white, brown, or toasted bread, some called two- and three-decker sandwiches, according to the number of slices of bread and butter or toasted bread employed in their composition.
Danish sandwiches are thick slices of a Vienna roll cut on the bias and cleverly arranged with an assortment of meats, salads, cheese and vegetables as a layer on the single slices of roll or crisp bread. (See Smörrebrod.)

Sangaree
Name of a punch, drunk in the West Indies, made with madeira wine, water, lime juice and sugar.

Sanglier (Fr.)
See Wild Boar, also Boar's Head.

San Si Yu Chi
A Chinese dish of sharks' fins. (See Sharks' Fins.)

Santos
Name of a Brazilian city which contributes some of the finest coffee to America, and in normal times to England.

Sapodilla (Sapote, Fr.)
The fruit of the tree from which chicle is obtained for chewing gum. It has the appearance of a cross between a new potato and a russet apple, with a soft, rough-grained, yellow to greyish pulp, and has a delicious flavour.

Sapota, White
A Mexican thin-skinned fruit, similar in appearance to a quince but slightly rounder. It has a cream coloured soft flesh and a sweet, pleasing flavour.

Saratoga Chips
First made by a negro chef at Morris Lake, Saratoga. Thinly sliced wafer potatoes washed free from starch and fried. Game chips or potato crisps.

Sarcelle (Fr.)
See Teal.

Sardine (Sardine, Fr.)
The name sardine was first applied to young pilchards caught off the coast of Sardinia. Since then, the name has been

applied to the young of herrings, anchovies, and other species of fish. So it would be as well to define them as follows :

Norwegian sardines are sprats.

Portuguese sardines are chiefly young pilchards.

American sardines are chiefly young herrings.

Need you wonder then, that the everlasting question constantly arises—what is a sardine ?

The sardines vary in goodness according to the quality of the oil used in canning them. Those are best which have been canned in good olive oil, and time allowed for them to mature well.

Sarrasin (Fr.)

See Buckwheat.

Sarsaparilla

A flavouring made from the dark-brown, bitter-flavoured roots of certain species of smilax used extensively in carbonated beverages which are sometimes classed as a tonic.

Sassafras

Name of a North American beverage made by an infusion of the bark, leaves and leaf buds of a laurel tree, used in some areas as a substitute for tea.

Satsuma Jiru

Name of a Japanese chicken soup, garnished with salt pork and diced root vegetables.

Sauce (Sauce, Fr.)

A liquid concentrate for serving with food. From the four mother sauces — Allemande, Béchamel, Espagnole and Velouté — almost all other sauces are derived, the exception being certain sweet sauces, and cold sauces made from oil, such as the mayonnaise sauce. Sauces for meat, fish, poultry and game are usually made from the extracts or broths of the foods and form a liquid seasoning to be served with the dish of food. Sweet sauces are generally composed of milk, sugar, eggs, cream and fruit flavourings. Cold sauces of the mayonnaise and Tartare variety are made from oil, egg yolks, vinegar and seasonings, cunningly blended together.

All sauces are served to improve the food's eating qualities and to give added flavour ; otherwise they are useless.

(Names of particular sauces will be found in their alphabetical order.)

Saucisse (Fr.)

See Sausage.

Sauerkraut (Ger., Choucroute, Fr.)

Finely sliced cabbage fermented with salt, caraway seeds and juniper berries, usually served with pork or sausages. A familiar garnish to almost all German dishes.

Sauge (Fr.)
See Sage.

Saumon (Fr.)
See Salmon.

Saumoneau (Fr.)
A small salmon.   (See Grilse.)

Sausage (Saucisse, Fr.)
The making of sausages goes well back into earliest Greek and Roman eras and is interwoven with romance and intrigue. Sausages are mentioned by Athenaeus in the Diepnoso-phists, A.D. 228, the oldest cookery book that has come down to us. He says : " Epicharmus mentioned saus-ages, calling them Oryae, a name by which he even entitles one of his plays, The Orya." This was written about 500 B.C. Aristophanes says, in " The Clouds " (423 B.C.) : " Let them make sausages of me and serve me up to the students." The Romans of Caesar's time made the eating of sausage such a ritual at their festivals, which soon turned into de-bauches of eating, that the Church banned the eating of sausage, as a sin.   But like so many such laws, it only served to develop a thriv-ing black market, and after several reigns the ban was lifted. (One might easily say the eating of sausages to-day is a sin !)

Sausage making really started as a means of preserving meat against spoilage, but soon be-came a highly developed art, which reached its height during the Middle Ages in Italy. Most of the varieties developed in these southern countries were richly spiced and of the harder, drier kind, now often called fancy sausages.   The northern countries developed the softer varieties.

To-day, America produces as many as 200 varieties, to suit the tastes of all the national-ities in that country, the most popular being the Frankfurters for " Hot Dogs ".

Saussiski (Rus.)
Sausage.

Sauté (Fr.)
A quick cooking process.   The foods are browned or cooked in little fat, in a sauté or frying pan, and tossed over a sharp fire or heat.   The process is usually applied to the quick cooking of sliced vegetables or diced meats when they are required to be browned prior to braising or adding to stews.

The process can be best illus-trated as being a type of shallow frying of any foods which require a sharp fire and quick cooking, tossed and turned, to be evenly browned and cooked on all sides.

Sauté Pan (Sautoise, Fr.)

A shallow pan, usually of tinned copper, used to sauté foods (see above).

Sauter (Fr.)

See Sauté.

Sauterne

A French white wine, much esteemed for culinary use. Made from grapes over-ripe, it is the best of the naturally sweet wines.

Savarin, Brillat

A noted French gastronome and author of culinary works, chiefly famous for his book " La Physiologie du Goût " (The Physiology of Taste). Born 1 April, 1755, died 2 February, 1826. He once stated : " Tell me what you like to eat and I'll tell you what you are." Such was his fame as a student of gastronomy. The well-known light, spongy yeast cake, made in ring form, is named after him, perhaps the favourite being Fraises Brillat Savarin, comprising a baked savarin border steeped in syrup, glazed with strawberry preserve and the centre filled with strawberries flavoured with curaçao.

Saveloy

Originally a sausage made of pig's brains. Now recognised as a highly seasoned, smoked pork sausage which is given its red colour by the addition of saltpetre in its preparation.

Savory

A small but hardy herb, possessing a strong agreeably aromatic smell and flavour. There are two distinct kinds, winter and summer savory. Its smooth leaves are used in soups, sauces and stuffings.

Savoureux (Fr.)

See Savoury.

Savoury (Savoureux, Fr.)

(1) The final course before the coffee. (2) Denotes an appetising, tasty dish.

Savoyard

Dishes of Savoy. Savoy—since 1860 a province of France. The Savoy cabbage originally came to us from Savoy, and when shredded and cooked in wine forms an agreeable garnish.

Savoy Bag

A V-shaped linen bag, used for holding cream, mashed potato, and such-like foods, when decorating with a large icing tube called a savoy tube.

Savoy Cabbage

A hardy, curly-leaved, winter cabbage. It has a milder flavour than the ordinary cabbage. Introduced to England from Savoy, France.

Savoy Cake

A light sponge cake, usually made in tall fancy-shaped moulds for use as tipsy cakes. (See Sponge Cake.)

Savoy Fingers
Small finger - shaped sponge cakes.

Scald
To pour boiling water over food and let it stand a few minutes. To scald milk is to bring almost to the boil.

Scallion
A young onion which has developed no bulb.

Scallop or Scollop (Pétoncle, Coquille Saint-Jacques, Fr.)
The scallop is something like a crab in taste, and can be used in many ways. It is never out of place in any fish pie.
They are in season from October to March and at their best for the first three months in the year, when the roe is full and of a bright orange colour. As with all such types of shellfish, select those with shells firmly closed and pick out the heaviest ones. Ignore those set out for display on the fishmonger's slab, and ask for some freshly opened ones while you wait. It will be worth the time.

Any housewife can open scallops, by the simple process of placing them for a moment on a warm stove, when they will open of their own accord. Remove the black part and gristly fibre, leaving intact the red coral, which is of fine flavour, being considered a great delicacy. Save the shells, which after cleaning well can be used again and again for all scalloped dishes.

Scaltheen
A potent beverage, at one time made in Ireland by brewing whisky and butter together.

Scarlet Runner
See Runner Bean.

Scarole
See Escarole.

Schmorbraten
A simple German dish, consisting of braised beef with a garnish of braised mixed vegetables and mushrooms.

Schnapps
Gin originally distilled at Schiedam, Holland. Sold in black bottles with flat sides and known equally as well under the title of " square-face ".

Schnitzel
An Austrian term for a thin slice of meat, usually egged, crumbed and fried, and served with fillets of anchovies and capers—as Wiener Schnitzel (Vienna schnitzel).

Schwarzbrod
German brown bread made from rye. See Rye Bread.

Schweins Sulz (Ger.)
An Austrian dish of jellied pork.

Scone
A variety of tea cake, at one time made from oatmeal and sour milk, originating from Scone, a parish in Scotland. Originally made as an imitation of the " stone of destiny " on which Celtic kings were crowned, and which at one time was at Scone before being conveyed to Westminster Abbey. Scotland boasts a large variety of this popular tea cake—oat, griddle, wheat, fruit, plain, etc.

Score, To
To cut narrow grooves or gashes.

Scotch Eggs
A dish comprising shelled hard-boiled eggs encased in sausage meat or savoury minced beef, which are then egged, crumbed and fried.

Scotch Kale, or Kail
Mutton stock in which sliced onions and leeks are cooked with a little barley, a liberal quantity of shredded cabbage is added when other ingredients are almost cooked. Scotch Kale like Kale Brose is a type of pot-au-feu of Scotland, but it differs from the French pot-au-feu in having only the green vegetables, from which it de-rives the name of " kale ". Use onions, leeks, and cabbage, and a little barley—no carrots, turnips, or the like.

Scotch Style (à l'Écossaise, Fr.)
For explanation see Écossaise, à l'.

Scotch Woodcock
A tasty savoury dish, com-prising toast spread with anchovy butter or paste, with a rich soft creamy scrambled egg on top. Garnished with an-chovy fillets and capers.

Scrapple
A mixture of pork carcase trimmings, ground maize, spices and sage, made into cakes and fried. A type of savoury sausage cake made from the trimmings at pig-killing times.

Scrod
A name given to young cod.

Scuppernong
The name given to the most widely cultivated of muscadine grapes. It is not a particu-larly good table grape, but is used in jelly, wine and as a grape juice.

Sea Beef
See Whale Meat.

Sea Bream (Brême, Fr.)
See Bream.

Seakale (Chou de Mer, Fr.)
This vegetable was found grow-ing wild near the sea and was first marketed in London in 1710, by the Rev. John Fremen, vicar of Sidbury. It is a very wholesome and easily digested vegetable if blanched properly ; unblanched it is useless.

Seal (Phoque, Fr.)
To the Esquimaux the seal is of vital importance, as bread is to a European. It is, of course, a mammal and not a fish. The liver is highly esteemed among sailors, being most agreeable when fried. The flesh of the seal forms most of the usual food of the Esquimaux. What fat is considered unedible is used as an oil in their lamps. The flesh may be fried, grilled, pot-roast, or braised.

Sear
To brown the surface quickly.

Seasoning (Assaisonnement, Fr.)
Spices, herbs or similar flavourings added to foods to make them more pleasing to the palate.

Sec, Sèche (Fr.)
Dry.

Séché (Fr.)
Dried.

Sèche or Seiche (Fr.)
See Squid.

Seigle (Fr.)
See Rye.

Seki Han
A Japanese dish of rice and red beans.

Sel (Fr.)
See Salt.

Self-raising
See Flour, Self-raising.

Selle (Fr.)
Saddle.

Selle de Mouton (Fr.)
See Saddle of Mutton.

Seltzer Water
See Mineral Waters.

Semmelklose
German bread dumplings.

Semolina (Semoule, Fr.)
Semolina consists of the small hard particles of wheat left in the bolting machine after the finer flour has passed through its meshes. It forms the basis of all Italian pastes from the finest vermicelli to the large type of macaroni called Zitoni. It also makes quite agreeable milk puddings. Another more creamy variety of semolina is made from maize or Indian corn.

Semoule (Fr.)
See Semolina.

Serviette (Fr.)
A table napkin.

Sévigné (Fr.)
Name of a French authoress who gave her name to a range of chicken soups. Consommé Sévigné is chicken consommé garnished with chicken quenelles. Potage Sévigné is a cream of chicken garnished with plain and chicken royale.

Shad (Alose, Fr.)
Shad is a salt water fish, not very highly esteemed in England, but more sought after in France and America, where it seems to take on a more pleasing flavour. It attains a length of 2 feet or more, and a weight of 10 lbs., the average market weight being about 4 lbs.

The body of the shad is of compressed shape, the back rounded and bluish, with a slight reddish tinge, and its sides are of silvery white. It is in season from March to June, and may be boiled, broiled, fried or baked. The shad roe, which is much sought after, is best from January to March.

Shaddock (Pamplemousse, Fr.) The grapefruit. Called shaddock in earlier times because it was originally brought from India to the West Indies by a Captain Shaddock and later to Florida where it was cultivated from a large coarse fruit to the normal size we enjoy to-day. (See also Grapefruit.)

Shallot (Échalote, Fr.) A small brown onion with a stronger, but mellower flavour than the common onion.

Shandy Gaff A drink for the initiatory ceremonies of teetotalers. Consisting of equal parts of ginger beer and ale. A long, cool and refreshing drink for cricketers and tennis players.

Sharks' Fins A delicacy much sought after in China, which consists of the parboiled fins being stripped of skin, bone and meat until only the soft yellow cartilage remains. It is then dried, when it takes on a seaweed-like appearance. When cooked, the fins become tender and gelatinous and absorb other flavours embodied in the dish, which usually comprise ham, chicken, onion, ginger and garlic. (See San Si Yu Chi.)

Shashlick Very young lamb, boned, cubed, steeped in oil and lemon juice from 4 to 5 days, and then placed on skewers, grilled and served with rice. Another form of the Indian Kebobs (which see).

Shchi The Russian national soup, erroneously spelt stechi and stehy. Made of fresh cabbage. Krapivnie shchi is made from nettles.

Shedder Crab See Crab.

Sheep's Milk This milk contains a higher percentage of fat and sugar than cow's milk. Rich yellow in colour, it is used in the manufacture of many French cheeses—as Brousses, Brocchio de Corse, Roquefort, Cachat and many others.

Sherbet A beverage of the East which consists of fruit drinks scented with rose water and flavoured with spices. England has taken on a cheap imitation consisting of certain chemicals mixed with pulverized sugar and flavoured with lemon. In America the term is given to a variety of flavoured water ices, from whence we get our sorbet.

Sherry

Sherry is made from white grapes grown in the Jerez district in the south of Spain. The best pale, dry sherries are usually sold under the names of Amontillado, Manzanilla and Vino de Pasto. The best dark, rich and full sherries are those usually sold under the names of Amoroso and Oloroso.

Sherry Cobbler

An American long drink consisting of crushed ice, sherry, sugar, slices of fresh fruit, topped with a maraschino cherry and served with straws.

Shin of Beef (Jarret de Bœuf, Fr.)

The forepart of the leg of beef. Due to its very gelatinous nature, it is used extensively for making broths and consommé.

Shirr

to break (eggs) into a dish with cream or crumbs and cook in the oven or on the fire.

Shortening

Any edible fat which, when added to flour to form a paste or dough, gives richness and renders it tender as a baked product.

Shot Pepper

Grains of Paradise or Mignonette Pepper, being pepper corns broken into granulated form. It takes its name of mignonette pepper from the fact that it looks the colour and is the size of mignonette seed. (See also Pepper, Mignonette.)

Shred

The action of slicing in small particles, which, due to the wafer-like ends, shrink a little, causing a curling effect ; as shredded suet or vegetables will do.

Shrewsbury Biscuits or Cakes

Crisp, crunchy, biscuit-like cakes made of a shortbread dough to which white of egg is added.

Shrimp (Crevette, Fr.)

There are several kinds of shrimp, the best known being the brown and red shrimps, the brown being the better flavoured of the two. The red shrimp, or rather the pale pink shrimp, rarely attains the size of the brown shrimp.

Shrimps form a common relish at provincial tea-tables, and when freshly boiled are excellent ; stale, they are indigestible. Boiled shrimps which are clammy to the touch should be discarded. When freshly boiled, their tails turn stiffly inwards, and are a bright colour. When stale, the tails go limp, the brightness of their colour goes off, and they become clammy.

Shrimps form an excellent garnish for most fish dishes, and are excellent in a sauce when served with turbot and sole.

Sikbaj

A sickly Arab stew, very gelatinous, owing to the long stewing of sheep's head which forms its base.

Sillbullar
A Swedish dish of herring croquettes.

Sillsillat
A favourite Swedish dish consisting of pickled herring. To be found on nearly every Swedish smörgäsbord. (See Smörgäsbord.)

Silverside
The joint of beef which is usually pickled in brine for the traditional " boiled beef and carrots ". It is cut from the round of beef and takes its name from the tissue on part of its side with a silvery sheen.

Simmer, To
To cook in liquid below the boiling point, about 185° F.

Simnel Cake
Originally this was a very heavy and stodgy confection, being a mixture of ingredients first boiled and then baked, until it resembled a baked plum pudding, being served to friends and visitors as a Lenten or Easter Cake. To-day, it is made quite differently, being a rich fruit cake with a layer of almond paste baked in its middle, with a ring of almond paste baked around its upper edge, the centre being suitably inscribed and decorated with a woolly chick and imitation eggs as an Easter or Mothering Sunday cake.

Singe, To
The burning off of the down and hairs of poultry or game birds after plucking. The operation is best carried out by a smokeless flame ; otherwise the delicate white flesh of some birds is blackened.

Sippets
Small morsels of bread, usually fried in hot fat.

Sirloin (Surlonge, Fr.)
See Sirloin of Beef.

Sirloin of Beef (Aloyau, Fr.)
The loin of beef which it is said was knighted by Henry VIII and so called Sir Loin, during one of the many court feasts which were quite a feature during his reign. Many French chefs ridicule this version and claim it is derived from the French " surlonge ". The truth is, the term Sir Loin was in vogue in England long before the French cooks could have introduced their derivation. Just one of those coincidences. The Anglo-Saxon " sur " was their equivalent for sour.

Sirniki
A Russian dessert sweet, consisting of cheese, sour cream and sugar, made into cakes and fried as fritters.

Sirop (Fr.)
See Syrup.

P

Skate (Raie, Fr.)

There are the long-nosed skate, flapper skate, and the blue or grey skate. The latter may be regarded as the most common and best known species, as it is found on all parts of the coasts of Great Britain and Ireland. Its ordinary size is from 2 to 4 feet, but examples have occurred in our seas weighing 200 lbs. A very fine specimen caught in the West Indies measured 25 feet in length and 13 in breadth. The snout is sharp, elongated and conical, the sides not being parallel ; the whole of the surface more or less granulated, the colour grey beneath with black spots.

The females cast their purses in May and continue doing so until September. In October, they are poor and thin, but begin to improve in November and grow gradually better till April, when they are at perfection.

This fish is nearly always sold cut into pieces or " crimped ". It is very rarely seen at the fishmonger's whole.

Skewers (Hâtelets, Fr.)

A pin of wood or metal for holding meat into shape while cooking. Aluminium skewers are said to be heat conductors and to assist in getting the heat to the centre of the meat.

Skillet

An American term for a cooking pot or pan.

Skilly

The gruel of Oliver Twist's days. A thin, watery porridge.

Skim Milk

Milk that is left after it has passed through the cream separating machine. The name is derived from the old-fashioned way of taking the cream off the milk by hand—skimming the cream off the milk—milk that has been skimmed of its cream.

Skinklada

Swedish ham omelette.

Slab Cake

Cake made into handy blocks for convenient baking, transportation and economical cutting. The shape enables the baker to pack his oven well, to avoid a thick crust and loss through evaporation.

Slapjack

See Flapjack.

Slaw

See Cole Slaw.

Sling

Name of a number of iced. alcoholic beverages made of spirits, water ice, sugar, sliced orange or lemon, with a touch of mint or borage.

Slip Sole

Small soles weighing between 6 to 8 ozs. each, are given this name. They are always cooked whole, usually by sprinkling lightly with salt and pepper, rubbed over with butter, and grilled. They need to be carefully watched, as being so thin they will soon become dry if cooked too long.

Sloak, Slook
See Laver.

Sloe (Prunelle, Fr.)
The wild plum or fruit of the blackthorn, small, dark purple in colour, with a yellow, very tart flesh. Large quantities are used on the Continent for various liqueurs and in this country for sloe gin.

Sloe Gin
A liqueur made by steeping sloes in gin.

Smelt (Éperlan, Fr.)
The smelt is nearly as forgotten a fish as the lamprey. The pollution of our rivers with death-dealing effluent and noxious smoke from riverside factories has left only the coarser type of fish, not to be compared with the delicate fish which once garnished the oriental majesty of salmon. The produce of the Dutch fisheries reach us with half their beauty faded and gone.

The scent emitted by smelts has been compared to that of green rushes, cucumbers or violets. Those found in the Medway are much esteemed. They are at their best from September to March.

In Scotland this fish is known as sperling or sparling.

Smetanick
A Russian pie made of ham and sour cream.

Smoked (Fumé, Fr.)
Foods pickled and cured in wood chip smoke to give added flavour after the brining process, as is the case with Findon haddock and smoked salmon. Oak chips are considered to give the best results.

Smolt
Smolt is the name given to salmon about 2 years old, when it first descends to the sea. At one time these young fish were caught and cooked as a great delicacy, but quite rightly this has been stopped, and it is now illegal to catch them in these Isles. This has been done to protect the salmon industry, which was suffering very badly from such vast quantities of these young fish being caught annually, before they had even reached maturity to spawn.

Smörgäsbord
The Swedish title for hors d'œuvre. Served at a side-table from which guests help themselves.

Smörrebrod
The name of those lovely Danish sandwiches. Open type sandwiches consisting of a slice of Vienna bread with an assortment of sliced foods on top like a salad.

Snail (Escargot, Fr.)

The best of the edible snails is known as the Burgundy "large white". Their shells vary in colour from greyish-yellow to grey-red with black markings. Most are gathered in vineyards, a few being raised on special snail farms. It is estimated that Paris consumes 80 to 90 millions a year, which is gradually declining as the modern taste sways away from their favour. The flavour is somewhat like that of an oyster and the food value very high.

Snipe (Bécassine, Fr.)

The name given to a large class of small game birds, which include the common snipe, pintailed snipe, great snipe, jack snipe and red-breasted snipe; and which somewhat resemble the woodcock. From the common snipe to the great snipe, the weight will vary from 2 ozs. to 10 ozs. per bird. They are considered one of the finest game birds gastronomically, and afford good sport for a quick shot.

Large numbers of these birds arrive in these islands during the autumn, but are little sought after. All the same, the Ministry of Food considered it desirable to fix a maximum retail price of 2/- per bird in 1942, but few were marketed. With modern canned meats and other fare available to the housewife of to-day, very few people can recall the flavour of this delicious morsel. It can be thoroughly recommended to those seeking adventure in the field of gastronomy.

Snipe, like woodcocks, when old have the feet hard and thick; when these are soft and tender the birds are both young and fresh killed. When the bills become moist and the throats muddy, they have been too long killed.

Snoek

Hardly any of the English had heard of this fish until the post-war period of World War II. In Australia and New Zealand it is very common, and known there as the Barracouta (not to be confused with the giant Barracuda, which is caught off the coasts of the U.S.A.)

The main supplies of canned snoek sent to this country come from South Africa, where it is caught and canned in great quantities. It seems well to place on record that when first introduced to this country, it was sold for 1/4½ per ½-lb. tin, and was officially stated to be cheap at this fantastic price. Its points value was 1 point per ½-lb. tin, as an inducement to buy it, but it never found favour.

Snow Eggs (Œufs à la Neige, Fr.)

See Neige, also Niverolle.

So Ba

Japanese black noodles.

Soda

Used for food, is known as bi-carbonate of soda or baking soda. In this form it is a by-product of washing soda. Soda added to vegetables quickly nullifies their vitamin C content.

Soda Fountain

A term applied to equipment from which flavoured and sweetened carbonated waters are dispensed from a pump and not a bottle. Embodied with modern equipment are all the requirements for dispensing milk shakes, iced drinks and a large variety of light refreshments.

Soda Water

See Aerated Water, Carbonated Water and Mineral Waters.

Soft-Shelled Crab

See Crab.

Sole, Dover

This noble fish, due to its selective habit of diet, loses very little flavour by a short delay between tide and table. It is extremely comforting to read that Carême approved of at least one thing in England. It was that he learned to re-move the skin of soles, and recommended the practice to his French pupils.

Lemon sole, megrims, witches, are all offered as substitutes for the true sole. Scotch sole and Torbay sole are megrims and, should never be accepted as a substitute for such a noble fish. The principal fisheries are on the south and west coasts, where the sole attains a large size. Those caught off the northern coasts are much smaller.

The shape of the body is a long oval, much rounded anteriorly, and the greatest width not amounting to half the length. The colour of the surface is nearly a uniform dark brown, having a reticulated appearance. The under side is white, and the side of the head opposite the eyes (which are on the right) is covered with a kind of villosity consisting of numerous soft papillae. It is placed on record that a sole appeared in Totnes market in 1826 which was 26 inches long, 11 inches wide, and weighed 9 lbs.

The sole is in season all the year round, being soft and watery only for a few weeks at the end of February and beginning of March, when in spawns. The lemon or French soles should never be confused with the true sole, if it be noted that the colour of the lemon sole is a mixture of orange and light brown, and is freckled over with light brown spots. Also, the under surface of the head is almost smooth, instead of presenting the papillae so re-markable in the true sole.

There are more ways of cooking a sole than any other fish, due to its great popularity with chefs of higher class establishments, who are always inventing new and better ways of presenting it.

The name Dover Sole is given to distinguish the real sole from its many inferior substitutes.

Solferino

An Italian village 5 miles west of the river Mincio, the scene of two battles between the French and Austrians. In celebration of these victories, many French dishes bear this name. Sauce Solferino consists of shallot reduced in madeira wine, blended with tomato purée and demi-glace. Consommé Solferino contains a vegetable garnish of carrots, turnips, diced tomato and quenelles.

Sommélier (Fr.)

Wine waiter.

Sorbet (Fr.)

The sorbet as we know it to-day originated from the Turkish iced sherbet (which see). Experiments were made in France to copy this fascinating fruit drink, but due to over-cooling or partial freezing the fruit juices became a soft water ice. Further experiments made the soft water ice into the delicious light fluffy water ice which to-day we call sorbet.

Sorghum

A title applied to a group of grains resembling Indian corn or maize. The plant grows 3 to 4 ft. in height, with a cluster like Indian corn at the top. It has a high percentage of sucrose and at one time experiments were tried to prove its value as a commercial source of sugar. Difficulties of crystallization and refining proved it an unprofitable proposition to compete with cane sugar.

Sorrell (Oseille, Fr.)

A perennial herb, not high in English favour. Used in soups, salads and mixed with spinach to enliven it. (see also Julienne.)

Soubise, Prince Charles

A celebrated French epicure, (born 1715, died 1787), who obviously must have been very fond of onions, for all dishes, sauces and garnishes which bear his name have onions embodied in some form. Sauce Soubise comprises onion purée mixed with rich cream sauce. As a garnish, stewed onions are pulped and used to mask the meat, poultry or game.

Soufflé (Fr.)

Food that is thoroughly beaten and made light by the addition of egg white. When baked it must be eaten immediately or else it will fall.

Soult
A favourite dish of South Africa, consisting of pigs' feet boiled with herbs and spices and allowed to mature for several days in the cooking liquid.

Sounds
Cod sounds are the air or swim bladder and are enjoyed by many as a delicacy. They are very gelatinous, which makes them rich eating.

Soup (Soupe, Fr.)
The most modern treatise on this subject is the " Master Book of Soups," published by Practical Press, 1949, and containing over 1,000 recipes covering every type of bouillon, borshch, clear, consommé, cream, potage and purée. The service and garnishings, together with a brief history of soups, are also fully dealt with. Soup as a food consists of water in which meat, fish, poultry, game, vegetables, or even fruits are stewed, to extract all the food value with the least possible loss of vitamins and flavour. Cereals and thickening agents are sometimes added to give body.

Soupe (Fr.)
See Soup.

Souper (Fr.)
Supper.

Souper de Bal (Fr.)
Ball supper.

Sour (Aigre, Fr.)
Acid, tart or sharp to the taste. Food or liquids which have become bad by long standing and fermentation.

Souse
A brine or pickling liquid. Pickled trimmings from a carcase of pork.

Soused Herring
See Herring, Soused.

Sowens
The Scotch term for flummery or furmenty, which is a kind of oatmeal jelly sliced and buttered.

Soy
A brown sauce obtained by long double fermentation of mashed steamed soy beans and pulverized, roasted wheat, together with water, salt, etc. It is an important ingredient of good quality Worcestershire Sauce (which see).

Soy or Soya Bean
For many centuries the soya bean has taken the place of meat in China, Japan and other parts of Asia. There, it is prepared in the form of a cottage cheese, and next to rice forms one of their main foods. Of recent years it has gained considerable favour in many other countries and is now recognised as one of the most nutritious legumes. Its protein is similar in composition and nutritive value to animal proteins and is a good

source of vitamins A, B and C. Because of their lack of starch, soya beans are a desirable food for diabetics. The bean has many uses and acts as many substitutes, in some countries even as a coffee substitute.

Soyer, Alex

Noted French chef who did much at the Reform Club, London, in the early 19th century, to bring about a change in English eating habits. Together with Carême, Francatelli and other prominent chefs of those times, a complete change was made in the style of garnishings and sauces in Court and West End dining rooms. It was of a lavish and heavy character, which has since been greatly modified to suit modern habits.

Spaghetti

A thin, fine kind of macaroni, made from hard wheat, but not hollow like macaroni. For full description of Italian pastes, see Vermicelli.

Spanish Juice

See Licorice.

Spare Rib

A term given to the ribs of pork when separated from the side before curing. A few spare ribs are given here and a few given there, as was always the case at pig-killing time in the country. " Spare a rib " was the poor man's cry when calling at the farmstead at pig-killing time.

Sparling

See Smelt.

Sparrowgrass

The country yokel's term for asparagus.

Spatchcock

A corruption of " the dispatched cock ". The cock killed at a fight, usually roasted or cooked on the spot for the guests assembled on the open moors. To-day, any bird split and flattened spread-eagle fashion has a more fancy name, for most poultry or game birds split in such fashion bear the title " à la Crapaudine ". (See also Crapaudine.)

Spatula (Spatule, Fr.)

A broad, flat, wooden spoon used for spreading food where it is undesirable for metal to come into contact with the food.

Spatule (Fr.)

See Spatula.

Spearmint

A smooth-leaved species of mint which bear a pale blue flower ; used extensively for culinary and medical purposes, and in the manufacture of chewing gum.

Speck

German word for bacon.

Spekelaar

Norwegian smoked mutton.

Spelt

A coarse type of wheat grown in some of the European countries, used very little for its flour, chiefly grown as cattle feed.

Sperling
See Smelt.

Spice (Épice, Fr.)
Aromatic vegetable condiments, whole ground, in paste or liquid form, used for imparting exciting flavour to foods.

Spinach (Épinard, Fr.)
A vegetable which has increased considerably in popularity during the 20th century. It was always considered to have certain medicinal qualities and when well cooked it is about as health-giving an article as can be imagined. It requires to be very well washed in many waters to rid it of sand and grit. In cooking, it requires no water, and thus cooks do not use bi-carbonate of soda, which is one reason why it can be consumed as a health-giving food.

Spirit
Alcoholic liquid obtained by distillation of various fermented liquors. Each type of potable spirit is distilled from some distinctive material ; gin and whisky from grain ; rum from sugar ; brandy from wine ; vodka from potatoes ; arrack from rice. In fact, there hardly exists a race of men who have not acquired the art of distilling alcohol after its formation during the fermentation of sugar. See also, Alcohol, Distillation and Still.)

Spit
An iron prong upon which meat is roasted in front of an open fire, usually fitted with a device to ensure its constantly revolving, such as a dog spit, being a cage in which a dog constantly walked to revolve the spit ; later revolved from the wind caused in the chimney. At one time, boys were employed to keep the spit on the move.

Split Peas (Pois Cassés, Fr.)
See Peas, Split.

Spongada
The Italian sorbet (which see).

Sponge Cake
Cakes made from well beaten eggs, sugar and flour. No fats are used as this would make a cake of a close-textured nature. Cake soft as sponge. (See also Savoy Cake.)

Spoonshell
See Gaper.

Sprat (Sprat, Fr.)
The sprat is of the same family as the herring, and has a limited popularity and a short season (October to March). Dried sprats are best eaten Continental fashion—skinned and raw. They make excellent appetisers among the hors d'œuvre.
It is important that the sprat be not confused with the young of the herring, as it has often been, even by professed naturalists. The ordinary length is from 5 to 6 inches, and the

colours are similar to those of the herring. Usually they are sold by measure, and not by weight. Sprats spawn in April, and usually appear on the market soon after the herring season is over.

Spread-eagle Chicken
See Spatchcock and Crapaudine.

Spring of Pork
The streaky flank or belly.

Sprouts, Brussels
See Brussels Sprouts.

Spruce Beer
Beer infused with the tips of the spruce fir and various spices.

Squab (Pigeonneau, Fr.)
The word squab in England is usually applied to young chickens small enough to cook for individual servings, which when appearing on the menu are termed poussins. There are squab chickens, squab guinea fowl, etc. In America, the term is applied to young pigeons, and these are at their best when about 4 weeks old. At this age, by special feeding, they will average 8 to 12 lbs. or more to the dozen, weighing sometimes as much as their fully matured parents. Their flesh damages very easily and they need handling with great care. Points to be observed when buying squabs are size, plumpness and light-coloured flesh.

Square Face
Hollands Gin. (See Schnapps.)

Squash
A term applied to a variety of edible fruits of many types of gourds of all shapes and sizes. The most common are the pumpkin and vegetable marrow. Also applied to juices extracted from citrus fruits by the action of splitting and squashing the fruits to facilitate the easier extraction of the juices.

Squid or Cuttlefish (Sèche or Seiche, Fr.)
Recipes for cooking squid have been asked for from the offices of " The Caterer and Hotel Keeper " when a stray one reaches our shores. The process is quite simple, for all recipes given for skate are suitable for cooking squid. Slice the bell-shaped body into $\frac{3}{4}$ inch thick slices, 2 or 3 inches wide, flour, egg and crumb and fry, either in deep fat or in clarified butter. The tentacles are sliced and cooked with vegetables, the liquor reduced and thickened for use as a sauce. Never attempt to boil squid, always fry it.

Squirrel (Ecureuil, Fr.)
Squirrels as food are not much sought after in England, although their flesh is quite tender and their flavour resembles that of the wild rabbit. During World War II squirrel pies and roast stuffed squirrels appeared on Soho menus, but never found favour, and it is safe to assume that further

available supplies were used as rabbit. Those seeking adventure in the culinary field might well try roast squirrel without suffering indigestion.

Stabiliser

A substance added to manufactured foods to provide against crystallisation and to give firmness or body—as in frozen ice cream usually gelatine or gum tragacanth are employed.

Staël, Madame de (Anne Louise)

A French novelist who gave her name to several French dishes as Tournedos Staël which consist of tournedos cooked in butter and garnished with grilled mushrooms filled with peas and served with Sauce Madère.

Star Apple

A tropical fruit about the size of the average dessert apple, with a skin varying in colour from white to purple. When cut crosswise its segments present a star-like appearance. The flesh is soft and sweet.

Starch (Amidon, Fr.)

All edible forms of starch are heat and energy producing foods and are to be found in nearly all plant life. The best known are those obtained from corn, wheat, rice, potatoes and arrowroot. Pure starch is a glistening white powder with a characteristic feeling when rubbed between the fingers ; when heated with liquids it swells considerably and is very useful as a thickening agent.

Starling (Étourneau, Fr.)

After many years of immunity, starlings were again marketed during World War II, and sold at 7/6 to 9/- per dozen at first, until the work entailed in preparing these tiny morsels was realised. Present-day cost of labour did not allow much profit when selling two to a portion at a controlled meal price of 5/- per head, which prevailed from 1942 onwards.

Steak

A slice, or cut of meat or fish. When the term is applied to meat, it generally refers to a slice from the choicest part of the animal. Fish are usually steaked by slices cut from the middle of the fish.

Steaming

Steaming as applied to domestic cookery is slower than boiling, but it is considered especially desirable for the cooking of small pieces of meat or pudding. The process is carried out with two vessels, the lower one containing the water and the upper vessel containing the food. The steam is allowed to pass to the upper vessel by way of perforations or tubes, and as the steam condenses it falls back into the lower compartment. Alternatively, if the vessel be big enough, a pudding may be steamed by standing it in a pan of water which rises no more than half-way up the pudding when it is lowered into the pan. Puddings should never be completely submerged in water, as it makes the outer shell soggy and slimy. A properly steamed pudding is lighter and more digestible than one cooked completely covered with water. In large catering establishments, proper steaming ovens are used, so that the water never comes in direct contact with the food.

Stearin
The principal constituent of solid animal fat, such as the kidney suet of mutton and beef.

Stechi, Stehy
See Shchi.

Steep
To soak in a liquid below boiling point.

Sterilize
To destroy micro-organisms. In cooking, usually effected by boiling in water or by steam.

Sterlet (Esturgeon, Fr.)
The sterlet is a small sturgeon, and very seldom seen in this country. When specimens do arrive, they are much appreciated by gourmets. The finest golden caviare comes from the roe of the sterlet. Any recipe given for sturgeon may be used for sterlet.

Stewed (Étuvé, Fr.)
Applied to foods that have been simmered in a small quantity of liquid. (See Stewing, below.)

Stewing

Stewing follows the same theories as boiling, for it is nothing more nor less than simmering foods in the smallest possible quantity of liquid. The meat, poultry or game and liquid are served together as a " stew ", instead of as in the process of boiling, where the meats are separated from the liquids. The one is served as boiled meat and the other used for soup or broth.

Stewing has many advantages from the nutritive and economic standpoints. It will render palatable and tender the coarser, older and cheaper types of poultry or game, which are always undesirable if grilled, roasted, or baked. The meat, poultry or game is usually browned in hot fat with vegetables, before being plunged into cold water, which is then gradually brought to the boiling point, the heat is then lowered to 180°F. to 190°F. (slow simmering) and the whole cooked until tender. It is essential that as little liquid as possible be used, to ensure that the goodness and flavour are not wasted in a lot of unwanted liquid ; also that the stew pot be covered during the whole process of cooking. Otherwise, the liquid will evaporate and more water will then have to be added.

Still
An apparatus for distillation of spirits in which the alcoholic liquid is separated from all or part of its water content by vaporisation. (See also Alcohol, Distillation and Spirits.)

Stilton
A popular English cheese which is reputed to have been made by a Miss Elizabeth Scarbrow at an inn at Stilton on the Great North Road about 1720. Stilton cheese, to be at its best, should mature in bulk and is usually ripe about Christmas time.

Stirabout
A type of porridge originating from Ireland.

Stock (Fond, Fr.)
Stock is the broth of beef, veal, chicken, fish, etc., kept " in stock " as its English name suggests, for instant use in soups and sauces.

Stove, To
To bake or heat in a stove— as stoved salt.

Strawberry (Fraise, Fr.)
Strawberries are 90% water and an excellent source of vitamin C with a small amount of calcium and iron. They are considered the most popular of fruits and their first appearance assures us that summer is here. There is a great range of berry, varying in size, shape and quality. They are extremely perishable if not handled with care.

Strawberry Brandy
Liqueur brandy flavoured with strawberries.

Strawberry Pear
A fruit common to Mexico and the West Indies. It is pear-shaped, with a bright red skin, with a whitish, slightly acid flesh.

Straw Wines (Vins de Paille, Fr.)
Wines obtained from the pressings of grapes which have been dried in the sun on straw mats.

Strega
A light golden Italian liqueur, not as sweet as most other liqueurs.

Stuffed (Farci, Fr.)
Meat, fish, fowl or vegetables filled with forcemeat. (See also Farce.)

Stuffing
The name given to all forms of forcemeat, usually cooked with the food but occasionally made into balls and fried or baked, to be served as a garnish.

Sturgeon (Esturgeon, F.)
Both in France and this country the sturgeon is regarded as a royal fish, that is to say, the property of the Crown. A provision still exists in the Statute Book that the Kings' escheater shall make diligent enquiry whether any sturgeon has been taken and withdrawn from the Crown. Now and again a sturgeon is taken, on average once in every three years, and then generally found entangled in

the salmon nets. The largest specimen recorded as having been caught in this country weighed 460 lbs.

Sturgeons are at once known by the elongated and angular body, defended by longitudinal rows of large indurated plates, of a pyramidal form, with the apex pointed. The snout is depressed and conical; the mouth tubular and without teeth, and placed on the underside of the head at some distance behind the extremity of the snout.

The sturgeon provides most of the caviare as known in this country. Its flesh is white, but hard, and requires a very good chef to make it acceptable. It should be hung 2 or 3 days to allow it to mature and soften a little, and then prepared in a marinade 24 hours before cooking. It tastes somewhat like veal.

In season September to March.

Succotash

A name borrowed from the native Indians, which they spelled " sukguttahash ". It is a stew consisting of green corn and lima beans.

Succulent

Mouth-watering, juicy.

Suchet (Fr.)

Name given to a rich white wine sauce, to which is added a julienne of young root vegetables; usually served with fish dishes.

Sucking Pig (Cochon de Lait, Fr.)

For those who would wish to read the most amusing and enlightening story of roast sucking pig, the author recommends the Essays of Elia, by Charles Lamb—" A Dissertation upon Roast Pig ".

Sucre (Fr.)

See Sugar.

Sucré (Fr.)

Sweetened.

Sucrose

The ordinary sugar of everyday use. The crystalline compound obtained from sugar cane, beet, maple, palm and sorghum-cane. (See Sugar.)

Suédoise, à la (Fr.)

Swedish style. Usually denotes a light soufflé of fish. As a hot sauce it comprises a white sauce flavoured with horse-radish and chili vinegar.

Suet (Suif, Fr.)

The hard fatty tissue which accumulates around the kidneys of an animal.

Sugar (Sucre, Fr.)

There are many kinds of sugar, principal of which are lactose, maltose, sucrose, fructose, glucose (dextrose)—which are explained under their respective headings. The main supplies are obtained from sugar cane, sugar beet, maple sugar, corn sugar. The most common forms produced are loaf, granulated, caster and powdered (icing). (See also Sugar Cane, and Barbadoes.)

Sugar, Pulled (Sucre Tiré, Fr.)
Sugar boiled almost to burning point, then coloured, stretched and pulled over hooks or poles till it takes on a silvery, silky sheen. With skilful manipulation baskets, fruits, flowers, etc. are formed almost true to colour and shape.

Sugar, Pulverised
Finely powdered icing sugar.

Sugar Cane (Bagasse, Fr.)
The sugar cane grows to a height of from 7 to 15 feet with a diameter of from 1 to 2 inches. It is considered ripe for harvesting at from 12 to 16 months growth, just before its flowering time, being then heaviest in juice. One ton of cane stalks will yield 2½ cwts. of sugar.

Sugar Melon
See Melon, Sugar.

Sughlio
Stock made of wine instead of water. A favourite method of cooking poultry, game, macaroni, etc., in Italy.

Suif (Fr.)
Suet ; tallow.

Suisse, à la (Fr.)
In Swiss style. Usually applied to a variety of iced puddings or moulds served on a sponge cake base and Swiss roll style.

Suki Yaki
Name of a Japanese beef stew containing bamboo sprouts, bean curd, Japanese curry powder, and served with rice.

Sultanas (Sultanes, Fr.)
Small, seedless, sun-dried grapes. Some of the best come to us from Turkey and Australia. The very pale golden ones from California are sulphur bleached, being better in appearance than flavour.

Sundae
Name of a variety of fancy ice creams first made in an American tuck shop as the proprietor's " Sunday special " for the teen-agers. By some fluke the name became " sundae ", and has now been taken to denote almost any ice cream served with a variety of fruits, sauces and syrups.

Suppe (Ger.)
Soup. Kohl Suppe, cabbage soup.

Supper (Souper, Fr.)
A light meal, the last of the day.

Suprême (Fr.)
Superb quality—delicate and refined.

Suprême Sauce
A rich flavoured cream sauce made from well reduced chicken stock to which fresh cream is added to ensure delicacy of flavour. Normal strength chicken stock is usually reduced to a quarter of its volume by rapid boiling, to ensure a really rich, gelatinous Sauce Suprême.

Sureau (Fr.)
See Elderberry.

Surloin
From the French surlonge—meaning " upper loin ". England claims the title " sirloin " (which see.)

Surlonge (Fr.)
See Sirloin and Surloin.

Swan (Cygne, Fr.)
Swans were consumed in large quantities in earlier times and were again marketed in quantity during World War II, more than once appearing on House of Commons menus.
To enjoy swan to the full, the young cygnet is best. Once a year, and in traditional style, cygnets are served at the Vintners' Hall in the City, amidst much pomp and show. When dressed, the swan has the appearance of a dark-coloured goose, but in no way tastes like one. It is well fleshed and carves well.

Swede
A large root vegetable of pleasing flavour. Sometimes referred to as the Swedish turnip. Its skin resembles that of a turnip and its flesh is of yellowish colour.

Swedish Sauce (Sauce Suédoise, Fr.)
See Suédoise.

Sweet
Tasting of sugar. Also the name given to all sweet dishes served at a meal, which in its correct form should be " sweetmeats ", which should be the right wording on the menu.

Sweetbread (Ris, Fr.)
The thymus and pancreas glands of the calf, lamb or any other animal. The glands are divided into the " throat sweetbread " and " heart sweetbread " (or breast sweetbread). The best are those obtained from a young sucking calf. They are very perishable and relatively high-priced, although in preparation for the table there is no waste to them.

Sweetened (Sucré, Fr.)
To make foods more agreeable by the addition of a sweetening agent as sugar, saccharine or syrup.

Sweet Herbs
This term is usually applied to the herbs most frequently used in cookery, such as basil, majoram, mint, parsley, sage, savory and thyme. Where a recipe recommends that a bunch of sweet herbs be used, it is usually understood that it refers to 6 sprigs of parsley, 1 sprig of thyme and a bay leaf, all being tied together. (See also Herbs.)

Sweet Pepper
See Paprika.

Sweet Potato
See Potato, Sweet.

Swift (Hirondelle, Fr.)
In the culinary world, the swift serves a useful purpose in providing the nest from which that highly over-rated Birds'

Nest Soup is made. Otherwise, the bird itself is not used for table purposes. The nests consist essentially of mucus secreted by the bird's remarkable salivary glands.

Swordfish (Espadon, Fr.)
The name which has been attached to this fish in nearly all languages indicates the most striking feature in its formation, namely the cutting and pointed blade, a projection of its muzzle, which threatens everything which approaches it. The swordfish attains a great size, and has been recorded as long as 18 to 20 feet. Specimens occasionally appear off our coasts weighing up to 100 lbs. and are often found stranded, a circumstance which has been explained by the allegation that these fish, being peculiarly exposed to the attacks of various parasitic animals which torment them beyond endurance, cast themselves ashore in despair, to rid themselves at once of their tormentors and their lives.

The colour of the upper parts of the body is a dusky blue ; of the under, a fine silvery-white ; the whole body being covered by a rough skin. It is more like beef than fish, and is dressed like cutlets. It has ever been considered of first-rate quality, is often salted, the tail and fins being most esteemed when fresh.

Syllabub
A light, frothy, whipped, milk punch.

Syrup (Sirop, Fr.)
The juice of fruits or other flavoured liquids saturated with sugar.

T

Tabasco
See Tobasco.

Table d'Hôte (Fr.)
To-day this title is given to a meal consisting of several courses served at a fixed price. Originally it was applied to the table at which the principal meal was served in any catering establishment. Hence the reason for its now being applied to a fixed price luncheon or dinner.

Table Napkin (Serviette, Fr.)
A small towel used at table to protect clothing and for use with the finger bowl at the end of the meal. Originally the dandy type of cuff handkerchief was used for this purpose.

Table Waters
Bottled, natural or mineral waters. See Aerated Waters, Carbonated Waters, Mineral Waters, all of which fall under the one heading of Table Waters.

Tafia
A spirit obtained from the sugar cane similar in character to rum.

Tagliarini (It.)
Very fine, strip-type Italian paste, a third the width of ordinary noodle strips.

Tagliati (It.)
A type of thin noodle paste cut into irregular-shaped pieces.

Tail (Queue, Fr.)
The tail of the ox is used for making what has become one of England's most famous soups, due to its rich gelatinous nature. It is also excellent when served as braised ox tail. Lamb's tail soup is also very rich and considering the number of lambs' tails available it is a wonder this soup is not better developed.

Taillevent
Name of a French chef and author of many culinary works. Taillevent is credited with writing the first treatise on soups which was published in France in 1456.

Talleyrand
Name of a noted old French ducal family, who gave their name to the well-known garnish which accompanies so many meat dishes. The garnish consists of spaghetti mixed with a julienne of truffle and foie-gras blended with Périgueux sauce.

Tallow (Suif, Fr.)
The fat of lamb or mutton. It is stronger in flavour than beef fat.

Talmouse (Fr.)
Name of small individual pastry-like soufflés served as a sweet or savoury course.

Tamale
A Mexican dish consisting of scalded cornmeal, rice or other cereal, chopped meat, sweet red peppers, garlic, wrapped in a plantain leaf, securely fastened and boiled.

Tamara
A form of Italian curry powder made of crushed cloves, cinnamon, aniseed, fennel and coriander seed.

Tamarind (Tamarin, Fr.)
The fruit of an East African tree now cultivated in Florida and many other tropical countries. It consists of a plump brown pod with a brittle shell about 1 inch in width and 8 inches long. The pulp, sweet yet acid in flavour, is the edible portion. Tamarind pulp is used in preserves, chutneys and sauces.

Tammy-cloth (Tamis, Fr.)
A fine linen cloth used for straining sauces and soups which refines them more completely than just passing them through a fine sieve.

Tangelo
A cross between the tangerine and grapefruit, with a well-balanced flavour of both fruits.

Tangerine

A small citrus fruit which has an orange-coloured skin more easily removed than in the true orange. They originated from China and many still refer to them as mandarins. The fruit has a juicy flesh of dark orange colour, with orange-like segments which are readily separated.

Tangoa

A tangerine brandy liqueur.

Tansy

A perennial herb which is little used now but at one time was appreciated as a flavouring for tansy tart.

Tapioca

Not to be confused with sago. A farinacious food made by heating the extracted starch from the manioc root (which see). As the starch is heated the granules burst into irregular pieces. It is then baked to remove all remaining moisture and is then known as flake tapioca.

Tarragon (Estragon, Fr.)

An aromatic herb ; the leaves of pungent flavour. It is employed for flavouring sauces, vinegar and French mustard.

Tarragon Sauce (Sauce Estragon, Fr.)

Espagnole sauce with chopped tarragon.

Tarragon Vinegar

An infusion of fresh tarragon with white wine vinegar.

Tart (Torte, Ger., Tourte, Fr.)

A disc of puff or short pastry baked in a concave tin, the pastry being filled in the centre with preserve or fruits. Tarts of puff pastry sometimes do not need a tin as individual support in baking.

Tartar Mustard

Mustard mixed to a smooth paste with horseradish vinegar.

Tartar Sauce (Sauce Tartare, Fr.)

The basis of this sauce is mayonnaise, to which are added chopped gherkin, capers and parsley. It is then reduced with red or white wine to a free-flowing consistency.

Tartlets (Tourtelettes, Fr.)

Small types of pastries filled with fruits, preserves or custards. Individual tarts.

Tasse (Fr.)

Cup. Consommé en Tasse—consommé served in cups.

Taste

Taste is influenced quite considerably by the temperature of the foods we eat. At low and at high temperatures no sensations of sweetness or bitterness can be experienced at all. Foods taken into the body at 108°F. (liquid or solid) will be tasted to better advantage than those at a higher temperature. Hot stewed fruit often appears too sweet, whereas it seems just right when cooled. Foods taken into the body at 130°F. or over are more likely to cause pain to the palate than pleasure. Ice cream cannot be tasted properly until the tongue has dissolved it to around 65°F. to 85°F. Below this temperature the palate is chilled and unable to function properly. (See also Appetite and Diet.)

Tea (Thé, Fr.)
Tea was introduced to England about 1659. We meet it in Pepys' Diary in 1660 when he tasted his first cup of tea at a cost of some 6 guineas per lb.— truly a staggering price when one considers what the pound sterling was worth in those days. It was not until well into the 18th century that it really began to make headway as the English breakfast beverage. To-day, we consume 50% of the world's exportable surplus of tea, which in 1948 amounted to 426,000,000 lbs., 8.03 lbs. per capita; in 1938 before World War II the consumption was 9.21 lbs. per capita.
All tea falls into one of three general classes—black or fermented, green or unfermented, oolong, or semi-fermented. Black and green tea may be picked from the same plants; the final difference is all due to the manufacturing process. (See also Pekoe.)

Teal (Sarcelle, Fr.)
The teal is a species of wild duck, beautiful in colour and highly esteemed for the table, although few will venture to buy it for the first time. It can be found in fair quantities in northern parts, and reaches the London market about November.
A full-sized bird will only afford a meal for two, and so proves expensive in use for the average housewife. Hence it has never become very popular. It is considered to be flavoured after the frost has set in, and is best from the end of September to January. It may be served according to any recipe given for wild duck, though less time will be required for cooking.

Tench (Tanche, Fr.)
The tench is more of a pond fish than a river fish, but is best when taken from rivers. It is similar to the carp, but smaller, as it seldom weighs more than 4 to 5 lbs.
Because of its love of muddy places, which impart an unpleasant flavour to its flesh, it is best turned into clear water for a day or two. If the fish be found difficult to scale, scald it 30 seconds in boiling water. In season October to May.

Tenderloin
The tender muscle found under the loin of beef, pork or mutton. In the younger animals it is very small.

Tendon

The white gristle, like that which is found in the breast of lamb or veal.

Tendron (Fr.)

See Tendon.

Terrapin (Terrapène, Fr.)

The small American turtle much used for soup. For recipe see page 279 of " The Master Book of Soups ". The diamond-back female is the only one used for food.

Terrine (Fr.)

An earthenware pot or jar used for foie-gras and other such pâtés or potted meats.

Tête (Fr.)

Head.

Tête de Veau (Fr.)

Calf's head.

Tétras (Fr.)

The French grouse, not so well flavoured as Scottish grouse.

Texienne, à la (Fr.)

Texas style. Usually denotes sweet corn or sweet potato as a garnish.

Thé (Fr.)

See Tea.

Theine

An alkaloid found in tea and now identified with caffeine.

Theobroma

A Greek word for chocolate, compounded from two words meaning " food for the gods ".

Theobromine

The stimulating element in chocolate and cocoa.

Thermometer

An instrument for registering cold or heat—zero 0°F. ; freezing point 32°F. ; boiling point 212°F.

Thickening (Liaison, Fr.)

In the culinary world this term is applied to all farinaceous substances capable of rendering liquids thicker. Liaison as generally applied in English kitchens usually signifies a mixture of cream and egg yolks used for thickening the richer type of sauces or soups.

Thon (Fr.)

See Tunny Fish.

Thornback (Raie, Fr.)

The thornback is one of the best known species of ray or skate. There is no chance of mistaking it, as it is at once known by being studded, at intervals, all over the surface, with oval or rounded tubercles which form the base of a strong curved spine. The tail is armed with from one to five rows of such tubercular spines, and a single row runs up the dorsal ridge.

The flesh of the thornback is held in good estimation ; it is in best condition for table September to February. The parts which are referred to as the wings should be cut in strips and laid in salt water for a day or two, to take away the coarse taste which is noticeable when freshly dressed. All recipes for skate are suitable for the thornback.

Thrush (Grive, Fr.)

The thrush was perhaps the most popular bird at feasting times in ancient Greece. When a girl married, she was sure of a brace of thrushes for her own special eating on her wedding day. In Rome, patrician ladies reared thousands of thrushes yearly, to be sold at the markets. The killing of the thrush for food in this country has long been frowned upon, just as killing larks for food is dying out.

When the meat ration dropped to 10d. worth per week in the post-war period, the housewife still found time to toss the crumbs from the breakfast table to these songsters. She never gave thought to their destruction, preferring their song to their death.

Thyme

A sub-shrub cultivated for its fragrant leaves, much used for flavouring, and with parsley and bay leaf is usually found in most stock pots for clear soups. There are many varieties and species, lemon thyme having a delicate lemon flavour and being much used for veal and turkey stuffing.

Tiffin

One-time name for mid-morning refreshment, originating from the Anglo-Indians. As the morning coffee habit grew, it was referred to as tiffin time.

Timbale (Fr.)

Thimble-shaped moulds of preparation of foods.

Tips

The initial letters of a notice usually displayed in old-time taverns, placed against a plate —To Insure Prompt Service. The guests in a hurry would patronise the plate as they came in (not on the way out) to gain priority in service.

Tipsy Cake

The true tipsy cake is made from a tall moulded shape of sponge cake, which is sliced, layered with cream and jam, and soaked in wine or spirit, according to the taste of the guests. It is then coated liberally with whipped cream, studded with blanched almonds, and sometimes decorated with a little preserve. If made properly and soaked well with wine, it will topple over of its own accord half-way through the dinner.

Tiré (Fr.)

Pulled.

Tiré Sucre (Fr.)

See Sugar, Pulled.

Tivoli

A town and episcopal province of Rome. Soups, sauces and garnishings bearing this name usually have semolina or raviolis embodied in their make-up.

Toad-in-the-Hole

The origin of this dish is said to have come about by accident. Many years ago a cook, having prepared a batter pudding, laid it at one end of the table while some cutlets were being chopped. One of the chops sprang up in the air (like a toad) and landed in the batter pudding, unnoticed as to where it had dropped. The pudding was eventually baked, when it was noticed a peculiar hole had been left in the centre and upon investigation the missing cutlet was found richly encased in batter pudding.

To-day we cannot spare cutlets, so we use sausages or any other spare meat.

Toast (Pain Grillé or Pain rôti, Fr.)

Slices of bread subjected to direct heat and crisply browned. In other foods, such as nuts or marshmallow, it means to brown by direct heat.

Tobasco

Name of a very pungent sauce used extensively in Mexico, India and countries of hot climate. Of recent years it has found favour in England to touch up vegetable juice cocktails such as the tomato juice cocktail. It is wrong to use it with oysters, as its pungency spoils the delicate flavour of the oyster.

Toddy

A type of rum punch made by the glass and not in a bowl.

Toffee

Hard-boiled sugar to which are usually added butter and flavouring ingredients.

Tokay (Tokai, Fr.)

A rich, sweet, aromatic Hungarian wine. It is regarded as the wine with the longest keeping qualities.

Tom and Jerry

Name of an American egg punch.

Tomato (Tomate, Fr.)

Tomatoes were first mentioned by a Netherlands herbalist as early as 1583, who described them as a vegetable to be eaten with pepper, salt and oil. In Italy it was called the golden apple, in France the apple of love, and in England the love apple. This title is said to have been originated by Sir Walter Raleigh, who initiated the custom of giving a tomato plant to one's sweetheart as a token of love, and he gave a very fine plant to Queen Elizabeth.

There are many kinds of tomatoes, ranging from the small currant tomato to large specimens weighing up to 1 lb. Tomatoes are low in food value, but are popular because of their piquant tart flavour and bright colour.

Tongue (Langue, Fr.)
Considered one of the most popular of meat delicacies. All types of animal tongues form excellent and tasty food. Canned luncheon tongue usually consists of the tongues of sheep or pigs. Ox tongue, as its name implies, is the tongue of ox or cow.

Tonic Water
Carbonated table water containing quinine, usually added to gin to make a long drink.

Tonka Bean
A dark aromatic seed pod of a South American tree. It has an aroma similar to that of the vanilla bean and is used extensively for cheap imitation essence of vanilla.

Topinambour (Fr.)
See Jerusalem Artichoke.

Torbay Sole
Just another name for lemon sole, when the true Dover soles are in short supply.

Torte (Ger.)
See Tart.

Tortillas
Very thin cakes prepared from ground manioc (which see) which are consumed as a form of bread in Mexico.

Tortue (Fr.)
See Turtle.

Tortue Claire (Fr.)
Clear turtle.

Tortue Fausse (Fr.)
Mock turtle.

Tortue Liée (Fr.)
Thick turtle.

Tortue Vraie (Fr.)
Real turtle.

Tot
A drinking vessel holding $\frac{1}{2}$ pint.

Tôt-fait (Fr.)
See Flapjack.

Toulouse, à la (Fr.)
Toulouse style. Toulouse is a city of south-western France, noted for its wine, grain, oil and farm produce. Vol-au-vents or Bouchées à la Toulouse are filled with a white stew of veal or chicken with mushrooms and truffles, or the mixture may be used as a garnish for other dishes.

Tourne-broche (Fr.)
See Turnspit.

Tournedos (Fr.)
Small fillet steaks cut thinner than filet mignon, so cut for quick cooking, and for this purpose they are usually cut from the tenderloin. (See Mignon.)

Tourte (Fr.)
See Tart.

Tourtelettes (Fr.)
See Tartlets.

Tourtière (Fr.)
A baking dish for covered pies or tarts.

Toxins
Poisons of bacterial origin. Virulent poisons causing ptomaine poisoning.

Tragacanth
See Gum Tragacanth.

Trail
The entrails or intestines.

Traiteur (Fr.)
Caterer in food.

Tranche, en (Fr.)
In slices.

Treacle
Molasses (which see).

Treble Palma
The finest quality in sherry.

Trenette
Italian macaroni paste cut in fine shreds, half the width of Fettuccelle.

Trianon, à la (Fr.)
Trianon style. A garnish for poultry and game consisting of three different-coloured vegetables served with demi-glace sauce, vegetables like carrots, peas and potatoes, or tomatoes, green beans and turnips.

Trichinosis
No matter what cut of pork you select, or by what method you cook it, there is one rule which you must observe, and that is, pork must always be cooked until it is white right through. Pink pork is always dangerous, because pork has an unfortunate tendency to be inhabited by tiny wormlike parasites, which cause the hog no apparent discomfort, but which may, if eaten, give one a dangerous and painful disease known as trichinosis. Cooking pork until it is white clear through kills the trichinæ and makes the meat entirely safe to eat. There is no danger of contracting trichinosis unless one takes stupid chances and eats pink pork. So remember, please, pork must always be thoroughly cooked until it is white right through.

Trifle
A dessert sweet, composed of sponge cake spread with jam and soaked in wine, interlayered with macaroons and topped with cream. There are many varied versions of trifle, such as sherry trifle, fruit trifle, chocolate, coffee, etc.

Trim
To cut away ragged or unsightly parts of the food before or after cooking, to improve its appearance for eye appeal.

Tripe
The fatty inner lining of the first and second stomachs of beef animals. That from the second stomach is more delicate. It is prepared by thorough cleaning and boiling. It lacks flavour, which is made up during the final cooking process. It should be thick, white and fat. If dark and thin it is of poor quality.

Tronçon (Fr.)
Small, dainty slice.

Tronçon de Saumon (Fr.)
Slice of middle-cut salmon.

Trout (Truite, Fr.)

River trout and sea trout both belong to a royal family of unquestioned greatness, who reign over every feast of distinction. There is the bull trout or grey trout, which is the largest next to the true salmon, often measuring between 2 and 3 feet and weighing from 5 or 6 to 20 lbs. It is not so elegant in shape as the salmon.

Next we have the salmon trout, or sea trout. This species rivals the salmon in the elegance of its form, and is almost as highly valued for the table.

Then we have the common trout. This beautiful species is among the most familiarly known of our fresh-water fish, and is distributed not only throughout our own island but over the whole of Northern Europe, and so plentiful that there is scarcely a collection of water of any extent, whether running or static, in which it does not occur in more or less abundance. Although its flesh has not the rich flavour of the salmon and sea trout, it is still in request as a highly palatable and wholesome food. The most striking characteristic of the common trout is the profusion of bright red spots with which its sides are speckled. These, in combination with its other brilliant hues, render it when newly taken from the water an exceedingly beautiful fish.

There are also the lake trout, which are distinct as a species from other trout.

As a rule, sea trout and the larger trout should be treated as salmon. Small trout of no more than 4 ozs. each should be fried in butter, as the only satisfactory method of dealing with them. (See also Salmon Trout.)

Truffle (Truffe, Fr.)

A variety of fungus which grows in clusters underground, with no part visible above ground. In addition to their excellent flavour, their black colour makes effective garnishings.

Truite au Bleu (Fr.)

Plain trout cooked to the turn. The essential point is that the fish must be alive when it reaches the kitchen for all its natural beauty to be retained. (See also Au Bleu.)

Truite Saumonée (Fr.)

See Salmon Trout.

Truss

To make fast the wings and legs of birds to the body by means of skewers and string—to draw tight and tie as a bundle.

Tubetti (It.)

Small hollow thin elbow shapes of macaroni, recognised as the thinnest elbow macaroni.

Tuica

A Rumanian liqueur flavoured with rum.

Tun

A large cask containing 210 imperial gallons.

Tunny Fish (Thon, Fr.)

Tunny fish seems to improve in a tin, from which it emerges with far more flavour than it possessed when fresh. It is familiar around the Mediterranean, and can be seen in the London markets from time to time, whither it is sent principally from Scarborough, where the sport of tunny fishing has been carried on for many years. The fish are so large when consigned to the London markets that quite a lot of difficulty and expense are experienced in transporting them, so as to make it hardly worth while to handle them. Usually they are used as a show piece, and finally end up on a manure heap, for want of buyers.

The flesh of this fish is of a red colour, like that of salmon, and is considered rich in flavour. When fried in the form of cutlets, it has the strongest resemblance to veal. Old males are sometimes taken weighing up to 18 cwts.

The form of the tunny is similar to that of the mackerel. The upper part of the body is dark blue, the corselet much lighter, the sides of the head white, silvery-spotted, the first dorsal, pectoral and ventral fins black, the tail paler, the finlets yellowish, tipped with black.

Turban

Ornamental dishes of fish, poultry, meat or game, formed in the shape of a turban for the centre to receive a garnish of some suitable mixture. Individual fillets of fish can be set in turban moulds and when cooked the centre is filled with shrimps, mussels, or the like.

Turbot (Turbot, Turbotin, Fr.)

Turbot should never be boiled, but poached, simmered or steamed. To enjoy at its best, cover with cold water (seasoned with herbs and a few drops of vinegar or white wine), bring to the boil and then stop the boiling at once, maintaining the temperature at just below boiling point until cooked.

The turbot spawns in autumn, and is best for the table during summer (April to August). It is considered an extremely choice food, and is most particular in its feeding habits. This occasions a good deal of trouble to fishermen, who are thus obliged to keep their bait always in a fresh state.

The ordinary length of the turbot is 18 inches to 2 feet, and the weight from 4 to 10 lbs. Individuals of 70 and even 190 lbs. have been met with. Small turbots are known as chicken turbots. The demand for this fish is quite extensive, due to its exquisite flavour. It is white, fat, flaky and delicate. It has exercised the skill and ingenuity of the great professors of gastronomy in a variety of culinary preparations from the time of Apicius down to that of the great Escoffier. Its favourite accompaniment is shrimp or lobster sauce.

Turbotin (Fr.)
Chicken turbot.

Turkey, Hen, Cock (Dinde, Dindon, Fr.)
Turkeys to be at their best should be hung fully a week before being dressed, if weather permits. During the process of hanging, if the weather be exceptionally cold, the bird should not be allowed to become frozen, or it will lose flavour.

The turkey is the most savoury of domestic poultry. It enjoys the singular advantage of assembling round it every class of society, and usually commands a high price, especially at Christmas, when rather extravagant prices are often asked and obtained for large well-fed Norfolk or Irish birds. They are in season from October to March and are at their best from December to end of January. However, modern refrigeration allows us to enjoy imported Hungarian and other European birds all the year round.

Incidentally, the true original turkey is what we now call guinea fowl, which was first introduced from West Africa long before the turkey (as we now wrongly call it) had been seen in Europe. When the turkey (which was then a much smaller bird) was eventually brought into this country, it was erroneously given the name already held by the guinea fowl. This no doubt came about by its similar feather markings, some considering it just a larger type of guinea fowl, until the difference in its flavour became well known.

It's turkey—it's good ! is a favourite expression. This expression can be traced back to the days when the vast Turkish Empire was a great commercial nation—as well as a fascinating one—and if something tasted extra good or looked beautiful, people in foreign countries readily believed that it came from Turkey. The first turkeys appeared in England when Cortez, the Conqueror of Mexico, sent some back to Charles V who, like most monarchs of that period, adored his stomach. It's turkey—it's good, was a slang phrase in those times.

Of the imported frozen kinds, undoubtedly the Hungarian are the best ; those imported from Ireland are mostly chilled and not frozen. Frozen birds are inclined to eat dry if cooked too quickly. It is wise to measure the oven before buying a handsome bird.

Turkey Poult (Dindonneau, Fr.)
A young turkey.

Turkish Delight
A sweetmeat of Turkish origin. A soft, jelly-like confection usually made in two colours and flavours, lemon and raspberry, cut into cubes and dusted with sherbet powder.

Turmeric (Curcuma, Fr.)
An aromatic rootstock of a plant grown in India and southern Asia. Its hard, resinous flesh when powdered forms the principal ingredient of curry powder. Its pigment is marketed as a dyestuff called curcumin.

Turn (Tourner, Fr.)
The expression to turn vegetables means to pare or trim them to a small size, especially where required for garnishing a dish.

Turnip (Navet, Fr.)
A common root vegetable of varying shape—long, round and squat—being white or yellow in colour. England favours the white turnip for the table, the yellow usually being referred to as the Swedish turnip. It has a pronounced flavour that blends well with chicken. Turnips are low in food value, being about 90% water, but their mineral content is good. Their iron, copper, calcium and phosphorus are in easily assimilated form.

Turnip Tops
Turnip leaves contain no oxalic acid. Quickly-grown turnip tops are excellent as greens and are particularly valuable for their minerals. They may be served raw as salads.

Turnspit (Tourne-broche, Fr.)
A revolving spit for cooking meat, fowl or game birds. Much used in olden times before the introduction of modern coal, gas or electric ovens. The meat was placed on a long iron prong and hung in front of the open fire.
Young boys were specially employed to keep the spit on the turn. Later, special revolving cages were built and basset hounds were used to keep these revolving, which in turn, turned the spit. Hence in some parts of France the tourne-broche is better known as the Basset (which see).

Turtle (Tortue, Fr.)
Turtle is not a fish, say the purists. However, it should not be confused with the land tortoise.
The turtle is much esteemed for its glutinous quality, which the Chinese prize so highly, and for definite reasons. Its aphrodisiac powers have been written about for many centuries. The green turtle is very much prized as a luxury and is used extensively for turtle soup (see the " Master Book of Soups ").

Turtles vary in weight from 30 lbs. to 500 lbs. and must reach this country alive to be of any use. Turtles which die on their way to this country, and are cold stored, are known in the trade as " angels ". The most prized of the edible portions of the green turtle are the outer circumferences of its two heavy shells—the upper known as " calipash " and the lower as " calipee ". That of the upper shell—so solid and tough that it adequately protects the living creature from any enemy save man—becomes in cooking the dull green, delicate, gelatinous substance which gives character and fame to " Green Turtle Soup ". Calipee is similarly gelatinous, but is lighter and yellowish. For fine soup, only the calipash and calipee are used. Only the " cow " green turtle is generally sought after, the shell of the bull not being considered worth while cooking, as its flesh is so coarse. The bull is easily recognised by its long tail. The best steaks are from the lean flesh under the top shell. The colour of the raw meat is somewhat like veal.

Green turtle eggs are considered a delicacy. (See also Mock Turtle.)

Tutti-frutti (It.)
An Italian term applied to fruits or vegetables cut small as for salad. In this country the term is confined to diced fruits served with ice cream.

Twelfth Cake (or Bean Feast)
For origin see Bean Feast.

Tyrolienne (Fr.)
Name given to a style of garnish consisting of fried onion rings and sliced tomatoes fried in butter. Also name of a cold, tomato-flavoured, mayonnaise sauce, used with fish.

Tzarine (Fr.)
Name given to a garnish for poultry which consists of small balls of cucumber cooked in cream sauce.

U

Ucha or Ouha
A Russian fish soup of which sturgeon forms the principal ingredient.

Udder
The cow's udder is indeed a most savoury dish. It should be prepared in the same manner as Escalopes of Veal and forms the most excellent Schnitzel. It is very easy of digestion. (See also Crepinette, Fr.)

Udo
An Oriental plant valued for its young blanced shoots similar in character to asparagus. They are sliced thin and allowed to soak in iced water for two hours, to reduce the pine flavour, and then served with French Dressing. They are very good keeping and can be stored for winter use.

Ullage
Meaning no longer full. A cask or bottle which has become defective and lost some of its contents.

Umble (Fr.)
See Ombre.

Umbre (Fr.)
See Ombre (Fr.) and Grayling.

Universelle, a l' (Fr.)
Universal style. This name, given to a sauce, comprises a highly spiced cold sauce for meats, poultry and game. Its foundation is mushroom ketchup mixed with port wine, vinegar, spices, chopped shallot and anchovy essence.

Usquebach
A potent Irish drink, made of highly spiced brandy left to infuse for a fortnight. Also the original Celtic name for whisky.

Uvaggio
A cheap Italian wine.

V

Vacuum Packed
Coffee, fats, oil, etc. which may lose their flavour by oxidation, are packed in cans from which the air is extracted and then hermetically sealed.

Vairon (Fr.)
See Minnow.

Valence (Fr.)
Valencia. Name of a maritime province of eastern Spain. Also the name of the capital of the province, noted for its oranges, onions and vineyards. It usually denotes that oranges form part of the dish.

Valenciennes
A town of northern France, which should not be confused with Valencia when wording menus. Valenciennes has extensive beetroot cultivation. Consommé Valenciennes is garnished with boiled rice, chervil, and served with grated cheese.

Van der Hum
A South African liqueur. Its chief flavour is obtained from the nartje or South African tangerine.

Vandoise (Fr.)
See Dace.

Vanilla (Vanille, Fr.)
The vanilla plant is of the orchid family ; its fruit is the vanilla bean. The beans are chopped or ground and allowed to stand in a solution of alcohol and water until the desired flavour is developed. This depends upon the quality of the beans, which are graded and sold from 50 to 60 lbs. per 1,000 beans in their original state, and which ultimately fall to as low as 12 lbs. per 1,000 by the time they reach the distillery.

Vanneau (Fr.)
See Lapwing.

Vatel
Name of a famous French chef who committed suicide rather than face his master, Louis XIV of France, when food for a special banquet was not ready to time. Certain fish dishes bear his name, such as the clear soup he perfected, consisting of rich fish broth garnished with crayfish royale and fillets of sole, flavoured with white wine. Fillets of Sole Vatel are fillets poached with Chambord sauce and garnished with cucumber chunks.

Veal (Veau, Fr.)
The dressed carcase of a calf, which has less fat than beef and much more connective tissues. Because of this, it requires more attention during cooking, which should be a slower process than cooking beef. The flesh should be pink and firm, the fat clear white, the bones red. A good milk-fed calf will weigh up to 135 lbs.; over this it is not so good.

Veau (Fr.)
See Veal and Noix de Veau.

Vegetable (Légume, Fr.)
If eaten fresh and cooked properly, vegetables as a whole are valuable for the minerals and vitamins they contribute to bone and tooth structure, for the bulk and acids which stimulate intestinal activity, for their laxative properties and for maintaining alkaline reserve in the body.
Beans, peas, beets, greens and potatoes are highly nutritious. Vegetables should find their way into soups, sauces, pies, stews, omelettes and salads. Long over-cooking should be avoided.

Vegetable Gelatine
See Agar-Agar.

Vegetable Marrow (Courge, Fr.)
A variety of squash. The best are 12 inches in length and 6 inches in diameter—more than this, they become woolly and lose flavour. If not over-boiled, its flesh is sweet, nutty and tender; over-cooked, it is valueless as a food and almost tasteless.

Velouté (Fr.)
With a smooth velvet finish, Velouté sauce being one of the four mother sauces which form the basis of all others. It is in fact a " Sauce Suprême ", being a very rich white sauce made from well-reduced chicken stock with added cream. Crème Velouté is a rich cream soup finished with a liaison of cream and egg yolks.

Venaison (Fr.)
See Venison.

Venison (Venaison, Fr.)

Venison is the culinary term for the flesh of all kinds of deer. That of plump, natural forest-fed animals is considered the choicest. Stall-fed venison is poor and coarse when compared with that brought in from its natural haunts. The meat of the deer is improved by moderate hanging, but care must be taken to see that it is not so old as to be stale. Indications of staleness are an offensive smell under the kidneys, the vein in the neck will be green or yellow instead of a bluish hue. Venison, to be kept, should be wiped dry and dusted with powdered ginger and hung cut end up, in a cool airy place. Flour may be used for dusting if the meat is to be kept for no longer than a week. A haunch of venison consists of the hindquarter—the leg and loin. The best-end neck piece is considered next in order of merit to the haunch. All other parts are best used for casserole or pies, being unsuitable for roasting. The head and trimmings make excellent soup. (See also Deer.)

Venitienne, à la (Fr.)

Venetian style. As a sauce, it is rich white, enriched with cream and yolks of egg, mixed with lemon juice, chopped parsley and mushrooms. Consommé Venitienne consists of cleared veal broth garnished with tiny cheese quenelles.

Verder

A type of milk punch, originating from the southern borders of France.

Verjuice (Verjus, Fr.)

The extracted juice of green or unripe fruit, usually applied to unripe grape or apple juice which flows with a green tint. In olden times, considered a pleasant beverage, but now used only for culinary purposes.

Vermicelli (It., Vermicelle, Fr.)

Vermicelli, spaghetti, macaroni and similar pastes, are considered as typical Italian foods. There are nearly 100 different varieties, varying in shape and thickness. The very finest shreds fall under the heading of vermicelli; next comes spaghettini, then spaghetti, foratini, forati, mezzanelli, mezzani, macaroni, and the large, tubular zitoni. In England we place them under the three headings —vermicelli, spaghetti, macaroni. (See Macaroni and Noodles.)

Vermouth

The two principal vermouths come to us from Italy and France and of the two the Italian is undoubtedly the better. The Italian is a white wine which possesses certain tonic qualities, as it is infused with certain aromatic herbs. French vermouth is cheap white wine infused with camomile flowers.

R

Véron (Fr.)
See Minnow.

Véronese (Fr.)
Verona style—Verona, a town of Italy. Veronese sauce comprises a blend of Béarnaise and Velouté sauces, with a dash of anchovy essence.

Vert, Verte (Fr.)
Green. Sauce Verte is a green herb sauce.

Vert-pré (Fr.)
Name of a green coloured sauce consisting of a cream sauce with plenty of green herbs. Also applied to green coloured garnishings as spinach purée or cream sauce blended with lettuce purée.

Viand (Viande, Fr.)
Article of food, the French word meaning meat.

Vichy (Fr.)
Name of a style of garnish consisting of sliced carrots cooked in cream.

Vichy Water
A natural mineral water obtained from springs in the valley of the Allier, near Vichy. The best type for the table is Vichy Celestins. Other types are drunk only on medical advice.

Villeroi (Francois de Neufville, (Fr.)
Famous marshal of France in the 17th century. Several dishes are named in his honour, sometimes misspelt Villeroy. Fillets of Sole Villeroi are fillets stuffed, rolled and poached, cooled, egg and crumbed and fried; served with tomato sauce.

Vin (Fr.)
See Wine.

Vinaigre (Fr.)
See Vinegar.

Vinaigre de Framboises (Fr.)
Raspberry vinegar.

Vinaigrette (Fr.)
A sauce or salad dressing made of oil, vinegar, salt and pepper.

Vin Blanc (Fr.)
White wine. Au vin blanc—with or cooked in white wine, as Sole au Vin Blanc.

Vinegar (Vinaigre, Fr.)
In French, " vin-aigre " means sour wine, from which all good vinegar should be derived. Most of the commercial product is a dilute acetic acid made from distilled alcohol or by fermentation with malt. Sweetened wine vinegar can be satisfactorily substituted for wine in any recipe where wine is stated. (See also French Vinegar.)

Vin Rouge (Fr.)
Red wine. Au vin rouge—with or cooked in red wine.

Vintage
The yearly gathering of grapes for wine.

Violet (Violette, Fr.)
Crystallized violets are used in large quantities for decorating cakes, chocolates and dessert sweets. When crystallized they retain their dark-blue colour and most of their delicate perfume.

Vitamins
The word implies a substance necessary to the maintenance of life. This food element is found in various forms in plants and animal fats and tissue.
Vitamin A is found in animal fats, fish oils and green, leafy vegetables, etc. ; vitamin B in cereals, animal tissues, fruits, nuts, etc. ; vitamin C in fresh vegetables and citrus fruits ; vitamin D in fats, liver, oysters, fat fish and sunshine. Vitamin E is found in nearly all types of food, especially so in wheat, corn, watercress and glandular organs ; vitamin G in most plant and animal life—milk, eggs, vegetables, fruit and meat.

Vitellin
The chief protein in egg yolk.

Vlattero
A sweet, very pleasing Greek liqueur, with a delicate, dried currant flavour.

Vodka
A potable spirit chiefly distilled in Russia from potatoes. It is colourless and practically tasteless. At one time only distilled from rye.

Voison
Name of a one-time Paris restaurateur who gave his name to a number of French dishes. Potage Voison is a mixture of purée of peas and carrots garnished with boiled rice.

Volaille (Fr.)
Poultry. A term used collectively for all domesticated birds. There is a mistaken idea that it only refers to all types of chicken. Poultry includes ducks, geese, chickens, turkeys, etc. Salade de Volaille, chicken salad.

Volatile
Easily vaporised.

Vol-au-Vent (Fr.)
A figurative expression applied to puff paste of the lightest type, baked in round or oval-shaped cases for receiving a rich combination of cream sauce with poultry, fish or game.

Volière, à la (Fr.)
The term applied to any poultry or game birds when cooked and dressed in their plumage, such as cock pheasant or peacocks.

Vraie Tortue (Fr.)
Real turtle. To distinguish the real thing from tortue fausse, mock turtle.

V.S.O.
The initials given to certain types of brandy, as Very Special Old Brandy.

V.S.O.P.
Very Special Old Pale Brandy.

V.V.S.O.P.
Very, Very Special Old Pale Brandy.

W

Wafer
A thin leaf of coloured rice mixture baked in wafer irons. Copied from the thin cake of unleavened bread used in the Eucharist. Its commercial production for the ice cream industry has grown tremendously. Made in oblong shape for ice cream sandwiches or in cone shape for ice cream cornets or cups.

Waffles
Rich, light, spongy batter confections baked between two electrically heated plates, which may be served with almost any type of food such as ham, syrup, eggs, beans, spaghetti, etc. The origin of this light confection is copied from the French gaufre, which was a similar mixture baked on irons, dipped into deep fat and fried.

Walewska
Name of a style of garnish for fish consisting of sliced lobster and truffles cooked in white wine. After a Polish lady of rank by whom Napoleon had a son.

Walnut (Noix, Fr.)
The nut of a green husked fruit with a brittle shell which is easily cracked. Walnuts are more astringent than other nuts and may discolour when combined with other foods. This discoloration is harmless but looks objectionable in creams and sauces.

Most of the walnuts which reach this country come from France or Italy. Those from France are generally known as Grenobles. The best Italian are the Sorrentos. The green whole nuts, gathered before the enclosed nut-shells harden, make excellent pickle or relish. Walnut shells are made into charcoal, which is used to a large extent by the vinegar industry as a clarifier.

Walnut Oil
An oil of nutty flavour used extensively in Germany and Switzerland in place of olive oil.

Wasabi
A Japanese plant the root of which is used in a similar manner to English horseradish, it having an agreeable, sharp taste.

Washington
Name given to a style of garnish consisting of sweet corn cooked in double cream.

Wassail Bowl
A beverage consisting of strong ale, roasted apples, ginger, nutmeg and other spices. At one time served specially on Christmas Eve to carol singers.

Water (Eau, Fr.)
Water is the second most essential factor for the continuance of life. Air is first. Without air, we can live but a few minutes, and it is interesting to note that air is all about us, requires little effort to get, and is free. We can live without water for a few days, and although it is not as free as air, it has, in its natural state, been free, close at hand, and relatively abundant. In fact, most life has been grouped about places where there was easy access to water. As our civilization has advanced, however, water made free of contamination, put into pipes, has become an item of considerable cost to many.

Chemically pure water is a compound resulting from the combination by volume of two parts of hydrogen and one part oxygen, constituting between 75% and 90% of all tissues. (See also Aerated, Carbonated and Mineral Waters.)

Watercress (Cresson de Fontaine, Fr.)
A semi-aquatic plant of pungent, spicy flavour, which makes it popular as a salad green. It is generally raised under cultivation with slowly moving water which must be free from any contamination. It is rich in mineral salts and vitamins A, B, C and G. First grown in Germany.

Water Hen (Poule d'Eau, Fr.)
See Moor Hen.

Water Melon
See Melon, Water.

Wedding Cake (Gâteau de Noce, Fr.)
A richly decorated cake provided by the bride's parents for the guests at a wedding, a custom which finds its origin in the Roman form of marriage, the essential feature being a cake made of flour, salt and water, and the holding by the bride of three wheat-ears symbolical of plenty (see Ceres). Later these cakes were made biscuit style and took the form of rectangular cakes containing spices and fruits which in time were coated with sugar until to-day we have cakes which are a real work of art, which are taking on colours away from the traditional white, a symbol of purity.

Weinbeeresuppe (Ger.)
Name of a German soup made of grapes, tapioca and yolk of egg.

Weinschaumsuppe (Ger.)
Name of a German wine soup.

Weissbiersuppe (Ger.)
Name of a German ale soup.

Welsh Rarebit or **Rabbit**
Dry cheese melted with beer or ale and spread on slices of toast. Seasonings are added as desired. If the cheese be too moist, it will not absorb enough ale, which is the secret of the rarebit.

Wensleydale Cheese

Wensleydale is considered by many as one of the most subtly flavoured of all the English cheeses; it has a honeyed after-taste. When in prime condition it should be quite spreadable and should readily melt in the mouth. Made in the vale of Wensleydale.

Westmoreland, Baron Neville

Awarded his earldom in 1397. Several dishes bear his name, which no doubt were created during the French expedition of 1380, in which he took prominent part.

Wether

A castrated ram.

Wey

As a measure of weight for food it equals 48 bushels oats, or 40 bushels salt or corn.

Whale Meat

Many people are not certain whether whale meat is fish or flesh. The whale is, of course, a mammal, and its flesh is classed as meat and not fish. Its proper name should be Sea Beef, which would dispel the confusion.

For those seeking advice on how to cook it to its best advantage, I give the following hints: The flesh of the whale should be frozen as soon as possible, and kept frozen right to the moment it is required for the cooking preparation. In this state, if pot-roasted, braised, or cut up and cooked in casserole, its flavour resembles that of beef. Otherwise, if it is allowed to thaw out too long in advance, it develops a fishy taste. In its early stages, this fishiness is pleasantly suggestive of salmon; if unchecked, it becomes over-strong. The flavour may be removed by immersing the raw meat in a solution of bicarbonate of soda, or by a preliminary parboiling with a sliced onion and then straining off any oil which it may emit. Remember—buy your whale meat in a frozen state, and keep it frozen till required, for best results.

Wheat

Next to rice, wheat is the most widely used grain for human consumption, due to the excellence of its flour for bread-making. The quality of a flour depends on the wheat selected. The hard wheats are heavy with gluten and yield a creamy-coloured flour. The soft wheats contain less gluten and give a whiter flour.

Flour was made in the Stone Age, 20,000 years ago, by crushing wheat between stones. (See also Flour.)

Wheatear (Cul Blanc, Fr.)

Wheatears are in season end of July to October. They should be dressed the same day as killed and treated like quails. They used to be trapped in considerable quantities on the Downs in Surrey, Sussex and Kent. They arrive quite early to this country and are soon busy nesting. The older birds are not such good fare, but before they migrate the first year birds will be found very good eating.

Whelk (Pou de Mer, Fr.)

Whelks should be procured alive and cleansed in fresh water for several hours. They are a large species of periwinkle, about the size of a hen's egg, and if too large are rather tough to eat.

Boil them in salt and water for 1¼ hours—or better still, take them out of their shells, dredge with flour, dip in well-beaten egg, roll into fresh breadcrumbs, and fry them. Take them up, sprinkle with salt, pepper and a little vinegar.

Whewer

See Widgeon.

Whey (Petit Lait, Fr.)

The uncoagulated product of milk remaining after the removal of casein, fat, etc. in the manufacture of cheese. It is a pale chalky colour, consisting of water and milk sugar chiefly, and forms a pleasing cooling beverage.

Whipped (Fouetté, Fr.)

Cream, eggs, jelly, or such liquid foods, beaten rapidly to incorporate air and produce expansion. (See also Cream, Whipped.)

Whisky (Eau-de-vie de Grain, Fr.)

A potable grain spirit obtained by the distillation of the fermented extract of malted grain. The Scotch and Irish are distilled from malted barley, Bourbon from maize, while others, such as rye whisky, are distilled from other grain.

Whitebait (Blanchaille, Fr.)

What is whitebait ? It is the fry of the common herring, a delicate morsel so highly esteemed by epicures. It is a small, silvery-looking fish, about 1 inch or more in length. It first makes its appearance in March, and is at its best in May, July and August. It needs to be procured perfectly fresh and in unbroken condition. If not to be used immediately, it should be rinsed in iced water and stored at 40°F. in the refrigerator.

Whitebait is served either fried or devilled, with cayenne, quartered lemons, and brown bread and butter.

Whiting (Merlan, Fr.)

Whiting when fresh is an excellent and delicate fish, tender and easy of digestion, but practically tasteless. It is obtainable all the year round, and at its best during the winter months, principally October to March, but unfortunately it is not a good keeping fish. When fresh, the eyes are bright and clear, the fish fairly rigid, and the colour a beautiful silver.

Whiting should not be marketed if more than 1½ lbs., the best being about 10 inches long. It is contrary to law to take the fish less than 6 inches long.

Whiting are occasionally boiled, but they are best when grilled or fried. It is usual to skin the fish before frying, and fasten the tail between its teeth or eye-holes.

Whortleberry (Airelle Myrtille, Fr.)

Another name for the bilberry or blaeberry (which see).

Widgeon (Macreuse or Canard Siffleur, Fr.)

The widgeon is a wild duck, about one-third larger than the teal, but smaller than the mallard. The common widgeon is still quite plentiful in Britain during the winter, and because of its clean feeding its flesh is quite good. The name widgeon is now given to both sexes, but at one time the female was known as the whewer.

It is in season from the beginning of August to the middle of March, but considered best in October and November, after which it becomes a little coarse eating, although the amount of flesh has increased in proportion to its bone.

Wiener Schnitzel (Ger.)

See Schnitzel.

Wild Boar (Sanglier, Fr.)

Wild boar hunting was a prominent sport of our forefathers and its flesh found its way on to all the principal banqueting tables. Boar's head was the pièce de résistance at the first banquet after each kill, and tradition has left us with the famous dish consisting of a domesticated boar's head served at principal hunt balls and prominent banquets. (See also, Boar's Head and Hûre de Sanglier.)

Wild Duck (Canard Sauvage, Fr.)

It has been said that a wild duck should be allowed only to fly through the hot kitchen before it is sent to table. This, of course, is an exaggeration. All the same, wild duck is considered to be in perfection only when it is well crisped and browned on the surface and so underdone that the gravy flows freely when it is cut. Notwithstanding the slightly fishy flavour of its flesh, the breast is a dainty morsel. The legs are best used in an entrée.

The wild duck in these Isles is, of course, the mallard. It is in season August to March, but in perfection in November and December, after which the flesh takes on a certain coarseness with its age and the fishy flavour becomes more pronounced. Because of this, only the breast is considered fit to serve as a roast, and as the wild duck is smaller than the fattened domesticated bird, allow 1 bird for 2 persons, or 2 birds for 5 persons.

For description for its recognition, see Mallard.

Wild Rice
See Rice, Wild.

Windberry
Another name for the bilberry or blaeberry (which see).

Wine (Vin, Fr.)
Fermented juice of grapes, which varies in colour and sweetness according to the colour of grape used and its sugar content. Wines made from grapes with a small sugar content are called dry wines. Climate and soil also have a deciding influence on its final quality.

Wintergreen
A low-growing shrub with evergreen leaves, from which a volatile oil is distilled employed in confectionery and medicine. Its leave are used sometimes as a substitute for tea (then known as mountain tea). Its red double berries are reputed to possess medicinal virtue as a tonic.

Witch (Carrelet, Fr.)
The witch has very many aliases, including witch flounder, witch sole and fluke, and is chiefly sold as plaice or sole, when these two fish are in short supply.

The body is very thin and the lateral line runs directly down the middle. The outline of the head inclines to circular ; the jaws are nearly equal and each is finished with a single row of small regular teeth. The length of this fish is much greater in proportion to the breadth than that of most flat fish. The fins are soft, the rays not projecting, and the dorsal and anal extend to the very root of the tail. The one side of the fish is a very light brown, the other white. The white side of the fish is very rough to the touch if the fingers be rubbed from the tail end to the head, in fact, so rough that even if fillets of this fish be sold as a substitute for plaice or sole, they can be detected blindfolded by the test described.

All recipes for sole are suitable for cooking witch, but do not expect the same flavour or softness of flesh.

Woandsu
A recently discovered food plant, native to tropical Africa, resembling the pea-nut, which furnishes a white flour, which when cooked has a pleasant chestnut flavour and considerable food value.

Woodcock (Bécasse, Fr.)
The woodcock has been described as the queen of the game birds and has excited the pens of French gourmets to the

highest raptures. Here is a rare bird highly treasured for its unusual flavour.

The woodcock still breeds in this country, but large numbers arrive from overseas in late autumn and stay here till March, when they become quite plentiful on the market. Woodcock, like snipe, are only good when they are fat, and are best October—November. They are held in high esteem when roasted, but the art in roasting a woodcock is to cook the legs well done and the breast under-done. This was easy in the days of the spit, for the birds used to be halted with their backs to the fire, to allow the legs to receive the heat while protecting the breast. To-day, with our press button stoves, we cover the breast with a blanket and leave the legs exposed, and so get the same result.

Woodcocks are not drawn, for the intestines are the most delicate part and paper should be used to secure them in the roasting process or they must be cooked on toast for it to receive them.

Wood Pigeon (Ramier, Fr.)

Wood pigeons need hanging till tender before being dressed. Only year-olds are fit for roasting. The older birds should be cooked en salmi (as a hash) or as steak and pigeon pie. They may be roasted and cooked in any manner described for the common dove-cote bird.

Woodruff

A small plant bearing white flowers. Its dried leaves possess a perfume suggestive of new-mown hay. It is used on a large scale in Germany for flavouring beverages.

Worcestershire Sauce

Ready - made, very dark - coloured, pungent sauce. If of good quality it contains soy as its chief character ingredient.

Wormwood

Said to be the bitterest of all herbs. Used in the manufacture of absinthe and in tonic bitters. In early times it was considered that an infusion of its dried leaves prevented drunkenness.

Wort

An infusion of any liquid in the incipient stage of fermentation.

Wurst

German name for all types of sausage.

X

Xanthurus or Yellow Tail

A fish found in the Caribbean Sea, which resembles the carp in appearance, and attains a length of about 3 feet.

Xavier, Francisco de

It has been said that Xavier should be regarded as the greatest of Christian missionaries since the 1st century A.D. A clear vegetable soup is named after him, which is garnished with tiny cheese quenelles.

Xeres

Name of a town near Cadiz, which gives its name to Vin de Xeres, a strong, deep-coloured, Spanish sherry.

Xymase

An enzyme which ferments sugar into alcohol.

Y

Yablouchni

Name of a Russian chilled apple soup, which is a great favourite in warm weather.

Yaghoust, Yogart

A product of Turkey and Armenia. A fermented milk often so thick that it is eaten instead of drunk. The milk is boiled to half its original volume before setting to ferment. It is then eaten with dates or bread.

Yam

The tuber of a climbing plant. Similar in appearance and taste to the sweet potato, although it belongs to a different family and grows much larger.

Yamadon

An oil extracted from a species of nutmeg.

Yaupon or Carolina Tea

A small tree with leaves of holly style which, when dried and boiled, produce a strong aromatic beverage not unlike very strong tea, containing 7% or 8% of tannin and about 1% of caffeine. Indians travel many miles to collect their yearly supply of the young twigs and leaves.

Yeast (Levure, Fr.)

A substance of vegetable nature being an aggregate of vegetable cells.

Yeast will ferment any food containing sugar but is destroyed by heat and retarded at low temperature. When yeast is added to bread dough it changes the starch in flour to sugar and the sugar is changed into carbon dioxide gas and alcohol; this gas increases the volume of the dough and lightens it, and the alcohol is evaporated during the baking process.

Yellow Tail

See Xanthurus.

Yolande (Fr.)

Name of a particular style of salad for cold meats consisting of carrots, celery, apples and beetroot cut julienne style and mixed with mint sauce.

Yorkshire Pudding

The famous batter pudding of Yorkshire. At one time served as the opening course to the meal and in some households the practice still holds good. Its success depends on thorough beating and amalgamation of flour, eggs and milk, and a good hot oven.

Young Bird

A bird taken or killed in the same year as bred.

Yupon

See Yaupon.

Yvette (Fr.)

Name given to a number of fish dishes finished, " fines-herbes " and garnished with chats stuffed with oyster forcemeat. Also, the name of a French liqueur distilled from violets.

Yvorne

A district of Switzerland noted for its fine wines of the same name which very rarely leave the country, being specially reserved for the busy tourist trade in the best hotels.

Z

Zabaione, Zabyajone or Zabaglione

An Italian wine cream or egg punch. A dessert sweet served in glasses and eaten with a spoon. It is well known all over the world, but in the course of its travels assumed so many different forms that in England it is looked upon as a kind of chocolate dessert sweet.

Zakouska, Zakouski, Zakuska

The Russian title for hors d'œuvre, meaning foretaste.

Zampino

A favourite dish prepared in Italy, consisting of boiled salt pork and French beans. Boned pigs' trotters are stuffed as a salami and are served cold in slices and bear the same name.

Zapotilla

See Sapodilla.

Zein

A protein found in maize (Indian corn).

Zeltingen, Zeltinger

A noted German white wine which, when infused with woodruff, makes very good cups.

Zéphire

Name given to small meat, fish or game forcemeat balls, which are simmered carefully and served in a well-reduced rich sauce.

Zest (Zeste, Fr.)

The thin, oily outer skin of citrus fruits which, when grated or cut thinly, forms delicious flavourings for many culinary dishes. One should avoid the pith immediately beneath, which is bitter in flavour.

Zeste (Fr.)

Flavoured with the zest of citrus fruit.

Zingara Sauce
Espagnole or game sauce blended with tomato purée, shredded truffle and smoked tongue. The name when applied to garniture consists of a julienne of tongue, mushrooms, ham, truffle in Sauce Madère blended with tomato purée.

Zitoni
The largest unfluted type of Italian macaroni.

Zitoni Rigati
The largest fluted type of Italian macaroni about ½ inch in diameter.

Zizanie
Another name for wild rice. (See Rice, Wild.)

Zoolak
A fermented milk, similar to Yaghoust (which see).

Zouave Sauce
Espagnole sauce blended with chili vinegar, tomato purée, flavoured with garlic and mustard.

Zubrowka
Green vodka. Made by the insertion of the herb zubrowka, which has a flavour similar to bitter almonds.

Zucchini
A squash of Italian origin. It is striped light and dark green or mottled with grey. The small ones are most sought after and are served like melon.

Zuppa (It.)
Italian name for soup.

Zuurkool
Dutch sauerkraut.

Zwieback
The German term for twice-baked bread. Made from ordinary bread dough to which eggs and butter are added. The loaves are baked, sliced and baked again, in a form of rusk, which are sometimes sugar coated.

Zymoma
Any ferment.

Zymometer
An instrument for measuring the degree of fermentation.

Zythos or Zythum
A beverage made by the ancient Egyptians from wheat, a type of beer, much appreciated by Diodorus.